COOKING VEGAN

VESANTO MELINA, MS, RD, and **JOSEPH FOREST**, Professional Chef

Book Publishing Company

Summertown, Tennessee

Library of Congress Cataloging-in-Publication Data

Melina, Vesanto, 1942-
  Cooking vegan / Vesanto Melina, Joseph Forest.
      p. cm.
  Includes bibliographical references and index.
  ISBN 978-1-57067-267-5 (pbk.) -- ISBN 978-1-57067-943-8 (ebook)
  1. Vegan cooking. I. Forest, Joseph. II. Title.
  TX837.M518 2012
  641.5'636—dc23

                                                      2011049761

Pictured on the front cover: Portobello Mushroom Burgers with Chickpea Topping, p. 148
Pictured on the back cover: Vegetable Kabobs, p. 140

We chose to print this title on sustainably harvested paper stock certified by the Forest Stewardship Council®, an independent auditor of responsible forestry practices. For more information, visit https://us.fsc.org.

FSC
www.fsc.org

MIX
Paper from
responsible sources
FSC® C005010

© 2012 Vesanto Melina and Joseph Forest
Photos © 2012 Book Publishing Company

Cover and interior design: John Wincek
Cover photo: Warren Jefferson

Printed in the United States of America

Book Publishing Company
P.O. Box 99
Summertown, TN 38483
888-260-8458
bookpubco.com

ISBN 13: 978-1-57067-267-5

18   2 3 4 5 6 7 8 9

CONTENTS

VESANTO:

To the inspirational leader Thich Nhat Hanh.
Thank you for the compassionate and mindful example you set.

JOSEPH:

To my mother, Louise Forest. Thank you for your
nourishing and unconditional Spirit of Love.

ACKNOWLEDGMENTS

Sincere gratitude to those who made this book possible: Bob Holzapfel, our publisher; Cynthia Holzapfel and Jo Stepaniak, our meticulous editors; and all the wonderful staff at Book Publishing Company.

We appreciate the careful recipe testing by Misuzu Noguchi and Dan Malloy. Thank you to our taste testers: Vesanto's wonderful neighbors at WindSong Cohousing Community, including Alan Carpenter, Chandra Carlson, Evan McFee, Gillian Allan, Howard Staples, Kayla Vierling, Jacob Wolfheart, Jessica Bustard, Leslie Wood, Linda Duarte, Michael Mogardo, Mina Mogardo, Miriam Evers, Oliver Bustard, Susan Collerman, Susan McFee, Trevor Erikson, Tricia Carpenter, Valerie McIntyre, and the Thursday Veggie Meal Club. Thanks also go to Tobias Leenaert and Melanie Jaecques of the Ethical Vegetarian Alternative in Gent, Belgium; Joseph's niece, Gillian Boehme; and friends Larissa Drozenko and Siripon Pittayakornpisuth.

Special thanks to Angelina Rogon for kitchen assistance, Cam Doré for computer assistance and inspiration, Cristina Viviani for manuscript review, Lars Warje for his baking expertise, and Maureen Butler for insightful editing help.

Love and gratitude to our families and dear ones who encouraged us throughout this project and understood when we went into hibernation to complete the manuscript: Vesanto's partner, Cam Doré, son, Chris Crawford, and daughter, Kavyo Crawford; Joseph's mother, Louise, brothers, Ray and Forest, and sisters, Donna and Nicole; teachers Jeffrey Armstrong, Sandi Graham and Sarah Webster; friends Lee Gross, Sandra Milena Arismendy, Savey Mattu, Sunrise Ranch, and Edenvale Retreat and Conference Center.

We would like to acknowledge the companies that provided us with their outstanding products: Asian Family Specialty Foods, Daiya Foods, Gardein, Grainworks, LeSaffre Human Care, Manitoba Harvest, Nature's Path Organic, Omega Nutrition, and Sunrise Soya Foods.

RECIPE ATTRIBUTIONS

Many thanks to the chefs and recipe innovators who generously allowed us to use or adapt their recipes for this book:

- BC Blueberry Board: Blueberry Mince Tart and Pie Filling (page 233)
- Jennifer Cornbleet: Mango-Strawberry Pie (page 236), inspired by recipes from *Raw Food Made Easy*
- Brenda Davis: Coconut Macaroons (page 225), from *Becoming Raw* by Brenda Davis and Vesanto Melina, and Cranberry-Pecan Muffins (page 228) and Lemon-Sesame Cookies (page 226)
- Valerie McIntyre: Pesto the Besto (page 82)
- David McKay: Garden of Plenty Salad (page 107)
- Cherie Soria: Green Giant Juice (page 106), from *The Raw Food Revolution Diet* by Cherie Soria, Brenda Davis, and Vesanto Melina
- Jo Stepaniak: Gooda Cheez (page 80) and Gee Whiz Spread (page 79), from *The Ultimate Uncheese Cookbook*

Welcome! This precious book is the creation of two people in food-related professions who have different areas of expertise: dietitian and chef. My collaboration with chef Joseph Forest began in 1991, when we met at a presentation by vegan writer and inspirational speaker John Robbins. Joseph and I soon became cohosts of a series of cooking classes that drew enthusiastic crowds and national media attention. Out of that grew our popular cookbook, *Cooking Vegetarian*, which is the forerunner to this volume.

As a dietitian, I was aware of the nutritional features of food but lacked the skills of a talented chef, who can present dishes that make people's eyes light up and cause everyone to lick their lips in anticipation. Joseph's gift of creating foods that appeal to the senses of sight, smell, taste, and touch drew me to new adventures in the world of food. I was intrigued when he shared with me experiences he had during his chef's training. For example, he recalled that in his apprentice cooking lab, ten budding chefs at ten separate workstations followed a set of identical recipes each day. At the end of every class, all of the prepared food was brought forward for the students to evaluate. Surprisingly, the food each student made tasted unique, even though they had all used the same recipes. Joseph's insights have helped me to understand that although we use the same culinary map, we may each arrive at different destinations. Preparing food, even when from a recipe, is truly a creative act that expresses the love and care we put into it. My cooking skills, along with my sensory appreciation of food, have flourished through years of association with my esteemed and capable coauthor.

My diet evolved from a North American pattern that was centered on meat, dairy products, and baked goods. My mother introduced me to the joy of cooking, both alone and with others. She emphasized good nutrition, as she understood it, and also physical fitness. My father was a physiology professor and did graduate work at the University of Toronto with the diabetes researchers who discovered insulin, Sir Frederick Banting and Charles Best. My parents' example led me to value the two main facets of food: the appetizing (making food look and taste good) and the academic (understanding the nutritional components of food).

After the birth of my children, I traveled around the world several times and learned a great deal about the production and preparation of many cultural foods, particularly vegetarian dishes. I loved learning about the origins and history of ingredients from near and far, and my first attraction to a plant-based diet came from enjoyment of the food itself.

In 1993, while writing the "Without Dairy" chapter for my first book, *Becoming Vegetarian* (with Brenda Davis), I came face to face with my own mistaken belief that dairy products were essential to human health. From a critical review of the scientific research, I soon learned that I could survive very well without any flesh or fluids of animal origin. Over time I learned about the profound impacts of our food choices on the environment, human health, human hunger, and the lives of animals. In doing the extensive nutrition research that is the foundation of our books, I came to see that a vegan diet could provide every nutrient that we need in recommended amounts and that such a diet makes sense for reasons that become more compelling every year. I came to appreciate how many of us are voting with our grocery dollars for good health, compassion for animals, and sustainable agriculture. My own dietary transition gave me an appreciation of the challenges and solutions that people encounter as they move along the continuum from nonvegetarian to vegan.

In recent years I have seen a great shift in attitude regarding vegetarian nutrition among those at the forefront of the dietetics profession. When I first taught university nutrition, the prevailing attitude was that vegetarian diets are nutritionally risky. Vegan diets were unheard of. With time, scientists have recognized that centering our diet on plant foods can significantly reduce our risk of chronic disease. After *Becoming Vegetarian* was published, I was awarded the prestigious Clintec Award for leadership in dietetics. I was invited to write sections on vegetarian nutrition for diet manuals and to coauthor the joint position paper by the Academy of Nutrition and Dietetics (formerly American Dietetic Association) and Dieticians of Canada on vegetarian diets. My vegan nutrition books are required reading for continuing education courses for health professionals.

I love to share with others the joy and fulfillment that comes from preparing food. It is a pleasure to see how, right from the start, young children will enjoy ingredients that are good for them. My son, Xoph (Chris), has a great appreciation for natural, healthful, and simple foods, and for ayurveda, and my daughter, Kavyo, now considers it very important for people to prepare and eat vegetables that they have grown. Producing one's own food can be empowering and can also create a deeper respect for and understanding of nature.

I have also enjoyed my role as a dietitian at Dr. Dean Ornish's San Francisco retreats, helping those with cardiovascular disease adopt diets that are both healing and delicious. It's deeply fulfilling to help clients and friends adopt ways of eating that support their health, and it is satisfying to reassure others that we have no need to subject "food animals" to the tortured lives and deaths they endure.

Joseph and I have had such fun creating this book. It has been a pleasure to test and retest the recipes so that each one is a gem. Welcome to a recipe collection that will support your well-being, satisfy your appetite, and inspire you to enjoy cooking!

Vesanto Melina, MS, RD
nutrispeak.com

A WORD FROM CHEF JOSEPH

The roots of my love for food go back to my youth in Edmonton, Alberta, where I lived with my parents and five siblings. My preference was to help my mom with the preparation of dinner rather than the dishwashing afterward. I didn't know it then, but the seeds of a lifelong interest in the nourishing properties of food were being planted in my psyche.

Many years later, when I finally made the decision to enroll in a yearlong culinary arts program, my primary intention was to work in a kitchen to pay for my university education. During the course of my chef's training, I had the very good fortune to be sent to the Vancouver Four Seasons Hotel (where I returned years later to work as a chef in the banquet kitchen). I was awestruck by the high standards of excellence there, and that initial experience changed the direction of my life. After graduation I embarked with enthusiasm on a career path that I have followed for nearly thirty years.

Highlights of my career include private catering with an emphasis on using whole foods, working as a consultant to several natural food manufacturers, assisting in the production and revision of two corporate cookbooks, and acting as a consulting chef for the opening of two natural food restaurants. Along the way I have had the honor of feeding international rock-and-roll personalities, political leaders, dignitaries, and numerous Hollywood celebrities.

My favorite achievement, however, has been cowriting the Canadian best-selling cookbook, *Cooking Vegetarian*, with registered dietitian Vesanto Melina. The nutritional knowledge I gained from working with Vesanto has been invaluable, and I consider my relationship with her to be one of the most rewarding associations of my professional life. We collaborated on a series of popular vegetarian cooking classes that received national media attention. Vesanto offered practical vegetarian nutritional theory, and I led hands-on cooking segments. We reached hundreds of people from all walks of life, and our students went home better informed and richer for the experience.

Beyond my formal training in classical French cuisine, I have studied Ayurvedic, diabetic, macrobiotic, vegetarian, and vegan diets during my many years of working with food. Through all of this, three personal perspectives have emerged:

1. Transitioning from one dietary lifestyle to another can take years. For lasting results, this important process requires time, knowledge, and patience.

Feeding the body is a lifelong process that can involve adjustments from one stage of life to another for a myriad of reasons.

2. Since each person is constitutionally different, no single diet can be considered the ideal for everybody (or every body). Although we all require carbohydrates, protein, vitamins, and minerals, the combinations and types of foods we choose to meet those needs vary among individuals and cultural groups.

3. We are all brilliantly tailored individuals guided by a deep source of inner intelligence. If we pay attention to that wisdom, we will be led to the dietary pattern that serves us best.

I am very pleased to collaborate with Vesanto on this book. It is our sincere wish that you expand your nutritional knowledge and increase your culinary repertoire for the purpose of sustaining your health (or regaining your health if it is compromised). As you work with and adapt this book to suit your lifestyle, may you find inspiration to eat well to be well.

Joseph Forest
josephforest.com

Food as a Spiritual Blessing

Food is sacred. It has long been perceived as a gift and a vehicle for spiritual blessing by cultures all over the world. Just think of the elevated role of wild rice by indigenous tribes in the Great Lakes region, and corn in the Aztec empire, the use of quinoa in South America, and the religious traditions of Jewish Passover, Christian communion, and numerous Hindu ceremonies. Countless beliefs, customs, and rituals have acknowledged foods' capacity to provide much more than vitamins, minerals, and antioxidants. Rather, they honor foods' ability to touch, heal, and nourish the human spirit.

When we prepare food with awareness of the sacred, it can become imbued with spirit, transforming the server and those who partake of it. The attitude and presence of mind that we bring to food preparation and consumption are important factors in generating health and well-being. Simply by cultivating thankfulness for food and its ability to provide strength and vitality, we become mindful that food is not strictly utilitarian but instead a source of blessing.

chapter 1

Vegan Nutrition

If you are like most people, you rely on ten well-loved recipes that you make over and over again. In *Cooking Vegan*, you will discover many more that will become lifetime favorites. Only the most healthful, delicious, and easy-to-make recipes have made the cut in this all-star lineup. Our mission is to help people with full and busy lives assemble appetizing and nourishing meals with readily available plant-based ingredients.

This book is designed to assist vegans—and other people who are interested in eating fewer animal-based foods—in pursuing optimal health. A well-balanced vegan diet can provide all the nutrients you need. In addition, this style of eating is the ultimate expression of compassion for the animals and concern for the environment.

A special feature of this book is that each recipe has a complete nutritional analysis that shows exactly how much of a particular nutrient is present. These analyses make it easy to see the number of calories and the amount of protein, fat, carbohydrates, minerals, vitamins, and even essential fatty acids per cup or serving.

The information in this chapter is provided to give you a basic understanding of vegan nutrition. Protein, fat, and carbohydrates are the macronutrients that provide us with calories. In contrast, micronutrients, such as minerals and vitamins, do not provide calories. Both the Institute of Medicine (IOM) and the World Health Organization (WHO) have established guidelines that specify the percentage of calories that should come from protein, fat, and carbohydrates. The recommendations from the two groups overlap but differ slightly. Table 1.1 blends and summarizes these recommendations.

TABLE 1.1. Distribution of calories from protein, fat, and carbohydrates

MACRONUTRIENT	RECOMMENDED INTAKE AS A PERCENTAGE OF CALORIES
Protein	10 to 20%
Fat	15 to 35%
Carbohydrates	45 to 75%

Source: Data from notes 1 and 6.

Protein-Rich Plant Foods

Vegans hear this question all the time: "Where do you get your protein?" The truth is that vegan diets deliver abundant protein. We can get all the protein we need, and then some, simply by eating a variety of plant-based foods, with the notable exceptions of fats, oils, and sugars.

Vegetables and grains are significant protein providers. Foods that are particularly rich in protein include legumes (such as beans, lentils, and peas) and soy products (such as tempeh and tofu). The quality of protein in these foods rivals that of animal-based products. Protein quality depends on digestibility and how closely a food's amino acid content matches the pattern of amino acids required by humans. Soyfoods, for example, contain excellent proportions of essential amino acids and are easily digested. Every essential amino acid originates from plant-based foods, and our bodies can build any other amino acids that we need from them, making it unnecessary to consume foods of animal origin.

Vegan Cooking for Everyone

This book will appeal to all sorts of cooks, from beginners whose priority is simplicity to gourmet chefs who seek depths and nuances of flavor. It is also designed for people who want excellent health and nutrition. Offering the best of both worlds, the recipes and menus in *Cooking Vegan* are suitable for people who:

- aspire to be vegan or are vegan;
- are interested in fitness and food choices that will deliver energy, power, and endurance;
- are on weight-loss diets;
- have diabetes and need to know the carbohydrate content of the foods they eat;
- have or are at risk for chronic diseases in which good nutrition can play a healing role;
- love simplicity and want readily available ingredients and easy-to-prepare recipes;
- want foods in which the six tastes are superbly balanced (see page 35);
- want their families and friends to enjoy comforting, familiar, and tasty foods;
- want to include more plant-based meals in their diets;
- want to know how many calories and how much protein, fat, iron, sodium, and other nutrients they are consuming.

Recommended Protein Intake Per Kilogram of Body Weight

The recommended dietary allowance for both men and women is 0.8 grams of high-quality protein per kilogram of body weight per day. This recommendation includes a safety margin to cover individual variation in protein requirements. If we add an extra safety margin to allow for the lower digestibility of some plant-based foods, the recommendation for vegans age fifteen and older is 0.9 gram of protein per kilogram of body weight.

To determine your recommended protein intake in grams, divide your weight in pounds by 2.2. A few examples of recommended protein intakes for people of different weights are shown in table 1.2.

TABLE 1.2. Recommended daily protein intakes* for vegan adults

WEIGHT (IN POUNDS)	WEIGHT (IN KILOGRAMS)	RECOMMENDED PROTEIN INTAKE (IN GRAMS)
110	50	45
132	60	54
155	75	68
176	80	72

* These recommendations are for people age fifteen and older. During pregnancy and lactation, recommended intakes for protein are further increased by 25 grams per day.

The idea from forty years ago that complementary proteins must be eaten at the same meal is no longer credited. Vegans easily get sufficient protein by eating an assortment of plant-based foods over the course of a day. As a bonus, protein-rich foods provide other valuable nutrients. For example, legumes tend to be high in iron and zinc, and fortified soymilk and tofu are abundant sources of calcium.

Recommended intakes for protein are stated in two ways: either as grams of dietary protein per kilogram of body weight (see table 1.2 above) or as calories from protein as a percentage of total calories in the diet. The nutritional analyses for the recipes in this book list both the grams of protein per serving and the percentage of calories in the recipe that is derived from protein.

Worldwide, protein contributes about 11 percent of total calories to human diets. Surveys show that in vegan diets, protein typically contributes 10 to 13 percent of calories. When people adopt weight-loss diets that are low in total calories, the percentage derived from protein increases.

PROTEIN FOR CHILDREN

Children require more protein per kilogram than adults, as can be seen by comparing tables 1.2 and 1.3. The values shown in table 1.3 include a significant safety margin. To determine protein needs for a child whose body weight

It's easy to get enough protein by eating a vegan diet, especially one that includes legumes and soyfoods. People who are unfamiliar with these ingredients may not realize how delicious they are or how easy they are to prepare and fit into menus. That's why this book features many recipes that provide simple and tasty ways to prepare beans, lentils, peas, and soyfoods in dips, entrées, soups, spreads, and other recipes on a daily basis. Plus, each recipe comes complete with a nutritional analysis that lists the amount of protein per cup or serving.

differs from the weights shown in table 1.3, adjust the recommended protein intake proportionally.

Whether or not a child is vegan, there is little room for candy, chips, and sweet beverages in a diet that meets recommended intakes for protein, minerals, and vitamins. Fortified nondairy milks are suitable beverages. Note, however, that fortified soymilk typically provides about 7 grams of protein per cup (250 ml), whereas rice beverages contain only about 0.5 grams of protein, and some other nondairy beverages can be similarly low in protein.

PROTEIN FOR VEGAN ATHLETES

For people who exercise regularly, 0.9 gram of protein per kilogram of body weight is a sufficient daily intake. Endurance and strength athletes need somewhat more, and the (US) Academy of Nutrition and Dietetics and Dieticians of Canada recommend 1.3 to 1.8 grams of protein per kilogram of body weight for vegan athletes. This is relatively easy to achieve since people who exercise a great deal tend to have high caloric intakes. Diets that include legumes; soyfoods; nuts, seeds, or their butters; and plenty of whole grains will automatically supply sufficient protein for vegan athletes.

Competitive athletes who want protein-rich breakfasts, lunches, and dinners need only scan the nutritional analyses included with each recipe in this book to find those that provide 15 to 20 grams of protein per serving. Hungry athletes can easily consume double or even triple portions.

TABLE 1.3. Recommended daily protein intake for vegan children

AGE (in years)	RECOMMENDED DAILY PROTEIN INTAKE (in grams per kilogram of body weight)	TYPICAL WEIGHT (in kilograms)	PROTEIN INTAKE AT TYPICAL BODY WEIGHTS (in grams)
1 to 2	1.6 to 1.7	11	18 to 19
2 to 3	1.4 to 1.6	13	18 to 21
4 to 6	1.3 to 1.4	20	26 to 28
7 to 10	1.1 to 1.2	28	31 to 34
11 to 14	1.1 to 1.2	46	51 to 55

Plant-Powered Athletes

Many vegan athletes inspire us with their achievements. Here are a few examples:

- Basketball champion: John Salley
- Bodybuilders: Jane Black, Robert Cheeke, Mike Mahler, and Kenneth Williams
- Cyclocross racers: Molly Cameron and Adam Myerson
- Ironman triathletes: Brendan Brazier and Ruth Heidrich
- Major League Baseball pitcher: Pat Neshek
- Marathon winners: Scott Jurek, Fiona Oakes, and Pat Reeves
- Mixed martial arts professional: Mac Danzig
- Professional ice hockey player: Georges Laraque
- Professional skateboarder: Ed Templeton
- Professional wrestlers: Bryan Danielson (also known as Daniel Bryan or the American Dragon) and Taryn Terrell
- Stuntwoman: Spice Williams-Crosby
- World record holder in high jumping: Weia Reinboud

Bodybuilders can require as much as 2 to 2.3 grams of protein per kilogram of body weight when they are adding to their muscle mass. For this purpose, they sometimes add protein powders made from soy, peas, or rice to smoothies. Even such high protein requirements can be met exclusively by plant-based foods. This fact is not surprising when you consider that large herbivores, including bulls and elephants, power up exclusively on plants.

A common challenge for athletes is to discover simple and practical ways to prepare protein-rich vegan foods to eat at sports events and while traveling. This can be accomplished by planning meals that include vegetables, seeds, nuts, cereals, breads, and pastas. Over half of the world's protein comes from grains, in which 8 to 16 percent of calories come from protein, so these foods should not be discounted. For menus that show high-calorie and high-protein variations, see pages 48 to 59.

> **@ A GLANCE**
>
> ### Protein Recommendations for Vegan Athletes
>
> - Endurance and strength athletes: 1.3 to 1.8 grams of protein per kilogram of body weight
> - Bodybuilders: 2 to 2.3 grams of protein per kilogram of body weight

Healthful Fats

 at is found in all plant cells and in every plant-based food. In lettuce, for example, 10 percent of the calories are derived from fat. So even if you don't spread your toast with margarine or cook with oil, your diet will contain some fats. The most healthful sources of fat are whole foods, such as avocados, nuts, olives, and seeds, rather than extracted oils that have lost essential fats, fat-soluble vitamins, fiber, and other nutrients.

The IOM recommends that diets contain between 20 and 35 percent of calories from fat, and the WHO recommends 15 to 30 percent of calories from fat. (These ranges are blended and summarized in table 1.1.) Many health experts advocate lower intakes such as 10 to 15 percent of calories from fat to reverse disease or reduce risk.

Two fat components are essential to life: an omega-6 fatty acid (linoleic acid) and an omega-3 fatty acid (alpha-linolenic acid). Each of these has derivatives that also are present in foods. Omega-6 fatty acids are present in grains (such as corn and wheat germ), nuts (such as butternuts, pine nuts, and walnuts), seeds (such as hempseeds, pumpkin seeds, sesame seeds, and sunflower seeds) soybeans, and in small amounts in many other plant-based foods. Omega-3 fatty acids are present in nuts (such as butternuts and walnuts), seeds (such as chia seeds, flaxseeds, and hempseeds), and in small amounts in green leafy vegetables and sea vegetables.

The body uses omega-6 and omega-3 fatty acids as raw materials for building cell membranes, the nervous system, and certain hormonelike substances. It is recommended that we get at least 5 to 8 percent of daily calories from omega-6 fatty acids and 1 to 2 percent from omega-3 fatty acids. In a vegan menu providing 2,000 calories, this means aiming for at least 9 grams of omega-6 fatty acids and 2.2 to 4.4 grams of omega-3 fatty acids. Nine grams of omega-6 fatty acids are easily obtained by eating a variety of plant foods, and 2.2 grams of omega-3 fatty acid can be found in 1 teaspoon (5 ml) of flaxseed oil. For more examples of omega-3 fatty acid sources, see Essential Extras, page 45.

Consuming the above ratio of omega-6 to omega-3 fatty acids supports good health. Because omega-6 fatty acids are added to many processed foods in the form of oils, most people eat too many of these and not enough omega-3 fatty acid.

You may choose to increase your intake of omega-3 fatty acids by supplementing with DHA (docosahexaenoic acid), which is a specific form of omega-3 fatty acid. Our bodies can make DHA from the omega-3 fatty acid we consume, although it is possible that supplemental DHA may be helpful for pregnant woman and for people who have diabetes. Further research is needed to clarify whether supplemental DHA can be beneficial on a wider basis. The vegan source of DHA is microalgae and is available in 200- to 300-milligram supplements. Note that fish oils are often promoted as sources of DHA; since fish obtain DHA by eating microalgae, there is no reason for vegans to worry that they are missing something by avoiding fish oil. In fact the supplements are missing the heavy metals and pesticides that can be present in fish.

@ A GLANCE

Essential Fatty Acids Recommendations

In a 2,000-calorie vegan menu, the following daily intakes are optimal:

- Omega-6 fatty acids: 9 grams
- Omega-3 fatty acids: 2.2 to 4.4 grams

Note that maintaining this ideal ratio of omega-6 to omega-3 fatty acids is important for good health.

Carbohydrates and Fiber

Carbohydrates are the body's most efficient source of energy, providing fuel for the brain, nervous system, and red blood cells. A vegan diet provides abundant carbohydrates. The recommended dietary allowance, or minimum daily carbohydrate intake, is 130 grams. Carbohydrates should provide between 45 and 75 percent of the calories in our diet.

The IOM recommends that the diet contains 45 to 65 percent of calories from carbohydrates, and the WHO recommends that 55 to 75 percent of calories come from carbohydrates. (These ranges are blended and summarized in table 1.1.) Both groups of experts agree that the best carbohydrate sources are the starches in whole grains, legumes, and vegetables; the simple sugars in fruits; and nuts and seeds (which have relatively small amounts of carbohydrates). These recommendations do not include the refined carbohydrates found in processed foods, such as sodas and sweets, which provide most of the carbohydrates in North American diets. These are the foods that unfairly give all carbohydrates a bad reputation.

> **Carbohydrate Recommendation**
>
> The recommended minimum daily carbohydrate intake is 130 grams.

FIBER

Fiber, a structural component in the cell walls of plants, is present in all whole plant-based foods but is absent in all animal-based foods. Fiber plays a major role in keeping waste products and toxins moving through the intestines so they can be eliminated. High-fiber foods allow carbohydrates to be released slowly into the bloodstream, thereby maintaining normal blood glucose levels and staving off hunger. Fiber is one of many important components that are present in whole grains but are lost when grains are refined. (Other losses are B vitamins, minerals, and protective phytochemicals.)

Recommendations for fiber intake vary with caloric intake. The suggested average daily fiber intake for women age fifty and younger is a minimum of 25 grams; for older women, the minimum is 21 grams. The suggested intake for men age fifty and younger is 38 grams; for older men, the minimum is 30 grams. The average fiber intake in North America falls far short of this at 15 grams per day. In contrast, vegan diets consistently meet and exceed suggested fiber intakes.

> **Fiber Recommendations**
>
> - Women age 50 and below: 25 grams
> - Women age 50 and above: 21 grams
> - Men age 50 and below: 38 grams
> - Men age 50 and above: 30 grams

Legumes are rich in a fiber that can cause flatulence; however, this potential problem can be avoided. For details, see the sidebar on page 15.

Minerals

The nutritional analyses that accompany each recipe in this book include all of the minerals in the following list. For recommended daily intakes for people of various ages, see Dietary Reference Intakes for Minerals, page 240.

Calcium. From advertising, you may have the impression that achieving good bone health is entirely reliant on the mineral calcium and eating dairy products. In truth, bone health is dependent on a number of nutrients, all of which can be found in a vegan diet: the minerals calcium, magnesium, boron, copper, zinc, manganese, and fluoride, and the vitamins D, K, C, B_{12}, B_6, and folic acid. In addition, physical activity plays a vital role in maintaining strong bones. For a list of calcium-rich plant-based foods, see the sidebar on page 9.

Iron and Zinc. Among nonvegetarians, vegetarians, and vegans alike, iron deficiency is the most widely recognized nutritional deficiency in North America. Women and children are particularly at risk. Vegans, like everyone else, should be aware of good iron sources. Foods that are high in protein also tend to be high in iron and zinc. For example, 1 cup (250 ml) of cooked beans, lentils, or peas or ½ cup (125 ml) of tofu provides 4 to 8 milligrams of iron and 2 to 4 milligrams of zinc. These can be compared with recommended daily intakes of 18 milligrams of iron for women of childbearing age and 8 milligrams for other adults; 8 milligrams of zinc are recommended for women and 11 milligrams for men.

One cup (250 ml) of cooked whole grains provides 1 to 4 milligrams of iron and 1 to 2 milligrams of zinc. Seeds, nuts, dried fruit (such as raisins, currants, and prunes), green vegetables (such as broccoli, green beans, and kale), mushrooms, and potatoes also are iron and zinc sources. Seeds and cashews are especially good sources of zinc. When iron-rich foods are eaten with a good source of vitamin C, absorption can increase greatly. Cast-iron cookware contributes iron to foods that are cooked in it. This is especially true of acidic foods, such as tomato sauce. Sprouting foods increases mineral availability, as does fermentation (which is part of the production of tempeh and miso).

Magnesium. Magnesium is the central atom in the chlorophyll molecule, so of course green vegetables are good sources. This mineral is also present in other vegetables, nuts, seeds, legumes, fruits, and chocolate.

Potassium. Though bananas have somehow become famous as a potassium-rich food, many fruits and vegetables are packed with greater amounts of potassium. In fact, mushrooms, tomatoes, potatoes, green beans, and strawberries each have more potassium per calorie than bananas.

Phosphorus. Phosphorus is present in seeds, nuts, whole grains, and legumes.

Sodium. While sodium is essential for life, most North Americans get too much rather than too little. Adults are advised to limit sodium intake to between 1,500

Calcium-Rich Plant-Based Foods

Vegan diets provide many good sources of calcium, including the following:

- almonds, almond butter, sesame seeds, and tahini
- blackstrap molasses
- calcium-fortified beverages, such as fortified soymilk, orange juice, and other nondairy beverages
- calcium-set tofu (note the amount of calcium listed on the label)
- figs
- greens, especially broccoli, collards, kale, mustard or turnip greens, napa cabbage, and okra
- white beans and black beans

Note that certain greens, such as beet greens, spinach, and Swiss chard, are not listed as calcium sources. This is because the calcium present in these foods is tightly bound by plant acids called oxalates and is unavailable for absorption.

and 2,300 milligrams per day. People age fifty and older should reduce the lower end of this range to 1,300 milligrams, and those age seventy-one and older should further reduce it to 1,200 milligrams. People who have high blood pressure should limit their sodium intakes.

Vitamins

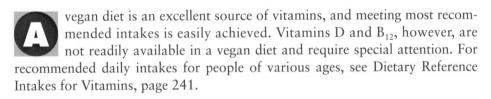 vegan diet is an excellent source of vitamins, and meeting most recommended intakes is easily achieved. Vitamins D and B_{12}, however, are not readily available in a vegan diet and require special attention. For recommended daily intakes for people of various ages, see Dietary Reference Intakes for Vitamins, page 241.

Vitamin B_{12}. We require a tiny amount of vitamin B_{12}, which is an essential nutrient that is produced by bacteria. Sources for vegans include fortified foods, nutritional yeast, and supplements. Plant-based foods, including tempeh, sea vegetables, and organic produce, are not reliable sources of vitamin B_{12}. For examples of vitamin B_{12} sources, see Essential Extras, page 45.

Vitamin D. Sources of vitamin D include sunlight, fortified foods, and supplements. Sensible sun exposure will trigger an adequate amount of vitamin D production in the body. For people with light skin, ten to fifteen minutes of daily sun exposure of the face and forearms can be adequate. However, many factors, including age, latitude, skin pigmentation, and time of exposure, can affect vitamin D production. People with dark skin may need up to two hours of daily sun exposure for adequate vitamin D production.

In many parts of the world, exposure to winter sun will not stimulate vitamin D production. At latitudes above 35 degrees north, there is little or no vitamin D production between November and March, and at 49 degrees north, the so-called "vitamin D winter" extends from October to April.

Where sunlight is not a reliable year-round source of vitamin D, fortified foods and supplements are necessary. In vegan diets, soymilk, orange juice and other nondairy beverages, cereals, infant formula are dietary sources of vitamin D (check labels). Grown in certain conditions, mushrooms contain a small amount of vitamin D but not enough to meet recommended amounts. Supplements provide either vitamin D_3, which is typically of animal origin, or vitamin D_2, which is vegan. Although there has been controversy about this matter in the past, it has been established that vitamin D_2 is equally as effective as vitamin D_3 in maintaining adequate blood levels of vitamin D. For more information about vitamin D, see Essential Extras, page 45.

For More Information

If you want additional details about vegan nutrition, including tables of the nutrient contents of individual foods and ingredients, we recommend the following books by Vesanto Melina and Brenda Davis:

- *Becoming Vegan*
- *The New Becoming Vegetarian*
- *Becoming Raw*

chapter 2

Vegan Ingredients

There is so much more to a vegan diet than fruits and vegetables. Vegans choose from a great variety of delectable foods, including grains, legumes, healthful fats, sweeteners, herbs and spices, and nondairy beverages. People often remark how liberating this style of eating is. Rather than being restrictive, it provides limitless options.

Granted, learning about unfamiliar foods can be daunting at first. We recently heard proof of this from an acquaintance who had decided to take greater responsibility for her health. She went to a large natural food store, looked around, and then walked out without making a single purchase. Why? She was simply overwhelmed by the number of new products she saw on every shelf.

If you are new to vegan cooking, this chapter is for you. Although our recipes call for whole-food ingredients and basic, easy-to-obtain items, here is some information to help you navigate the grocery store aisles. In addition, this chapter includes a shopping list (see pages 30 to 32) that contains staples and other products you will need from time to time. We hope you find it useful.

Whole Grains: The Staff of Life

True grains, such as corn, rice, and wheat, are members of the botanical family of cereal grasses. However, there are many other foods that are not true grains even though we prepare and eat them just like grains. We call these "pseudograins." For example, buckwheat is the seed of a plant in the rhubarb family, quinoa is from a botanical group that includes spinach and sugar beets, and wild rice is actually a grass. Pseudograins have gained popularity because many people are sensitive to wheat and other gluten-containing cereal grains, and pseudograins don't produce the same troubling symptoms.

Grains and pseudograins are excellent sources of energy, protein, and B vitamins, and throughout this book we generally include pseudograins when referring to grains.

Grains are made up of four distinct parts. Protein is present in all four parts, although it is not evenly distributed. The outer layer, called the husk, surrounds the kernel and protects it from the elements during its growth. Because it is indigestible for humans, the husk is removed and discarded. Next is the bran—a thin layer that is rich in protein, vitamins, minerals, and fiber—that surrounds the endosperm, the biggest part of the grain. The endosperm stores most of the grain's food energy in the form of complex carbohydrates, or starch.

A tiny but very important portion of the grain is the germ, or embryo, which abounds with essential fatty acids, minerals, and vitamins. Unfortunately, along with the bran, the germ is removed during milling and refining because its oils can become rancid during storage. In the case of wheat, for example, refining results in pure-looking white flour with a long shelf life. However, because the bran and germ have been removed, the flour has lost much of the grain's original wealth of essential fatty acids, fiber, minerals (such as calcium, chromium, magnesium, and zinc), protective phytochemicals, and vitamins (such as vitamin B_6). Although four of the B vitamins (folate, niacin, riboflavin, and thiamin) and iron are added back during in the enrichment process, much is lost.

CHOOSE INTACT WHOLE GRAINS

The best way to eat grains is the way nature grew them: completely intact. Whole grains, such as barley, brown rice, Kamut berries, millet, oat groats, quinoa, spelt berries, and wheat berries, can be cooked as breakfast cereal (page 69) or eaten at lunch and dinner in casseroles, pilafs, soups, and stews.

Other great choices are grains that have been minimally processed, such as those that are cut, rolled, or stone ground, with little or nothing added or removed. These methods of processing do relatively little damage to the grain, and although nutrient losses occur, they are minimal.

If you need to choose a processed grain, such as flour for baking, whole wheat flour is more nutritious than refined wheat flour or unbleached all-purpose flour. Refined flours produce a light, appealing texture in baked goods. To add nourishment to muffins, pancakes, and other items made from refined flour, mix dried fruits, nut butters, nuts, or seeds into the batter before baking.

GENERAL GUIDELINES FOR COOKING GRAINS

The size of the pot you choose will determine your success when cooking grains. Use a deep pot to ensure that the grain is covered with water for as long as possible during the cooking process. In addition, use only pots with tight-fitting lids to ensure that very little steam escapes.

Generally speaking, grains take less time to cook than legumes and do not require soaking before cooking. To cook grains, put the water in the pot and bring it to a boil before adding the grain. Once the water has come to a boil, add the grain, cover the pot, and wait for the water to return to a boil before decreasing the heat to low.

Always bring the water to a boil before adding grains, unless you want a sticky product. Stickiness occurs because cold water draws some of the starch from the grains into the surrounding water. When the water boils, the starch slightly thickens the water, making the final product sticky. This is particularly true for grains in which the bran has been removed, such as white basmati rice.

The grain is cooked when all the water has been absorbed and the grain is soft and no longer crunchy. If the heat is too high during cooking, too much water will be lost through evaporation and the rice will not get tender. If that happens, add a small amount of hot water to the pot to complete the cooking. Do not stir the grain while it is cooking or while it is still hot. Grains bruise very easily, and stirring will make them sticky. Once the grain is cooked, remove the pot from the heat and let the grain rest for five minutes before serving. If moisture remains on the bottom of the pot after the grain is fully cooked, open the lid slightly and drain off the excess water.

Table 2.1 below shows the amount of water to use, the cooking time, and the yield for cooking 1 cup (250 ml) of dry grains or pseudograins. Generally speaking, 1 cup (250 ml) of dry grain will yield two servings; however, the number of servings depends on how hungry the eaters are and the amounts of other foods served. Leftover grain can easily be reheated, incorporated into soups,

TABLE 2.1. Cooking grains: water, time, and yield

DRY GRAIN (1 CUP/250 ML DRY)	WATER	COOKING TIME (IN MINUTES)	APPROXIMATE YIELD
Amaranth	3 cups (750 ml)	20 to 25	2½ cups (625 ml)
Barley, pearl	4 cups (1 L)	50 to 60	4 cups (1 L)
Buckwheat (kasha)	2 cups (500 ml)	12 to 15	4 cups (1 L)
Cornmeal	4 cups (1 L)	10	4½ cups (1.125 L)
Kamut berries	3½ cups (875 ml)	60 to 70	3 cups (750 ml)
Millet	2½ cups (625 ml)	25	4 cups (1 L)
Oats, rolled, old-fashioned	2½ cups (625 ml)	20	2¼ cups (560 ml)
Quinoa	1½ cups (375 ml)	15 to 20	3½ cups (875 ml)
Rice, brown basmati	2 cups (500 ml)	40	3¼ cups (810 ml)
Rice, brown long-grain	2 cups (500 ml)	45	3½ cups (875 ml)
Rice, white basmati	2¾ cups (685 ml)	18 to 20	4 cups (1 L)
Rice, wild	4 cups (1 L)	50 to 60	3 cups (750 ml)
Spelt berries	3½ cups (875 ml)	60 to 70	3 cups (750 ml)
Wheat berries	3½ cups (875 ml)	60 to 70	3 cups (750 ml)

made into salads, used in International Roll-Ups (page 144), or served as a pudding for dessert (as in Creamy Rice Pudding, page 238).

Legumes: Protein Powerhouses

Legumes (beans, lentils, and peas) are of prime importance in vegan diets because they are rich in protein, iron, zinc and other minerals, folate and other B vitamins, and fiber. Soybeans are superstars, with about 36 percent of their calories coming from protein, similar to that of eggs or beef. Soybeans, however, have the advantage of having less fat and no cholesterol.

SOAKING BEANS AND PEAS

When beans, lentils, and peas are harvested, they have a high moisture content. Before they are sold, they are dried to prolong their shelf life. Reconstituting legumes by soaking them for eight to twelve hours considerably decreases their cooking time. Note, however, that lentils and split peas do not need to be soaked before cooking, whereas beans and peas do. Soaking draws out oligosaccharides, which are potentially problematic carbohydrates that pass into the large intestine, where they are acted upon by bacteria. A by-product of this bacterial activity is intestinal gas, which can produce discomfort in the lower bowel and be embarrassing. Because oligosaccharides are water soluble, discarding the soaking liquid and rinsing beans before they are cooked goes a long way toward reducing intestinal gas.

Soaking beans increases their nutritional value to us because the minerals in soaked beans become more available for our use. When beans are soaked, the calcium, iron, and zinc they contain are released from a mineral-phosphate complex known as phytate, allowing more of these and other minerals to be absorbed by the body.

It can be a good idea to pick through beans and peas before soaking to remove any dirt, small stones, or twigs that may have come in from the field. To remove these unwanted materials and shriveled or chipped beans, arrange the beans in a single layer on a baking sheet and inspect them in good light. After you have picked through the beans, rinse them well.

Cover the beans with triple their volume of water and let them soak for eight to twelve hours at room temperature or in the refrigerator. As they soak, dried legumes will expand and become two to three times greater in size, so make sure the bowl or pot you use for soaking is large enough. After the beans have soaked, drain and rinse them. Then put them in a large pot and add enough fresh water to cover the beans by two to three inches. Follow the cooking guidelines in table 2.2 (page 16) and cook the beans until they are soft.

If you forget to soak beans overnight or don't have time, you can still salvage your dinner plans. Pick through then rinse the beans and put them in a large pot. Add three times as much water as beans and bring to a boil. Decrease the heat

The Gas Crisis: Four Simple Solutions

Try these techniques to minimize the production of intestinal gas that can be caused by eating legumes and other problematic foods:

1. Begin by adding small amounts of legumes to your diet and increase amounts gradually. Start with smaller legumes (lentils and split peas) and tofu, which are easier to digest. Soak dried legumes, discard the soaking water, and rinse the legumes before and after cooking.

2. Identify the specific foods that cause trouble for you. For example, eating sugar in combination with certain foods may cause gas. For some people, large amounts of cabbage can be a concern.

3. Don't overeat: Excessive amounts of undigested food can become fodder for bacteria.

4. Adopt the gas-reducing methods used by international cooks. For example, the Japanese add the sea vegetable kombu to foods, especially soups. Latin Americans use an herb called epazote, the French add fennel seeds, and Indians add cumin or asafetida.

to low, cover, and simmer for five minutes. Remove the pot from heat and let the beans rest for one hour. Drain and rinse the beans. Then return them to the pot and add enough fresh water to cover the beans by a two to three inches. Follow the cooking guidelines in table 2.2 (page 16) and cook the beans until they are soft.

GENERAL COOKING GUIDELINES

Drain and rinse soaked legumes before cooking. Discard the soaking liquid and use fresh cold water to rinse. Put the legumes in a large pot and add enough fresh cold water to cover them by two to three inches. Bring to a boil, decrease the heat to low, cover, and cook, stirring occasionally, until the beans are tender. Rinse cooked beans before using them. (For cooking times, see table 2.2, page 16.)

When cooking legumes, it is important to gently simmer them because vigorous boiling can burst their skins. In addition, simmering prevents the water from evaporating before the legumes have a chance to cook completely. Some legumes produce foam after the water comes to a boil. If this happens, use a ladle or big spoon to skim off the foam once or twice during the first five to ten minutes of cooking. If the water is absorbed or evaporates before the legumes are cooked, simply add more water to cover the beans by an inch or two (2.5 to 5 cm).

Do not add salt at the beginning of the cooking process. Salt toughens the outer skin of legumes, making it more difficult for water to penetrate them and increasing the cooking time. Adding about 1/4 teaspoon (1 ml) of salt per cup (250 ml) of

TABLE 2.2. Cooking times and yields for legumes

LEGUME (1 CUP/250 ML DRY)	COOKING TIME (IN MINUTES)	APPROXIMATE YIELD
Adzuki beans	35 to 45	3 cups (750 ml)
Ancient ancestor beans (Anazazi)	50 to 60	2⅔ cups (670 ml)
Appaloosa beans	45	2⅔ cups (670 ml)
Black beans	45 to 55	2½ cups (625 ml)
Black-eyed peas	45 to 60	2 cups (500 ml)
Cannellini beans	60 to 70	2⅔ cups (670 ml)
Chickpeas	45	2¾ cups (685 ml)
Fava beans	40 to 50	2¼ cups (560 ml)
Great northern beans	45	2⅔ cups (670 ml)
Kidney beans	35	2½ cups (625 ml)
Lentils	25 to 35	2¼ cups (560 ml)
Lentils, red	20	2 cups (500 ml)
Lima beans, small	55 to 60	3 cups (750 ml)
Mung beans	25 to 30	3 cups (750 ml)
Navy beans	50 to 60	2⅔ cups (670 ml)
Pinto beans	45	2⅔ cups (670 ml)
Split peas	45 to 60	2 cups (500 ml)
Swedish brown beans	60 to 70	2⅔ cups (670 ml)
Yellow-eyed beans	50 to 60	2½ cups (625 ml)

Note: All yields are based on 1 cup (250 ml) of dried legumes cooked in 3 cups (750 ml) of water following an 8- to 12-hour soaking time (except for the lentils and split peas, which do not require soaking).

dried legumes toward the end of the cooking period develops the overall flavor of legumes and decreases the need for salt in the recipes in which they are used.

Legumes are cooked when they are no longer crunchy or grainy when bitten. Test a few—some may have finished cooking before others. Let legumes cool in their cooking liquid to keep the skins from splitting, which occurs when hot cooked legumes come into contact with cooler air.

Additional Tips for Cooking Legumes

The general cooking guidelines and table 2.2 provide most of the information you need to cook legumes. However, certain factors can affect cooking times and outcome. For example, older legumes take longer to cook. In addition, legumes may take longer to cook at higher elevations: At sea level, the boiling point of water is 212 degrees F (100 degrees C), and at higher elevations, the boiling point is lower. Boiling is a function of atmospheric pressure, and since the pressure is lower at higher elevations, more time is required to cook and bake food.

Soyfoods

In China, soybeans are known as *tatou*, the greater bean, and with good reason. For thousands of years, soybeans have been highly valued in Asia for their versatility and high protein, oil, and mineral content. Scientists have discovered the excellent amino acid profile of soybeans and have recognized that highly digestible soyfoods, such as tofu, compare favorably with other forms of protein, including animal-based foods. In addition, the isoflavones in soy function as antioxidants. Add soy to your diet, and you may lower your risk of cardiovascular disease.

TOFU: MANY TEXTURES, MANY USES

In the tofu-making process, hot soymilk is blended with a coagulant to form a curd. At this stage, soft tofu is poured directly into its package. Soft tofu has relatively greater amounts of water and less protein and minerals when compared with the firmer varieties. Traditionally, the coagulant used to make tofu was a sea vegetable extract called nigari; however, in modern processes, magnesium or calcium salts are often used. Calcium-set tofu is an excellent source of calcium (check the label).

When medium, medium-firm, firm, and extra-firm grades of tofu are being made, the curd is poured into a mold, pressed to form a block, cut, and packaged. The amount of pressure applied and water expelled determines the tofu's consistency. Because the textures vary, each type of tofu has specific uses in recipes.

Pressed tofu. Even though a certain amount of water is expelled from tofu before it is packaged, the water content may still be too high for certain recipes, such as Curried Sandwich Spread (page 78) and Scrambled Tofu (page 70). If you were to make these recipes without pressing the tofu first, the liquid would weep into the bread or onto the serving plate. To press tofu, remove it from the package and put it on a dinner plate. Put another plate, or a cutting board, over the tofu, and then carefully put a 4- or 5-pound (2 kg) weight, such as several cans of food or a bag of grain, on top of the plate. Let the tofu drain for fifteen to twenty minutes. About ½ cup (125 ml) of liquid will pool on the bottom plate. Discard the liquid, transfer the tofu to a bowl, and proceed with the recipe.

Silken tofu. Silken tofu, of Japanese origin, is particularly silky in nature. Like other types of tofu, it is available in textures ranging from soft to extra firm. Mori-Nu brand silken tofu is sold in aseptic cartons and needs no refrigeration before opening. It's handy for camping trips and to keep on the shelf for use when company arrives and you want to whip up a quick dessert. Recipes that call for silken tofu include Lem-Un-Cheesecake with Crumb Crust (page 232) and Pumpkin Spice Pie (page 237).

Tempeh. Tempeh is a fermented soy product that originated in Indonesia, where it has long been consumed as a source of protein. It is made using a fermentation process that binds the soybeans into cakes or blocks. Unlike many other soy products, tempeh is made using the whole soybean, which gives it more fiber and a slightly higher protein content. In Indonesia, tempeh is principally made using 100 percent soybeans; however, in the West, tempeh often includes other legumes, grains, and vegetables. Look for it in the refrigerated or freezer sections of large supermarkets and natural food stores.

GOOD FATS FROM WHOLE FOODS

Fat is an essential nutrient. We all need fat to live, yet it has a bad reputation. However, only some of the fats that we eat undermine human health. The highest-quality fat is that which is naturally present in avocados, olives, nuts, seeds, soybeans, and other plant-based foods. There is simply no contest between the fats found in these fresh foods and the chemically altered fats found in margarine, shortening, and other hydrogenated vegetables oils or the highly saturated fats found in animal-based foods. Furthermore, whole foods are far more nutritious than the oils that are extracted from them because they retain valuable essential fatty acids, fiber, minerals, phytochemicals, protein, sterols, and vitamins. In our recipes, nuts, seeds, and other whole foods add healthful fats while providing rich, creamy textures.

AVOCADO

Most people associate avocados with fat, and for good reason. One cup of cubed avocado contains 240 calories and 21 grams of fat. However, the fats in avocados are primarily monounsaturated fatty acids, which have been shown to reduce total cholesterol while increasing HDL, or "good" cholesterol, when eaten in moderation. Plus, avocado has other bragging rights: 1 cup (250 ml) of cubed avocado impressively has 7 to 10 grams of fiber and 2 to 3 milligrams of vitamin E.

COCONUT

Coconut has been a staple in the cuisines of Asian countries and the Pacific Islands for centuries. The oil of coconuts is high in saturated fats; however, these

Correcting Omega Fatty Acid Imbalance

Standard American diets typically contain as much as ten times the amount of omega-6 fatty acids as omega-3 fatty acids. Because many foods and oils are rich in omega-6 fatty acids but not omega-3 fatty acids, this ratio can climb as high as ten, twenty, or even forty parts omega-6 fatty acids to one part omega-3 fatty acids. Such imbalances are found in both vegan and nonvegan diets and contribute to common degenerative diseases. Researchers believe this excessive imbalance plays a significant role in the rising rate of inflammatory disorders in North America. Omega-3 fatty acids have been shown to reduce inflammation in the body.

fats are medium-chain saturated fatty acids (MCFAs) that break down differently than the long-chain saturated fatty acids typically found in animal-based foods. MCFAs digest more easily, are found in breast milk, and are preferentially used by the liver as a source of fuel to produce energy. Coconut's predominant fatty acid, lauric acid, appears to raise HDL to an even greater extent than it raises LDL, or "bad" cholesterol. Consequently, the overall effect of lauric acid on the ratio of total to HDL cholesterol is consistently favorable. Although coconut is high in total fat, like other nuts and seeds it contains respectable amounts of the minerals copper, iron, manganese, phosphorus, selenium, and zinc, making it much more nutritious than coconut oil.

Young coconuts contain a soft, gel-like meat and more coconut water than mature coconuts, which are firmer. Coconut milk is made by blending coconut meat, coconut water, and additional water, if needed. (For instructions on how to break open a coconut and make fresh coconut milk, see page 113). Besides being used to make milk, pieces of fresh coconut can simply be eaten as a snack or blended into a smoothie. Fresh coconut can also be grated and sprinkled over breakfast cereals or any other foods that it complements.

NUTS

Nuts are high in monounsaturated fats, low in saturated fats, and free of trans-fatty acids and cholesterol. Almonds are particularly high in calcium, cashews are high in zinc, and walnuts are rich in valuable omega-3 fatty acids. Nuts are great sources of antioxidants, including selenium (especially Brazil nuts) and vitamin E, and are good sources of protein and fiber. Important trace minerals, such as chromium, copper, magnesium, potassium, and zinc, are found in nuts.

Nuts add nutrition, flavor, and texture to a variety of dishes, such as the Sprouted Lentil Salad Plate (page 119) and Brown Rice, Mushroom, and Walnut Pilaf (page 207). Nuts are also great as snacks and are very portable. Pack them on their own or combine them with raisins, dried blueberries, or dried cranberries and take them along when biking, camping, or traveling.

OLIVES

There are many varieties of olives, and all of them are high in monounsaturated fatty acids. Most olives are cured or pickled in salty brine before they are sold. This means that in addition to healthful fats, ¼ cup (60 ml) of pickled olives provides 250 milligrams of sodium, or about one-sixth of the daily recommended intake. The key is eating olives in moderation or seeking lower-sodium options. Because raw foods are increasingly in demand, raw olives that are not high in salt are now available.

SEEDS

Chia seeds, hempseeds, poppy seeds, pumpkin seeds, sesame seeds, and sunflower seeds are all good sources of omega-6 fatty acid. Even more important is the fact that chia seeds, flaxseeds, and hempseeds are high in hard-to-get omega-3 fatty acids. Seeds vary in their protein content, ranging from 12 to over 30 percent of calories. They are among the richest sources of vitamin E and contain an impressive variety of other vitamins, minerals (including zinc), phytochemicals, and fiber.

It is important to remember that one gram of fat contains nine calories whether it is found in whole foods or extracted oils. Just because avocados, nuts, olives, and seeds are better eaten whole does not mean they are meant to be eaten in unlimited amounts. Typically, ¼ cup (60 ml) of nuts or seeds provides 1 tablespoon (15 ml) of oil.

Flaxseeds. Flaxseeds, also known as linseeds, offer a significant advantage for vegans as their oils have the greatest omega-3 fatty acid content of any commonly eaten food, averaging about 57 percent omega-3 fatty acid. They also contain a little of the more easily obtained omega-6 fatty acids. Flaxseeds and flaxseed oil are valuable because they can help bring the ratio of these essential fatty acids to the more desirable two or four parts omega-6 fatty acids to one part omega-3 fatty acids. For that reason, flaxseeds can go a long way toward correcting essential fatty acid imbalances in the modern diet (see sidebar, page 18).

Flaxseeds are very high in soluble fiber, which is the type of fiber that lowers blood pressure, cholesterol, and triglyceride levels. Flaxseeds can also improve blood sugar response in people with diabetes and may improve immune system and inflammatory disorders.

Because flaxseeds are so small and hard, they can pass into the stomach without being broken open by chewing and may not be digested. Consequently, the seeds are best ground before being consumed. Here is an easy way to incorporate flaxseeds into your diet: Process 1 cup (250 ml) of whole flaxseeds in a blender or coffee grinder and store the ground flaxseeds in the refrigerator or freezer. Mix 1 to 2 tablespoons (15 to 30 ml) of ground flaxseeds into a smoothie or salad dressing or sprinkle them over steamed vegetables or cooked rice. You can even use ground flaxseeds as a garnish for soup. (For instructions on how to use ground flaxseeds as an egg replacer, see the sidebar on page 29.)

Hempseeds. Hemp is a crop that holds a lot of nutritional promise. Like other oil seeds, hempseeds typically contain about 31 percent fat by weight. The ratio of omega-6 fatty acids to omega-3 fatty acids in hempseeds (or hempseed oil) is ideal at 3:1.

Shelled hempseeds are used in the Banana-Blueberry Power Drink (page 64) and Green Smoothie (page 65). They provide abundant nutrition and long-lasting energy for children, adults, and athletes. Hempseeds are very versatile and can be eaten raw; made into nondairy milk; turned into hummus; sprinkled over noodles, salad greens, or pizza; used to thicken salad dressings; added to most baked goods; or incorporated into raw pie crusts.

Pumpkin seeds. Pumpkin seeds are nutritional powerhouses that supply a host of nutrients, including iron, magnesium, potassium, and zinc. Most of the fatty acids in pumpkin seeds come from monounsaturated fats and polyunsaturated fats in the form of omega-6 fatty acid. One-quarter cup (60 ml) of pumpkin seeds has 184 calories, 12 grams of fat, and 10 grams of protein. They have slightly less fat than sunflower seeds and 30 percent more protein.

Sesame seeds. Sesame seeds are primarily grown for their rich and flavorful oil content; however, they are even more valuable as a whole food. Sesame seeds are abundant in the minerals calcium, copper, iron, magnesium, and manganese. In addition to these key nutrients, sesame seeds contain lignans, which have antioxidant properties that help fight cancer.

Sesame seeds add a nutty taste and crunch to foods. However, like flaxseeds, sesame seeds are so small, they will not be digested properly unless they are ground. To solve this problem, grind 1 cup (250 ml) of seeds in a blender or coffee grinder for five to seven seconds, or until they are mostly broken apart. Store the partially ground seeds in the refrigerator or freezer and add them to smoothies; sprinkle them over cooked grains, salads, and steamed vegetables; or add them to pie crusts. Tahini is made of ground sesame seeds and is highly digestible. It can be eaten as a spread on bread, drizzled over pancakes, used to make a dressing or sauce, or used to thicken soups. Try it in the much-loved Heart-Healthy Hummus (page 81).

Sunflower seeds. Mild and nutty, sunflower seeds can be eaten as a protein-rich snack between meals or easily incorporated into the main meal. These seeds are a rich source of vitamin E, a powerful antioxidant that neutralizes free radicals in the body and has an anti-inflammatory effect. Sunflower seeds are also a good source of B vitamins and the minerals copper, iron, manganese, selenium, and zinc. One-quarter cup (60 ml) of sunflower seeds contains 6 grams of protein.

Start the day by adding sunflower seeds to the Banana-Blueberry Power Drink (page 64) and Green Smoothie (page 65), and try the Sunflower-Sesame Spread (page 83) with the Raw Vegetable Platter (page 86) as a snack.

Good Fats from Oils

The best way to achieve the daily recommendation for fat is to eat whole plant-based foods that are rich in the oils that the body requires. Though an increasing number of people prefer to get their fats exclusively from whole plant foods, the oils that are extracted from these foods also play a role in the diets of most people. Given the extensive variety of oils that line grocery store shelves, choosing the right oil for food preparation can be confusing and overwhelming. The following information is provided to help you understand how most cooking oils are made, which may be useful as you make your selections.

HOW OILS ARE PROCESSED

The majority of edible oils are made using one of two extraction methods: expeller pressing or solvent extraction. Both processes generate high temperatures that strip the oil of most of its nutrition, including omega-3 fatty acids, which are extremely sensitive to heat.

In the expeller-pressed method, seeds are cooked for up to two hours to soften the cells that contain the oil. Then the seeds are pushed against a press head, where enormous pressure generates temperatures of up to 200 degrees F (95 degrees C). The heat damages the essential fatty acids in the oil, and light and oxygen also contribute to deterioration. Expeller-pressed oils are then filtered, bottled, and may be labeled as "cold-pressed," "natural," or "unrefined."

The solvent extraction method is the predominant method used today to produce oil from seeds, nuts, and legumes. The principal solvent is hexane, a highly flammable by-product of the petroleum industry and a known carcinogen. Solvent-extracted oils may be mixed with mechanically pressed oils and labeled as "unrefined."

Refined oils are further subjected to heat—as much as 200 degrees F (95 degrees C) to 480 degrees F (250 degrees C) for up to one hour, chemicals (such as caustic soda and phosphoric acid) are added to remove gums such as lecithin, bleaching (to remove naturally occurring pigments), and deodorization. Several synthetic antioxidants are added to replace those that were removed in processing. Inert refined oil can keep on the shelf for years.

HYDROGENATION

The shelf life, stability, and smoke point (see sidebar, page 23) of liquid oils can be increased by turning them into solid or semisolid fats (such as margarine, oil for deep-frying, and vegetable shortening) through a process called hydrogenation. Hydrogen atoms are added to unsaturated oil at high temperatures, which drastically changes the shape of the oil molecule and how it is processed in the body. The resulting hydrogenated fats, which are harmful to human health, are also known as trans fats. The principal danger associated with trans fats is an elevated risk of coronary artery disease. Other diseases, such as cancer, diabetes, and obesity, have also been linked to the consumption of trans fats.

Hydrogenated and partially hydrogenated fats are used by the ton in processed foods, snacks, and fast food. These fats keep cakes moist, cookies crisp, chips crunchy, and breads soft. The Food and Drug Administration requires food manufacturers to list trans fats on food labels; however, levels of less than 0.5 grams per serving can be listed as 0 grams trans fats on labels. Health advocates strongly believe this small amount is still harmful and recommend that people avoid trans fats altogether. The National Academy of Sciences has concluded there is no safe level of trans fat consumption.

COLD-PRESSED OILS

Cold-pressed oils are produced within a narrow temperature range that protects the nutritional integrity of vital omega-3 fatty acids and vitamin E, a powerful antioxidant. Oils that are valued for their content of omega-3 fatty acids (such as flaxseed or hempseed oils) are pressed at between 80 and 92 degrees F (27 and

We do not recommend cooking foods at high temperatures or deep-frying, nor do we feature these methods in this book. However, understanding the concept of "smoke point" may be helpful when choosing cooking oils. An oil's smoke point is the temperature at which it starts to break down and gives off a bluish smoke that may contain carcinogens. If an oil is heated above its smoke point, its flavor and nutritional properties will be greatly diminished.

Highly refined oils have higher smoke points than cold-pressed oils because vulnerable components that can smoke and become damaged, including fatty acids, protective phytochemicals, and vitamins, have been removed. Unrefined, cold-pressed coconut oil will smoke at 375 degrees F (190 degrees C), whereas refined coconut oil will not smoke until it is heated to 450 degrees F (230 degrees C). Extra-virgin olive oil will smoke at 325 degrees F (160 degrees C), whereas more refined olive oil will not smoke until it is heated to 420 degrees F (216 degrees C).

33 degrees C). Cold-pressed coconut oil and extra-virgin olive oil are pressed at or below 120 degrees F (49 degrees C).

Consumers may believe that cold-pressed oils have been extracted by mechanical pressure and without heat; however, it is important to note that the term "cold-pressed" is not subject to regulation in the United States. The lack of regulation leaves it up to the consumer to determine which oil producers make genuine claims on their labels. Some oils that are labeled cold-pressed are actually pressed at temperatures as high as 200 degrees F (95 degrees C) or mixed with oils that are refined.

You can expect to pay more for cold-pressed oils because the methods used for extraction yield less oil than processes that involve higher temperatures or solvents. When shopping for oil, read labels carefully. Manufacturers that produce high-quality oils will provide sufficient information to let you know that you are holding a premium product in your hands. The extra cost is worth it.

Another valuable feature of cold-pressed oils is flavor; their complex aromatic fragrances and taste profiles are preserved, adding layers, depth, and variety. Cold-pressed oils may be added to salad dressings, sprinkled over grains or steamed vegetables, tossed with cold or hot noodles, or used to garnish soups. Remember, however, that whole foods that contain oils (such as avocados, nuts, olives, and seeds) can be even better choices.

Cooking and Salad Oils

We use a variety of oils in our recipes, depending on how the recipes will be prepared and how they'll complement the flavors of the ingredients. The two principal cooking oils are coconut oil and extra-virgin olive oil. Two oils that should never be heated are flaxseed oil and hempseed oil, which are both excellent sources of omega-3 fatty acids and great for making salad dressings.

Coconut oil. Coconut oil can be used to sauté vegetables or to replace liquid oil in baking if it is heated just enough to become liquid. If all remaining recipe ingredients are at room temperature, the warmed liquid coconut oil will remain liquid and incorporate well into the recipe.

Flaxseed oil. Flaxseed oil must be stored in the refrigerator or freezer. It should never be used for cooking, because heat destroys omega-3 fatty acids. Some people initially dislike the taste of flaxseed oil but later grow to appreciate its rich flavor. To get your omega-3 fatty acids for the day, include 1 to 2 teaspoons (5 to 10 ml) of flaxseed oil.

Hempseed oil. Hempseed oil is green in color and has a pleasant nutty flavor that some people even compare to fresh grass. You can get your day's supply of omega-3 fatty acids from 1 tablespoon (15 ml) of hempseed oil or ¼ cup (60 ml) of hempseeds. Like flaxseed oil, hempseed oil should never be used for cooking.

Olive oil. Oils that are obtained directly from the fruit of the olive without the use of solvents are classified as "extra-virgin olive oil," "virgin olive oil," "refined olive oil," and "olive oil." Oil producers are required to list one of these designations on their food labels. Of these varieties, extra-virgin olive oil is superior in terms of nutrition and flavor. It can be used for cooking when it will not be heated above its smoke point (see page 23). Other grades of olive oil are more refined, and the more refined they are, the more nutritional damage has occurred and the less flavor they have.

Pomace oils are treated with solvents in an attempt to extract every last drop of oil. Ground olive pulp and pits, known as pomace, is what remains after olive oil has been extracted from the fruit. Pomace oil is cheap and inferior due to the solvent method used to extract it.

Other Good Oils for Special Use

Sesame oil. In this book, unrefined sesame oil and tahini, the delicious butter made from whole sesame seeds, are used in salad dressings (such as Asian Dressing, page 125). When sesame seeds are toasted and pressed, an aromatic amber oil is produced, which adds a delicious, nutty flavor to Asian stir-fries, marinades, and salad dressings. Because its flavor is intense, toasted sesame oil should be used in small quantities.

Sunflower seed oil. Sunflower seed oil is used for cooking and baking and also in salad dressings. It has a higher smoke point than many other oils, making it more stable when heated.

Vegan buttery spread. There are a growing number of vegan buttery spreads available, and the best ones are nonhydrogenated and free of genetically modified ingredients. These spreads give baked goods a buttery taste without a trace of dairy, and they can be used in all kinds of baking whenever butter or shortening is called for. One popular brand is Earth Balance.

Sweeteners

Sweeteners vary widely, both in terms of their source and their cost. Because a variety of sweeteners could be used in our recipes with equally good results, we often leave the choice to you. If you're trying to use less sweetener, recipes like Baked Stuffed Apples (page 218) contain only ½ teaspoon (2 ml) per apple. Here's another tip: You can use less sweetener if you chew food well. The starch-breaking enzyme amylase in saliva creates sugars from the complex carbohydrates in many plant-based foods, so chewing in itself can satisfy a sweet tooth.

Certain sweeteners, such as blackstrap molasses or maple syrup, offer a wealth of flavor in addition to their inherent sweetness. Granulated sweeteners, such as brown or golden sugar (which are white sugars with some added molasses), dehydrated cane juice, raw sugar, and unbleached sugar, are all flavorful but offer minimal nutrition. Some sweeteners, such as rice syrup, contribute very little flavor.

Sweeteners can be granular (such as various sugars), or liquid (such as syrups), or somewhere in between (such as applesauce, dates, fruit juice concentrate, or mashed bananas). If you want to substitute one type for another in a recipe, you may need to adjust the amount of other wet or dry ingredients. Here are a few other things to consider when you choose a sweetener.

NUTRITION

If health is your priority, fruits have the most to offer as sweeteners. Top marks go to fresh or frozen fruit. For inspiration, see Fresh Fruit as Dessert (page 215), Vegan Dazs Ice Cream (page 217), and Watermelon and Fresh Fruit Sculpture (page 216). Dried fruit can give extra sweetness, as in Banana-Blueberry Power Drink (page 64), Design-Your-Own Muesli (page 67), and Mango-Strawberry Pie (page 236). (For a list of naturally sweet foods, see page 39.)

It makes sense to choose organic products for the environment and for health. Blackstrap molasses is rich in the minerals that are stripped from sugar cane; however, it can also be a concentrated source of pesticides and herbicides, so be sure to choose organic blackstrap molasses.

ETHICS

Some people make purchases based on ethical concerns. For example, buying fair trade sugar can reflect a desire to provide a living wage for farm laborers and their families. Also, environmentalists may not buy sugar because they object to the large quantities of fossil fuels that are used to process and transport sugarcane and sugar.

For vegans, compassion for animals tends to influence purchase decisions, including which sweetener to choose. Most vegans avoid cane sugar that has been filtered through bone char (charcoal made from animal bones). Though this practice is diminishing, some sugar cane refineries still use bone char to purify and whiten sugar. Note that beet sugar, which also may be simply labeled "sugar," is never produced using bone char. In the past, maple syrup was treated with a small amount of lard (pig fat) or other animal fat to reduce the foaming that occurs during production. Today, synthetic defoamers or vegetable oils are more commonly used. Honey is not a vegan product. See vegsource.com/jo/qa/qahoney.htm for more information.

Herbs and Spices

Herbs and spices create the magic in many recipes and are essential for developing flavor. Herbs are leafy parts of plants that are prized for their ability to season food and often for their medicinal qualities. Spices come from different parts of plants. For example, cinnamon is tree bark, cumin is ground from seeds, ginger is a root, peppercorns are berries, and saffron comes from a flower. In addition to providing flavor, spices are used to color food. Examples include saffron and turmeric.

Aromatic oils in herbs and spices impart flavors in cooking. These oils are volatile and can easily evaporate if not stored properly. Store herbs and spices in dark glass jars or opaque containers with tight-fitting lids to keep out damaging light and oxygen. Avoid storing herbs and spices near or above the oven, as heat quickly dissipates the valuable oils. Instead, store them in an enclosed dark space, such as a cupboard. Excess supplies can be stored in the freezer. Replace herbs that have lost their color and ground spices that no longer have a vibrant fragrance. Whole spices will keep indefinitely if stored properly.

Herbs and spices are best purchased where there is a high turnover and the products are fresh. It is also best to buy whole spices whenever possible, because until they are bruised, crushed, or ground, whole spices retain their oils. Turning spices into powder increases the surface area, exposing valuable oils to air, so ground spices immediately begin to lose potency. An inexpensive coffee grinder used solely for grinding spices, or a mortar and pestle, is a good investment that will allow you to grind spices, and tougher herbs like rosemary, as needed, allowing the full strength of their oils to emerge in a prepared dish.

Fresh herbs may be used instead of dried herbs in recipes provided the amount is adjusted. Use 1 tablespoon (15 ml) of fresh herbs to replace 1 teaspoon (5 ml) of dried herbs, and vice versa. For a list of the herbs and spices used in this book, see the Shopping List on page 30.

Nondairy Milks

It is important to select nondairy milks that are fortified (enriched) with vitamins B_{12}, vitamin D, and calcium. Nondairy milks are often the sole source of vitamin D in a vegan diet. The addition of vitamin D is permitted in just a few foods, such as milk, margarine, orange juice, and breakfast cereal. Be sure to check labels: The form added to some nondairy milks is vitamin D_2 (ergocalciferol), which is vegan, whereas others have added vitamin D_3 (cholecalciferol), which is of animal origin.

Although it is possible to get sufficient calcium from greens, including non-dairy milks in your diet will make it easier for you to reach a daily target of 1,000 to 1,300 milligrams (see page 240). For example, you can get 150 milligrams of calcium from either ½ cup (125 ml) of fortified nondairy milk or 1⅔ cups (420 ml) of kale. Nondairy milks that are labeled as "natural" typically are not fortified (check labels).

Nondairy milks can be made from almonds, hempseeds, oats, rice, or soybeans. In many recipes, different varieties of nondairy milks may be used interchangeably, with only slight differences in the final result. Soymilk is often recommended for children because its protein content is relatively high.

Commercial soymilk is made either from whole soybeans or soy protein isolate. For the former, whole soybeans are washed, soaked, ground, and cooked. The fibrous part of the mash, called okara, is filtered out and discarded, and the remaining soymilk is packaged with or without added flavoring and fortification.

Soymilks that are made from soy protein or soy protein isolate (check labels) are processed using a series of steps in which fractions of the whole soybean are extracted, often using acids, alkalis, and the solvent hexane. For that reason, you may prefer to use a soymilk that is made from whole soybeans.

Thickeners

Starches are the most common thickening agents. There are a number of plant-based thickeners, including ground flaxseeds, gums (such as xanthan gum), pectin, and sea vegetable extracts (such as agar). Most of these ingredients do not change the flavor of the final product, though some do. Examples of thickeners that do alter flavor include browned flour in a gumbo or seed or nut butters in a soup or salad dressing. Here are brief descriptions of the thickeners that are used in this book, along with instructions for how to use them.

AGAR

Agar, also known as agar-agar, is a sea vegetable extract that can be used as a substitute for gelatin, which is derived from the bones of cattle and horses. Agar

Using Agar as a Thickening Agent

Different amounts of agar flakes and agar powder are used to thicken the same amount of liquid. One tablespoon (15 ml) of agar *flakes* will thicken 1 cup (250 m) of liquid, and ½ teaspoon (2 ml) of agar *powder* will thicken 1 cup (250 ml) of liquid. Gooda Cheez (page 80) includes agar as an ingredient.

comes in several forms, including bars, flakes, and powder, and has valuable characteristics, such as the ability to gel liquids at a wide range of pH and temperatures. Agar is readily available in larger natural food stores and, generally for a much lower cost, in Asian markets.

Since agar bars, flakes, and powder differ considerably in density, be sure you are using the correct form specified in a recipe. For instance, if you were to use an equal measure of agar powder in a recipe that calls for flakes, the end product would likely resemble a rock-hard hockey puck, since agar powder is much denser than agar flakes. If an equal measure of agar flakes were used in a recipe that calls for agar powder, the end product would not gel properly.

Agar needs to be thoroughly dissolved in a hot liquid for it to gel. Agar bars may be crumbled before measuring and can then be measured as flakes. Thickening power may vary from one brand of agar to another. If you find that the specified amount of agar results in a product that is either too soft or too firm, take note and make the appropriate adjustment during your next attempt.

ARROWROOT STARCH

Arrowroot is a perennial tropical plant that produces a large rootlike stem from which a starch is extracted. Arrowroot starch is used to thicken custards, gravies, puddings, and sauces. It is also useful in thickening fruit pie fillings.

Arrowroot starch, which has a very delicate taste and is easily digested, can be used interchangeably with cornstarch. Arrowroot starch is the better choice when a transparent end result is desired, such as with a fruit sauce, rather than an opaque one. Because it is gluten-free, arrowroot starch is used in baking mixtures that replace wheat flours and other flours that contain gluten. Blueberry-Orange Sauce (page 178) includes arrowroot starch as an ingredient.

CORNSTARCH

Cornstarch is extracted from a large component of the corn kernel called the endosperm. Corn is falling out of favor with a growing number of consumers as more and more of the North American crop includes genetically modified organisms. To use cornstarch as a thickener, follow the same instructions provided for arrowroot starch (see below).

Using Arrowroot as a Thickening Agent

One tablespoon (15 ml) of arrowroot starch will thicken 1 cup (250 ml) of liquid. Before adding arrowroot starch to a recipe, dissolve it thoroughly in cold liquid to prevent clumping. Bring the liquid that is to be thickened to a boil and slowly but steadily pour the arrowroot starch mixture into the liquid while constantly stirring with a spoon or whisk. Do not simmer more than ten minutes, as overcooking or overmixing can cause the thickened liquid to become thin again.

Using Ground Flaxseeds as an Egg Replacer

A mixture of ground flaxseeds and water can be used to replace eggs in baking. Here is the recipe:

1 tablespoon (15 ml) ground flaxseeds

3 tablespoons (45 ml) water

Put the ground flaxseeds and water in a small bowl. Stir until well combined. Let rest for 5 to 10 minutes, until thickened. Use in baked goods as a substitute for one egg.

FLAXSEEDS

Ground flaxseeds are commonly used to thicken smoothies. See Liquid Gold Dressing (page 126) to see how they can be used to increase the viscosity of a liquid. They also can be used as an egg replacer to help bind ingredients in baked goods. Soaking ground flaxseeds in a small amount of water creates a gelatinous mixture similar to egg whites that can be used in recipes such as muffins, pancakes, waffles, and in most baking that calls for one or two eggs (see above). Alternatively, ground flaxseeds can simply be added to the wet ingredients as directed, as in the recipe for Apple Spice Cake (page 220).

To grind flaxseeds, put 1 cup (250 ml) of whole flaxseeds in a blender or coffee grinder and process for 30 seconds, stopping after 15 seconds to stir the seeds, or until the seeds are ground. Ground flaxseeds can be stored in a tightly sealed jar in the freezer for up to one year.

NUTS, SEEDS, AND THEIR BUTTERS

Ground nuts, seeds, and their butters make excellent thickeners for cheeselike toppings and rich salad dressings and soups. Tahini and cashews impart unique flavors and are particularly effective thickening agents that are used in Lemon-Tahini Dressing (page 134) and Cashew Cheese Lasagne (page 170). Peanut butter (made from peanuts, which are legumes rather than nuts) is another good thickener and is used in African Chickpea Stew (page 152).

VEGETABLES

The consistency of a liquid can thicken and change when vegetables are added. One common example is the use of tomato paste to thicken a sauce or soup. The starch in root vegetables also can be an effective thickener, as in the Ginger, Carrot, and Yam Soup (page 94). Winter squash and roasted chestnuts also can be used as thickeners when pureed.

Using soft, grated vegetables that have a high water content is a novel way of thickening a liquid. In Cucumber-Dill Dressing (page 128), the grated cucumber and zucchini give the dressing body and consistency, significantly decreasing the amount of oil that is normally used for that purpose in salad dressing.

WHEAT FLOUR

Wheat flour is classically used to make a roux to thicken hot liquids. Equal parts of oil and white flour are combined to thicken soups, sauces, and gravies. The use of flour makes a very smooth end product, and for this reason it has been used in French cuisine since the mid-seventeenth century. However, as more people become allergic, intolerant, or sensitive to wheat, other thickening agents are becoming common. Light Mushroom Gravy (page 186) and Rosemary Gravy (page 188) are thickened with flour.

Shopping List

The following shopping list is a convenient resource that itemizes both the staples used in our recipes and ingredients that may be used only occasionally or for recipe variations. You may wish to photocopy the list and include additional items of your own. Buy fresh produce as needed and in season. Dry ingredients can be purchased in appropriate amounts and stored indefinitely in sealed containers in a cool, dry place. For the best price, look for sources that offer grains and legumes in bulk.

VEGETABLES

Asparagus

Avocados

Beets

Bell peppers (green; orange; red; yellow)

Bok choy

Broccoli

Cabbage (green, napa; red, savoy)

Carrots

Cauliflower

Celery

Collard greens

Corn (on the cob; fresh or frozen kernels)

Cucumbers

Eggplant

Fennel bulb

Garlic

Ginger

Green beans

Kale

Lettuce (butterhead; leaf; romaine)

Mushrooms (cremini; portobello; shiitake; white)

Onions (green; red; white; yellow)

Parsley

Parsnips

Potatoes (gold; red-skinned; russet; yellow nugget)

Radishes (daikon; red; watermelon; white)

Snap peas

Snow peas

Spinach

Sprouts (alfalfa; lentil; mung; mustard; radish; red clover)

Sweet potatoes

Tomatoes

Turnips (young)

Winter squash

Yams

Zucchini

FRUITS (FRESH)

Apples

Bananas

Blueberries

Lemons

Limes

Mangoes

Oranges

Papaya

Pineapple

Raspberries

Strawberries

Watermelon

FRUITS (DRIED)

Blueberries

Coconut (unsweetened shredded)

Cranberries

Currants

Dates

Mango

Raisins (dark; golden)

Tamarind pulp

GRAINS AND GRAIN PRODUCTS

Amaranth

Barley

Buckwheat

Flour (unbleached all-purpose; whole wheat pastry, spelt)

Kamut berries

Millet

Oats (old-fashioned rolled)

Oat groats

Pita bread

Quinoa

Rice (brown; short-grain brown; white basmati, arborio)

Spelt berries

Sticky (sushi) rice

Wheat berries

Whole wheat burger buns

Wild rice

LEGUMES

Adzuki beans

Black beans

Cannellini beans

Chickpeas

Great northern beans

Green split peas

Lentils

Lima beans

Mung beans

Pinto beans

Swedish brown beans

White beans

SOYFOODS

Miso (dark; light)

Soymilk (fortified)

Tamari

Tempeh

Tofu (soft; medium; firm; extra-firm)

Tofu, silken (firm; extra-firm)

Vegan meat alternatives (deli slices; wieners, Gardein Chick'n)

NUTS, SEEDS, BUTTERS

Almond butter

Almonds

Cashews

Coconut (unsweetened shredded)

Flaxseeds (whole or ground)

Hempseeds (shelled)

Peanut butter

Pumpkin seeds

Sesame seeds

Sunflower seeds

Tahini

Walnuts

FATS AND OILS

Coconut oil

Extra-virgin olive oil

Flaxseed oil

Hempseed oil

Sunflower seed oil

Toasted sesame oil

Unrefined sesame oil

Vegan buttery spread

© *Cooking Vegan* by Vesanto Melina, MS, RD, and Joseph Forest, Professional Chef

HERBS AND SPICES

Allspice (ground)
Basil (dried; fresh)
Bay leaves
Cardamom (ground)
Cayenne
Celery seeds
Chili paste
Chili powder
Cilantro
Cinnamon (ground)
Cloves (ground; whole)
Coriander (ground; whole seeds)
Cumin (ground; whole seeds)
Curry powder
Dill weed
Fennel seeds
Garam masala
Garlic powder
Lemongrass
Marjoram
Mint
Mustard seeds
Onion powder
Oregano
Paprika
Pepper (ground black; ground white)
Peppercorns
Red chiles (fresh)
Red pepper flakes
Rosemary
Salt
Thyme (dried)
Turmeric (ground)
Yellow mustard (dry)

BAKING SUPPLIES

Active dry yeast
Baking powder
Vanilla extract

BEVERAGES

Almond milk (fortified)
Apple juice (unsweetened concentrate)
Hempseed milk (fortified)
Orange juice concentrate
Pineapple juice
Rice milk (fortified)

DRY GOODS

Breadcrumbs
Lasagna noodles
Macaroni
Nutritional yeast flakes
Sun-dried tomatoes

JARRED OR CANNED PRODUCTS

Artichoke hearts
Capers
Dijon mustard
Kalamata olives
Olives (black; green)
Patak's Mild Curry Paste
Pesto
Pimientos
Salsa
Thai curry paste
Yellow mustard

MISCELLANEOUS ITEMS

Agar (flakes; powder)
Arrowroot starch
Coconut milk
Mayonnaise (vegan)
Nori
Refried beans
Sake
Shiitake mushrooms (dried)
Tomato paste
Tomato sauce
Tomatoes (canned)
Tortillas
Vinegar (balsamic; cider; rice)
Vegetable stock (cubes; powder; liquid)
Wasabi

SEASONINGS

Almond extract
Chipotle chiles
Spike (a brand-name seasoning)

EXTRAS
(for recipe variations)

Almond extract
Barley flakes
Celeriac
Corn pasta
Pickled ginger
Pickles
Rice flakes
Rice pasta
Rye flakes
Water chestnuts
Whole wheat flakes

© *Cooking Vegan* by Vesanto Melina, MS, RD, and Joseph Forest, Professional Chef

chapter 3

Vegan Cooking

Cooking is both an art and a science. As with any art, there are unlimited ways of assimilating, blending, and combining materials—whether they are food ingredients, musical notes, or watercolors—to produce a new and satisfying result. In this chapter, we'll explore the artistic side of cooking and how to use all your senses in the kitchen. In addition, we'll discuss the six tastes that will be your palette: astringent, bitter, pungent, salty, sour, and sweet.

When you pair your creativity with an understanding of culinary science and cooking procedures, you can produce unforgettable meals. Every process and technique used in the kitchen today can be understood and explained by science. The good news is that you don't need a degree to make a spicy soup or tangy vinaigrette. You need only understand basic culinary techniques to advance your cooking skills and eliminate errors in the kitchen. We will share these basics and some of our favorite tips in this chapter.

The Science of Nutrition

In addition to the science of cooking, there is the science of nutrition. Nutrition can be summarized as the study of nourishment, or the act of taking nutrients into the body for the purpose of building and maintaining health. Nutrition proponents have been advising humans how to eat for hundreds of years. In 400 BC, Hippocrates, the father of modern medicine, told his students: "Our food should be our medicine. Our medicine should be our food." He also said: "A wise man should consider that health is the greatest of human blessings."

Nutrition research tells us how much of a particular nutrient is present in any given food, why we need specific nutrients, and the amounts we need to maintain or regain health. Knowing what nutrients your body needs and the food sources of those nutrients is a foundation for well-being.

For some people, food is a central theme in enjoying life. Sometimes referred to as foodies, these folks delight in discovering new ingredients, cooking, and eating. For them, there simply aren't enough meals in a day to prepare all the foods they want to try. Their kitchens are full of staples and gadgets, and their refrigerators are overflowing with items for the next dinner party. Their travel plans are built around sampling exotic cuisines. Closer to home, visits to the market are adventures in themselves, where colors, aromas, and sounds are all part of a culinary wild carpet ride.

For people at the other end of the spectrum, food is just another commodity. Preparing and eating it is a chore that takes time away from more important things. In contrast, these folks have mostly empty refrigerators, except for a few bottles of sauce just in case they are forced to make a meal. For them, cooking is a chaotic struggle that ends in frustration, disappointment, and a renewed resolution to buy prepackaged entrées or eat out more often.

If you are a foodie, this book may serve you by extending your love of food into the vegan arena. If preparing food is more of a utilitarian act for you, this book may broaden your interest in cooking, enhance your relationship with food, and rouse your appreciation for home cooking.

This book is designed to assist vegans, and others who are interested in eating plant-based foods, in pursuing optimum health. Ensuring that your diet is well balanced and provides all the nutrients you need will keep you and your family in excellent health and may also inspire others to eat more vegan meals.

The Science of Perception: The Physical Senses

To expand your awareness, skills, and confidence in the kitchen, engage all five senses. Hearing, seeing, smelling, tasting, and touching are the physical means by which you perceive the physical world. Your ears, eyes, nose, tongue, and hands help you navigate through your life; in the kitchen, they are indispensable tools.

By employing all five senses when you prepare food, you can improve your dexterity, enhance your timing, stimulate your creativity, and unleash your intuitive abilities. Enter the kitchen without being attuned to your senses, and you are more susceptible to disorganization, frustration, mistakes, and possibly even injury.

"We eat with our eyes first" is a common expression that demonstrates how our senses can be transfixed by food before we even sample a morsel. Indeed, our senses are engaged long before we assemble ingredients on the kitchen counter—they are essential when we shop for food.

Consider the sensory feast you experience during a trip to the local market. This input determines your choices. You handle avocados, lemons, and peaches to find out how ripe they are. Sniffing a tomato can tell you the same. You tap a watermelon, listening for the right thud. Bending fresh green beans in search of a crisp snap tells you if they are fresh. You nibble a free sample in the deli section and follow the scent of freshly ground coffee beans or newly baked bread. Conversely, when a bad food odor repulses, you steer away from a questionable item.

USING YOUR SENSES IN THE KITCHEN

The same senses you rely on when shopping can guide you in the kitchen. Here's how to hear, see, smell, taste, and touch your way to culinary success.

Hearing. Pay attention to the sounds around you as you cook. Listen to the sizzle of onions in the skillet, the turbulent roil of boiling water, and the popping of pumpkin seeds roasting in the oven. Follow important cues. For example, when you hear a saucepan lid rattling, the liquid is simmering too strongly and you need to decrease the heat. Cooking sounds are loaded with information. Often, they indicate the need to move on to the next step of the recipe.

Seeing. The recipes in this book tell you how long each step will take. Many times, a visual cue is also provided. For instance, the instructions to "cook the onions for 3 minutes, or until soft," or "cook the pancake for 3 minutes, or until the bottom is crispy brown" include visual cues. By looking for and becoming familiar with these indicators, you can relax and not be fixated on the clock, timer, or recipe instructions.

Smelling. Use your sense of smell to connect with food. Occasionally move your nose closer to the cutting board and sniff the food as you work with it. Zero in on the scents of chopped garlic, freshly cut herbs, spices in the grinder, and grated lemon zest. Bend your head over a skillet or soup pot and take a deep whiff.

Tasting. There are six tastes (see below) that play important roles in balancing a dish on its own or in relation to the whole meal. A dish or meal is well balanced when all six tastes are activated during the course of eating. For lists of foods categorized by taste, see pages 36 to 37.

Touching. How a kitchen tool feels in your hand can tell you a lot about the food you are preparing. For example, when you pierce a vegetable with a sharp knife to test for doneness, assess the ease with which the blade moves. As you cook, use your mouth to evaluate doneness. For instance, bite into a green bean or noodle to check if it is tender or al dente. Professionals often use the term "mouthfeel" to describe the quality that a food has in the mouth. Wine tasters use this term to describe the qualities of wine.

THE SIX TASTES

Taste buds are specialized cells in the mouth that detect six basic tastes: astringent, bitter, pungent, salty, sour, and sweet. Western science recognizes only four tastes (bitter, salty, sour, and sweet), with a fifth taste, umami, more recently discovered, but Eastern schools of thought recognize two more (astringent and pungent).

Astringent. Astringent tastes can make the mouth feel dry, puckered, and constricted. These sensations are caused by tannins, substances in some foods and wine that tighten mucous membranes, contract tissues, and decrease inflammation. Tannins have a cleansing effect on the palate, which is why many people enjoy drinking wine with meals. Astringent foods can cause difficulty swallowing. The drying effect of astringent foods can balance out the excessive salivation or perspiration caused by pungent foods. Astringent foods tend to be more alkaline, whereas sour foods are more acidic.

Examples of astringent foods include cranberries, green bananas, leafy greens, legumes (beans, lentils, peas, and soyfoods), pomegranates, potatoes, and turmeric. For a more complete list of astringent foods, see page 38.

Bitter. Bitterness is detected at the very back of the tongue. Because many poisonous substances in nature are bitter, the tongue acts as a gatekeeper, providing a warning if a potentially toxic substance is about to be swallowed. However, not all bitter foods are bad; often, the reverse is true. For example, bitter foods are a valued part of each meal in Japan, where people recognize their role in supporting good health. Bitter foods have an alkalinizing effect on the blood, acting as a buffer and balancing acidity. They also stimulate digestion and immediately wake up the palate, creating a desire for balance with other tastes.

Foods we find bitter, such as grapefruit, green tea, or leafy greens, contain health-promoting phytochemicals. Examples are the glucosinolates in broccoli, cabbage, cauliflower, kale, and other cruciferous vegetables, which have cancer-preventive properties.

Overcooking bitter vegetables can make them more bitter, so eat them raw or lightly steamed or cooked. Add bitter vegetables to soups, stews, or stir-fries at the end of the cooking process, heating until they are just cooked and tender yet firm.

Examples of bitter foods include Brussels sprouts, chocolate, cumin, and plums. For a more complete list of bitter foods, see page 38.

Pungent. Pungent tastes are acrid, biting, hot, spicy, and strong. In small amounts, pungent tastes stimulate digestion, clear the sinuses, dispel gas, and help detoxify the body. Too much can cause excessive salivation, leading to a dry mouth and increased thirst. Shortly after consuming pungent foods, the body heats up and may perspire. This is a natural cooling mechanism and the reason that pungent foods are consumed in large quantities in hot climates.

Examples of pungent foods include chiles, citrus zest, garlic, mustard greens, and onions; pungent spices include black pepper, cayenne, cinnamon, and ginger. For a more complete list of pungent foods, see page 38.

Salty. Salt is nature's true and original flavor enhancer. It adds depth, strength, and vigor to food and stimulates the appetite by activating saliva and other digestive juices. Salt can enhance the flavor of food; however, when used in excess, salt can overwhelm the other flavors in a dish.

Examples of salty foods include salt (naturally), bottled sauces, bouillon cubes or powder, and tamari. For a more complete list of salty foods, see page 39.

Sour. Sour foods sharpen the senses, stimulate the appetite, and promote digestion. They also have a cleansing effect on the palate and body. A sour food added at the end of a recipe makes it bright by accentuating and sharpening the inherent top notes (see page 40). Sourness enhances other flavors, adds intensity, and can decrease the need for salt. Balancing the acid content of a dish is critical to its success.

Examples of sour foods include lemongrass, lemons, molasses, and vinegar. For a more complete list of sour foods, see page 39.

Sweet. In whole foods, such as fruits and root vegetables, a sweet taste is provided by naturally occurring sugars. In many prepared foods, sweetness is created by the addition of extracted sugars from beets or cane sugar, or agave nectar, barley malt, maple syrup, or other processed sweeteners. However, foods can be sweet even without added sugars: when the long chains of complex carbohydrates are broken down into their constituent glucose molecules by the action of salivary amylase in the mouth, a sweet taste results. For example, when you chew a mouthful of brown rice twenty to thirty times before swallowing, the rice will release an inherent sweetness that can be discerned by the taste buds. In short, chewing can be a sweet experience in itself.

Like salt, sweeteners enhance the flavor of food. They accentuate desserts the way salt accentuates savory foods. In addition, sweetness can balance or smooth out the other tastes and take the edge off any harsh tones. Sweetness is soothing and relieves thirst.

Examples of sweet foods include apricots, corn, nuts, rice, seeds, and many herbs and spices. For a more complete list of sweet foods, see page 39.

Putting It All Together

The word "flavor" is often used as a synonym for "taste." In truth, flavor has a broader meaning, encompassing what we perceive through the nerves in our mouth, nose, and other sensory organs, including the eyes. Other nonphysical factors, such as frame of mind (mood), environment (romantic atmosphere), social conditioning (belief systems), and personal thoughts (judgments), all determine how flavor is perceived by an individual at a particular time. Flavor is very subjective, and the final verdict rests with each person.

Flavors are routinely synthesized in laboratories and added to practically every processed food on the market to enhance the appeal of products and create uniformity. In our recipes, however, flavor is derived from natural, unadulterated food.

Taste, on the other hand, is less subjective than flavor, although individuals vary physically and genetically in their ability to perceive various tastes. Good cooking may be viewed as the ability to bring the six tastes into harmony, assembling astringent, bitter, pungent, salty, sour, and sweet foods to create balanced and appealing flavor combinations.

There are good reasons why recipe ingredients are not all combined at once in a bowl or saucepan, stirred together, and served. Instead, there are steps to assembling most recipes. Cooking is a process of building layers; for the best results, develop and complete each layer before starting the next one. Base flavors

Foods Grouped According to the Six Tastes

Examining each list that follows will deepen your understanding of how the tastes can be combined with harmonious results. Note that some foods are found in more than one category; these foods typically have a primary taste and a different secondary taste.

ASTRINGENT FOODS	
FRESH AND DRIED FRUITS	Apples, apricots, blackberries, cranberries, lemons, plantains, pomegranates, raspberries, strawberries
VEGETABLES	Alfalfa sprouts, asparagus, collard greens, kale, lettuce, okra, potatoes, Swiss chard, turnips
BEANS	Adzuki beans, bean sprouts, black beans, black-eyed peas, chickpeas, kidney beans, lentils, lima beans, navy beans, pinto beans, soybeans, tempeh, tofu
MISCELLANEOUS	Black tea, turmeric, walnuts, white wine

BITTER FOODS	
FRUITS	Grapefruit, lemons, plums
VEGETABLES	Alfalfa sprouts, artichoke hearts, arugula (rocket), bean sprouts, beet greens, beets, bitter melon, broccoli, brussels sprouts, collard greens, cucumbers (under some circumstances), dandelion greens, eggplants, endive, fennel stalks, garlic, horseradish, kale, lettuce, mustard greens, parsnips, radicchio, radishes, rapini, rutabagas, spinach, Swiss chard, turnips
HERBS AND SPICES	Basil, cilantro, coriander, cumin, hops, nutmeg, parsley, peppermint, thyme turmeric
BEVERAGES	Beer, black tea, coffee, tonic water
MISCELLANEOUS	Chocolate, cocoa, dulse, extra-virgin olive oil (some brands), molasses, seeds (such as flax, hemp, sesame, and sunflower)

PUNGENT FOODS	
FRESH AND DRIED FRUITS	Citrus zest (grapefruit, lemon, orange)
VEGETABLES	Arugula, garlic (raw), ginger (fresh) mizuna, mustard greens, savoy cabbage, watercress
FRESH AND DRIED CHILES	Green chiles (chipotle, jalapeño, and serrano), red chiles (including cayenne, crushed red pepper flakes, and paprika)
FRESH AND DRIED HERBS	Basil, bay leaf, chives, cilantro, dill, green onion, marjoram, mint, parsley, rosemary, safflower, sage, tarragon, thyme
SPICES	Allspice, anise, asafetida (hing), caraway seeds, cardamom, celery seeds, cinnamon, cloves, coriander seeds, cumin, curry powder, fennel seeds, fenugreek, ginger (ground), mustard seeds, peppercorns, saffron, star anise
CONDIMENTS	Chili paste, chipotle chiles in adobo sauce, curry paste, Dijon mustard, extra-virgin olive oil (some brands), garlic paste, horseradish, wasabi

SALTY FOODS	
CONDIMENTS	Bragg Liquid Aminos, miso, salt, shoyu, tamari
SNACKS	Chips, crackers, popcorn
FLAVORINGS	Bottled sauces, bouillon cubes, marinades, vegetable stock powder, yeast extract
PROCESSED FOODS	Olives, ready-to-eat entrées, sea vegetables (dried)

SOUR FOODS	
FRESH AND DRIED FRUITS	Apples, blackberries, blueberries, cherries, cranberries, grapefruit, grapes, lemons, limes, mangoes, oranges, pineapples, pomegranates, raspberries, rhubarb, sour cherries, spinach, strawberries, tamarind, tomatoes
HERBS AND SPICES	Asafetida, caraway seeds, coriander, dill, fennel, fenugreek, hibiscus, lemongrass, sorrel, tarragon
CONDIMENTS	Capers, olives, pickles, sauerkraut, vinegar
MISCELLANEOUS	Beer, black olives, bread (rye, sourdough, and pumpernickel), galangal, miso, molasses, pickles, red wine, sauerkraut, vinegar

SWEET FOODS	
FRESH AND DRIED FRUITS	Apples, apricots, avocados, bananas, blackberries, blueberries, cherries, cranberries, currants, dates, figs, grapefruit, grapes, honeydew melons, kiwifruit, mangoes, oranges, papayas, peaches, pears, pineapples, plantains, plums, pomegranates, prunes, raisins, raspberries, strawberries, watermelons
VEGETABLES	Asparagus, beets, bell peppers (especially orange, red, and yellow), cabbage (cooked), carrots, cauliflower, chestnuts, corn, cucumbers, garlic, leeks, okra, onions (especially red), parsnips, peas, potatoes, pumpkins, sweet potatoes, tapioca, tomatoes, winter squash (acorn, butternut, and kabocha), yams
GRAINS	Amaranth, barley, basmati rice, brown rice, buckwheat, bulgur, corn flour, cornmeal, kamut, millet, oatmeal, quinoa, rice, risotto, spelt, wheat, wild rice
NUTS AND SEEDS	Almonds, cashews, chestnuts, coconuts, pecans
HERBS AND SPICES	Allspice, basil, cardamom, cinnamon, fennel seeds, nutmeg
PREPARED FOODS	Breads, cakes, cookies, crepes, ice cream, muffins, pancakes, pasta, pies, waffles
SWEETENERS	Agave nectar, barley malt, brown rice syrup, brown sugar, confectioners' sugar, date sugar, fructose, malt, maple syrup, molasses, raw sugar, stevia, sucanat, turbinado sugar, white sugar
MISCELLANEOUS	Licorice, nutritional yeast flakes, roasted vegetables

are developed then built upon with ingredients that have middle and top notes. A single ingredient is blended with another, and then another, until they all come together to create a satisfying symphony of tastes.

One classic combination is onions, carrots, and celery, three aromatic vegetables that provide a base for sauces, soups, stews, and stocks. Other classic combinations include onions, garlic, and tomatoes in pasta sauce; ginger, curry powder or paste, and coconut milk in soup; and ginger, green onion, and tamari in dipping sauce.

Once a concentrated flavor base is developed, the next step is to add the main flavor ingredient of a dish. Examples include cauliflower or split peas in a soup, black beans or tomatoes in an entrée, and cranberries or plums in a chutney or relish.

The top notes in a recipe contains flavors that are a bit more subtle. You can detect a hint of them, but you can't quite identify them. This is the flavor that helps bring the whole dish to a peak of satisfaction. Top notes can be added at the very end of the recipe, for example, as fresh lemon or lime juice (see Savory Black Bean Soup, page 102); freshly cut herbs or chiles (see Baked Yams with Lemon and Green Chiles, page 198); or a combination of flavors, such as tamari and balsamic vinegar (see Portobello Mushrooms with Marjoram and Balsamic Vinegar, page 199).

Just before serving a dish, it is important to taste it and adjust the seasoning if required. This means more than just adding salt or pepper. Finer tuning may be needed to tweak the final taste and bring it into balance. Once you have a sense of how foods are categorized into different tastes, you will be more adept at adjusting seasonings.

Kitchen Organization: The Key to Success

Some rudimentary organizational skills can maximize your productivity and efficiency in the kitchen. The key to success is organization, which the French refer to as *mis en place*, meaning literally "everything in place." The following steps can help you attain positive results when using this book and a more enjoyable experience in the kitchen.

Following a Recipe

Recipes are similar to paint-by-number kits: every detail is laid out to help users reach a consistent and favorable result. Follow the steps diligently, and the same image or product that the creator had in mind will emerge for you.

Some people follow recipes exactly. Others, however, refer to recipes for inspiration or to ascertain the ratio of ingredients before they improvise. Once you understand how food ingredients interact with each other, you can start to assemble them in complementary ways according to your creative enthusiasm, culinary ability, and dietary preferences.

1. Read the recipe before starting. This step cannot be overemphasized. Develop the habit of reading recipes from beginning to end. This will give you an overview of the ingredients and equipment you will need, the recipe procedures, and the culinary techniques. If you don't understand a particular part of a recipe, review the procedure before you start rather than in the middle of preparing a dish. Furthermore, if a recipe points to important information on another page, examine that material before you begin.

2. Gather all needed equipment. This may include a cutting board, a food processor, knives, mixing bowls, measuring cups, pots, spoons, and so on. This step may prompt you to read the recipe again, so you don't miss anything. Reading the recipe a second time can further deepen your understanding of what you are about to achieve, especially if you have not made the recipe before.

3. Gather all the ingredients. Knowing up front that you have all the ingredients eliminates the frustration of discovering halfway through a recipe that you didn't replenish an important staple during your last shopping trip. This step also saves time. When you gather all the ingredients and have them in front of you before you begin, you will assemble a recipe more quickly than if you periodically stop cutting or measuring to return to the refrigerator or cupboard to look for the next item. This step also allows you to be more efficient. While you are preparing ingredients for the recipe, you may boil water for pasta, preheat the oven, or warm the skillet or soup pot on low heat.

4. Set up the counter space. This is not so much a step as a pattern to follow each time you prepare a dish. How you arrange and organize the ingredients and equipment just before cooking determines how smoothly and quickly the recipe takes shape. As an example, here is how I prepare Stir-Fry 101 (page 138).

First I clear the counter, removing everything I do not need. Then I lay down a damp dishcloth and set my cutting board on top to prevent slipping (a valuable safety tip when using sharp knives). I select the kitchen utensils I need from a wicker basket that holds spatulas, spoons, whisks, and so on. I gather all the ingredients and arrange them to the left of the cutting board, and I wash the items that require it. I heat the skillet on the lowest heat setting. (Heating a pan, pot, or skillet on the lowest setting distributes the heat so that when I increase the temperature, it comes up to medium heat in a very short time.) As I cut vegetables, I put them in separate piles on a baking sheet or large plate to the right of the cutting board. I measure all of the dry herbs and spices and put them in small bowls. I return ingredients that I no longer need to the cupboard or refrigerator. Finally, I proceed to the stove, where I am poised to cook.

How you set up your space is partly determined by how much you have to work with. If you are short on counter space, consider bringing a portable table, such as a TV tray, into the kitchen when you need an additional surface on which to organize ingredients.

When all ingredients are prepped and gathered within reach, cooking becomes a much easier task, whether you are stir-frying or making a soup. You won't have to worry about burning the onions while you're still cutting carrots. Your counter space will be much clearer, and with everything you need right at hand, you can simply focus on cooking. Being organized is the key to avoiding kitchen chaos.

Kitchen Equipment List

Consider kitchen equipment an investment in your health. Working with good equipment of any kind makes you feel capable and increases your willingness to perform the task at hand. Following is a basic inventory of the tools you will need to prepare all of the recipes in this book, though you may begin with a few of these items and add to your collection once you gain experience.

If your budget is limited, browse thrift stores, where you may be able to find many gently used items at affordable prices. Splurging on new high-quality kitchen knives is recommended. Visit a store that specializes in kitchen knives to acquire basic knowledge on how to purchase and use a knife and how to maintain a good edge. Serious cooks will want to purchase both a sharpening steel and stone for the best results.

COOKING UTENSILS

Baking dish, 13 x 9-inch (33 x 23-cm)

Baking sheets (2)

Muffin pans (2)

Pie pans (2), 8-inch (20-cm)

Pizza pan, 12-inch (30-cm)

Pots with lids (3), small, medium, large

Skillets (2), small and large

Steamer basket

Stockpot with lid, 12-quart (36-L)

Wok

ELECTRIC APPLIANCES

Blender

Coffee grinder (for grinding spices)

Food processor

KNIVES

Chef's knife, 10-inch (25-cm)

Paring knife

Serrated bread knife

Sharpening steel

Sharpening stone

HANDHELD TOOLS

Can opener

Pancake turner

Rubber spatulas (3), small, medium, large

Slotted spoon

Soup ladle

Spring-loaded tongs

Vegetable peeler

Vegetable scrub brush

Whisks (2), small and medium

Wooden spoons (2)

STORAGE ITEMS

Aluminum foil

Canisters and jars for grains, legumes, and other dry goods

Freezer containers

Plastic wrap

Storage containers with lids in many sizes

MISCELLANEOUS

Citrus juicer

Coffee grinder for grinding herbs and spices (optional)

Colander

Cutting boards (2), large and small

Food grater

Funnels (2), small and medium

Kitchen timer

Measuring cup set

Measuring cups, medium and large

Measuring spoon set

Mixing bowls (3), small, medium, large

Mortar and pestle

Rolling pin

Scissors

Strainers (2), small and medium

Zester or food rasp

chapter 4

Vegan Food Guide and Menus

This chapter features a Vegan Food Guide (see table 4.1, page 46), information about essential extras, and twelve menus that will help you meet your nutrient needs on a daily basis. The menus are all based on recipes in this book along with other plant-based foods.

We hope this information helps keep you on course—and in excellent health. Of course, we don't expect you to follow these suggestions rigidly. You don't need to meet the minimum intake from every food group every single day, but you should shoot for meeting intakes when averaged over time. Eating patterns can vary greatly and still meet recommended intakes.

The Vegan Food Guide combines servings of foods from different food groups that meet recommended intakes for all of the nutrients you need. It also emphasizes foods that will help you get sufficient amounts of calcium. Following the table are suggestions for getting other essentials, including omega-3 fatty acids, vitamins B_{12} and D, and iodine.

The Vegan Food Guide can help with meal planning for families, individuals or couples, people who want to lose weight, older adults whose energy requirements have decreased with age, raw food vegans, and athletes with high energy requirements. Following is some information about the food groups featured in the guide.

Vegetables. Vegetables are particularly nutrient-dense, meaning that they contain more vitamins (especially vitamins A and C and folate), protective phytochemicals, protein, and minerals per calorie than any other food group.

Fruits. Fruits, nature's healers and protectors, are rich in antioxidant vitamins, phytochemicals, and potassium but are lower in protein than vegetables. In the nutritional analyses that follow each menu in this chapter, fruit provides most of the sugar.

Legumes. This food group includes beans, lentils, peas, and soyfoods. Legumes, the protein powerhouses of the plant kingdom, are rich in iron and zinc, and important providers of the amino acid lysine. Whole legumes are the most concentrated natural sources of fiber in the diet, whereas highly processed vegan meat alternatives are low in fiber and tend to be relatively higher in sodium. If few legumes are included in the diet (for example, for people who choose a raw vegan diet), intake of nuts and seeds should be increased.

Grains. This food group includes breads, cereals, and pastas. These foods provide energy (especially whole grains and whole-grain products) and are excellent sources of carbohydrates, fiber, protein, and most of the B vitamins (but not vitamin B_{12}). People who have relatively low caloric requirements, wish to lose weight, or eat more raw food may opt for few servings from this group. Athletes or others with high energy needs can choose much higher intakes (for example, twelve servings).

This food group also includes corn, millet, rice, and the gluten-free pseudograins that are botanically not grains (such as amaranth, buckwheat, quinoa, and wild rice). Starchy vegetables provide similar amounts of energy as grains, so people who avoid grains could consume starchy vegetables, such as parsnips, potatoes, squash, sweet potatoes, turnips, and yams. Starchy vegetables have the advantage of being higher in potassium and vitamin A. Grains, however, are higher in B vitamins.

Nuts and Seeds. Nuts and seeds, and butters made from nuts and seeds, contribute copper, selenium, vitamin E, and fat. Seeds and cashews are especially rich in zinc. Chia seeds, flaxseeds, hempseeds, and walnuts provide omega-3 fatty acids. Sesame seeds and almonds are good sources of calcium. Brazil nuts are high in selenium.

Peanuts are technically legumes, but we also include them in our listing of nuts and seeds. Like other legumes, peanuts are high in protein, the amino acid lysine, iron, and zinc, but like nuts, they are high in fat and other nutrients. In general, nuts and seeds have less protein than legumes.

Calcium-rich foods. The Vegan Food Guide (see table 4.1, page 46) dedicates an entire column to featuring the calcium-rich foods within each food group. Each serving in the third column of the guide provides 100 to 150 milligrams of calcium. As you select from the food groups, take care to include calcium-rich foods that can meet multiple nutrient needs. For example, either ½ cup (125 ml) of fortified soymilk or calcium-set tofu counts as a serving from the legumes group and also counts toward your calcium-rich foods quota. If you prefer not to consume calcium-fortified beverages or tofu, adding a calcium supplement is a very good choice. Note that beyond the items listed in the calcium-rich foods column, small amounts of calcium are found in many plant-based foods. For more information about calcium rich foods, see page 9.

Nondairy milks. Choose nondairy milks that are fortified with calcium and vitamin D. Nondairy milks made from nuts, seeds, and grains, such as almond milk, hempseed milk, and rice milk, are excellent sources of calcium and vitamin D. However, they don't have as much protein as soymilk. It is fine to include these nondairy milks in your diet as long as you get protein from other sources. This can be especially important when designing children's diets.

Number of servings. The guide may seem to recommend a lot of "servings," and you may wonder if it's possible to fit all these servings into one day. Our answer is yes, it is. Here's why: people usually eat more than one "serving" from a particular food group at a meal. For example, a person may eat 3 ounces of a vegan meat alternative (three servings); 1 cup (250 ml) of fortified soymilk or oatmeal (each two servings); or 2, 3, or even more cups of salad (two, three, or more servings). Don't let the number of servings alarm you.

The Vegan Food Guide is designed so that most calories come from wholesome, nutritious foods. Although you might occasionally include other foods that are high in sugar or fat but lack important nutrients, there is not a lot of room for such items in any diet that meets recommended intakes.

Essential Extras

In addition to choosing foods from all of the food groups described in table 4.1 and monitoring your calcium intake, be sure to include sufficient amounts of the following essential extras. Omega-3 fatty acids, vitamins B_{12} and D, and iodine are important components of a healthful vegan diet.

OMEGA-3 FATTY ACID

Greens and soyfoods provide some omega-3 fatty acids. To meet your daily requirement, include at least *one* of the following more concentrated sources:

- 2 tablespoons (30 ml) of ground flaxseeds or chia seeds
- ¼ cup (60 ml) of hempseeds or walnuts
- 1 teaspoon (5 ml) of flaxseed oil
- 1 tablespoon (15 ml) of hempseed oil
- 2 tablespoons (30 ml) of canola oil

A vegan DHA or DHA with EPA supplement is optional and may be beneficial for some individuals, such as pregnant women or people with diabetes.

VITAMIN B_{12}

Be sure to include *one* of the following:

- 2 to 3 daily servings of vitamin B_{12}-fortified foods, such as nondairy milks, vegan meat alternatives, or breakfast cereals that are fortified with a total of 4 micrograms of vitamin B_{12} or 100 percent of the daily value (check the label)
- Per day, 2 tablespoons (30 ml, or 8 grams) of Red Star Vegetarian Support Formula nutritional yeast flakes
- A daily supplement that provides at least 25 micrograms of vitamin B_{12}
- Twice a week, a supplement that provides at least 1,000 micrograms of vitamin B_{12}

TABLE 4.1. Vegan Food Guide

FOOD GROUP, SERVINGS PER DAY	FOODS IN THIS GROUP, WITH SERVING SIZE	CALCIUM-RICH FOODS, WITH SERVING SIZE (Choose 6 to 8 servings per day.)	NOTES
Vegetables, 5 or more servings	• ½ cup (125 ml) raw or cooked vegetables • 1 cup (250 ml) raw leafy vegetables • ½ cup (125 ml) vegetable juice	• 1 cup (250 ml) cooked bok choy, broccoli, collard greens, napa cabbage, kale, mustard greens, or okra • 2 cups (500 ml) raw bok choy, broccoli, collard greens, napa cabbage, or kale • ½ cup (125 ml) calcium-fortified tomato or vegetable juice	Include at least 2 daily servings of calcium-rich greens. Choose from the full rainbow of colorful vegetables: blue, green, orange, purple, red, white, and yellow.
Fruits, 4 or more servings	• ½ cup (125 ml) fruit or fruit juice • ¼ cup (60 ml) dried fruit • 1 medium fruit	• ½ cup (125 ml) calcium-fortified fruit juice • ¼ cup (60 ml) chopped dried figs • 2 oranges	Make these your sweet treats! Fruits are excellent sources of potassium. Choose from the full spectrum of colorful fruits.
Legumes 3 or more servings	• ½ cup (125 ml) cooked beans, lentils, tofu, or tempeh • ¼ cup (60 ml) peanuts • 2 tablespoons (30 ml) peanut butter • 1 cup (250 ml) raw peas or sprouted lentils • 1 ounce (30 g) vegan meat alternative	• ½ cup (125 ml) fortified soymilk or soy yogurt • ½ cup (125 ml) calcium-set tofu (look for calcium-sulfate on the label), cooked soybeans, or soynuts • 1 cup (250 ml) black or white beans	Legumes are powerful providers of iron, zinc, and protein, with 7 to 9 grams of protein per serving. Include a selection from this group at most meals.
Grains, 3 or more servings	• ½ cup (125 ml) cooked cereal, pasta, quinoa, rice, or other grain • 1 ounce (30 g) ready-to-eat cereal • 1 slice of bread • ½ cup (125 ml) raw corn or sprouted buckwheat, quinoa, or other grain	• 1 ounce (30 g) calcium-fortified bread or cereal • 1 calcium-fortified tortilla	Select whole grains as often as possible. Adjust the number of grain servings to suit your energy needs. Some fortified cereals and tortillas are particularly high in calcium (check labels).
Nuts and Seeds, 1 or more servings	• ¼ cup (60 ml) nuts or seeds (including peanuts) • 2 tablespoons (30 ml) nut or seed butter	• ¼ cup (60 ml) almonds • 2 tablespoons (30 ml) almond butter or tahini	Nuts and seeds contribute copper, fat, selenium, and vitamin E. Include nuts and seeds that are rich in omega-3 fatty acids (see page 44).

Sources: See notes 3, 4, and 5 on page 242 for information about table 4.1 and the essential extras described on pages 45 to 47.

VITAMIN D

You can get vitamin D from sunlight, fortified foods, a supplement, or a combination of the following:

Sunlight. On a clear day (except in winter), exposing your face and forearms to warm sunlight between 10 a.m. and 2 p.m. without sunscreen may provide your daily supply of vitamin D. Sufficient daily exposure times are fifteen minutes for light-skinned people, twenty minutes for dark-skinned people, and thirty minutes for people age seventy and older.

Fortified foods or supplements. Use vitamin D supplements or fortified foods if your sun exposure is insufficient. The recommended vitamin D intake is 15 micrograms (600 IUs) for adults age seventy and younger or 20 micrograms (800 IUs) for older adults. Amounts of vitamin D as high as 1,000 IU for adults (and 2,000 IU for older adults) also are considered suitable and safe. Note that 5 micrograms of vitamin D is equivalent to 200 IU of vitamin D.

IODINE

You can get your daily recommended intake of 150 micrograms of iodine by taking a combined vitamin and mineral supplement or by consuming about ⅓ teaspoon (2 ml) of iodized salt. (A teaspoon of iodized salt provides 400 micrograms of iodine.) Sea salt is typically not iodized. Sea vegetables, such as kelp, contain iodine, though amounts vary greatly. In a vegan diet, iodine intake can be insufficient or vary considerably, as it will depend on the amounts of iodine in the soil where plant-based foods were grown. So it is essential to make sure you are getting enough of this nutrient.

Tempting Menus That Meet Recommended Intakes

⦿ n pages 48 to 59 you will find twelve menus that can be used in conjunction with the Vegan Food Guide (see table 4.1, page 46). The menus are nutritionally adequate at three caloric levels: the standard 2,000 calories, 1,600 calories (for a small person or for weight loss), and 2,500 calories (for a larger or more active person). Caloric intakes can be further increased (for example, for an athlete) with larger servings of the listed foods.

The first menu is suitable for families with children, the second provides healthful vegan versions of typical North American favorites, the third is designed for someone who has few cooking skills or little time for food preparation, and the fourth is entirely raw. The menus that follow offer an array of tempting ethnic tastes: Asian, French, Indian, Italian, Japanese (this menu also is gluten-free), Mexican, and Middle Eastern. The final menu includes more complex dishes that are appropriate for celebrations or holiday meals.

Feel free to alter the menus. For example, it's okay to swap lunch foods for dinner foods and vice versa. You can also replace recipes with simple plant-based foods that involve little or no preparation if they are nutritionally similar. Many of the menus can be gluten free, depending on your choices of ingredients, and others can be easily modified. Though it takes a little time to adapt to any new dietary pattern, creating a balanced and nutritionally adequate vegan diet is easier than it may appear at first glance.

Note: In addition to the foods listed, all menus require vitamin D sources (fortified foods, supplements, or sunlight) and supplementary vitamin B$_{12}$.

① Children's and Family Favorites Menu

A great way to entice children and teenagers to eat vegetables is to set out a raw veggie platter and a nutritious dip. When the starving hordes return from school or play, they are likely to prefer this colorful array over steamed broccoli at dinnertime. The high intakes of B vitamins come from the nutritional yeast in the Gee Whiz Spread. For alternative sandwich ideas, see page 88. Small children can get 1,000 calories and twice as much protein as they need by eating half portions of the foods listed here.

BREAKFAST

1 cup (250 ml) Good Morning Granola (page 68) or cooked or ready-to-eat cereal

1 cup (250 ml) fortified soymilk

½ cup (125 ml) blueberries

LUNCH

Sandwich: 2 slices of bread with 2 tablespoons (30 ml) of almond butter

½ cup (125 ml) carrot sticks

1 cup (250 ml) grapes

½ cup (125 ml) fortified soymilk

DINNER

1 Timesaving Taco (page 159)

1 cup (250 ml) fortified soymilk

SNACKS AND DESSERTS

½ cup (125 ml) Gee Whiz Spread (page 79), with 1 teaspoon (5 ml) of flaxseed oil stirred in

2 cups (500 ml) Raw Vegetable Platter (page 86)

1 cup (250 ml) Vegan Dazs Ice Cream (page 217)

1 Blueberry-Cornmeal Muffin (page 227)

Nutritional analysis of menu: calories: 1,949, protein: 66 g, fat: 65 g, carbohydrates: 300 g (113 g from sugar), dietary fiber: 39 g, calcium: 1,368 mg, iron: 18 mg, magnesium: 479 mg, phosphorus: 1,940 mg, potassium: 4,447 mg, sodium: 1,620 mg, zinc: 12 mg, thiamin: 7.5 mg, riboflavin: 8 mg, niacin: 58 mg, vitamin B_6: 8 mg, folate: 585 mcg, pantothenic acid: 6 mg, vitamin B_{12}: 7.6 mcg, vitamin A: 847 mcg, vitamin C: 179 mg, vitamin E: 17 mg, omega-6 fatty acid: 17 g, omega-3 fatty acid: 3 g

Percentage of calories from: protein 13%, fat 28%, carbohydrates 59%

VARIATIONS

- For a 1,600-calorie menu with 59 grams of protein, have ¾ cup (185 ml) of the granola and eliminate the muffin.

- For a 2,500-calorie menu with 80 grams of protein (appropriate for a hungry athlete or teenage boy), have 1½ cups (375 ml) of the granola, two tacos, and two muffins (or increase menu options as desired).

2 North American Menu

This menu is packed with nutritious versions of North American favorites. The high levels of B vitamins, including vitamin B$_{12}$, come from the nutritional yeast in the Scrambled Tofu. Note that including condiments, such as mustard and vegan mayonnaise, will significantly increase the amount of sodium in this menu.

BREAKFAST

½ cup (250 ml), ½ serving Scrambled Tofu (page 70) made with calcium-set tofu

1 slice toast with jam or marmalade

1 cup (250 ml) calcium-fortified orange juice

LUNCH

1 cup (250 ml) Multicolored Bean and Vegetable Salad (page 117)

3 cups (750 ml) Salad Bar (page 137), including broccoli, napa cabbage, romaine lettuce, and other vegetables

2 teaspoons (10 ml) flaxseed oil or hempseed oil in dressing

2 tablespoons (30 ml) sunflower seeds

DINNER

1 Portobello Mushroom Burger with Chickpea Topping (page 148)

1 whole wheat hamburger bun

Mustard or vegan mayonnaise (optional)

Leaf lettuce and slices of cucumber, red onion, and tomato, as desired

6 Seasoned Potato Wedges (page 206)

SNACKS AND DESSERTS

1 slice Lime Pie (page 235) with Almond, Date, and Coconut Pie Crust (page 230)

2 oranges or other pieces of fruit

Nutritional analysis of menu: calories: 1,996, protein: 70 g, fat: 72 g, carbohydrates: 296 g (119 g from sugar), dietary fiber: 55 g, calcium: 1,219 mg, iron: 19 mg, magnesium: 571 mg, phosphorus: 1,460 mg, potassium: 5,919 mg, sodium: 2,190 mg, zinc: 13.6 mg, thiamin: 9 mg, riboflavin: 9 mg, niacin: 72 mg, vitamin B$_6$: 9 mg, folate: 1,037 mcg, pantothenic acid: 8.5 mg, vitamin B$_{12}$: 6 mcg, vitamin A: 760 mcg, vitamin C: 532 mg, vitamin E: 19 mg, omega-6 fatty acid: 17 g, omega-3 fatty acid: 6 g

Percentage of calories from: protein 13%, fat 31%, carbohydrates 56%

VARIATIONS

- For a 1,600-calorie menu with 65 grams of protein, omit the pie.
- For a 2,500-calorie menu with 79 grams of protein, have two mushroom burgers with buns or two pieces of pie. Further increase the protein with a full serving of scrambled tofu.

❸ Super Simple Menu

This is a nutritionally adequate menu for someone who is busy or whose food preparation skills are minimal. The only item that requires preparation is a stir-fry with rice. Trail mix is a snack that requires some combining but no cooking. For variety, the canned soup may be replaced with another bean or lentil soup or Stovetop "Baked" Beans (page 150). Note that sodium levels can vary greatly among brands of soup. The stir-fry may be replaced with Black Beans with Coconut and Mango (page 153).

BREAKFAST

2 slices whole-grain toast

2 tablespoons (30 ml) almond butter

1 cup (250 ml) calcium-fortified orange juice

LUNCH

2 cups (500 ml) canned black bean soup

1 banana or other fruit

DINNER

2 cups (500 ml) Stir-Fry 101 (page 138)

1½ cups (375 ml) brown rice

SNACKS

Trail mix: ¼ cup (60 ml) walnuts, ¼ cup (60 ml) almonds or cashews, and ½ cup (125 ml) dried figs or other dried fruit

1 fresh or canned peach

Nutritional analysis of menu: calories: 2,009, protein: 61 g, fat: 71 g, carbohydrates: 307 g (94 g from sugar), dietary fiber: 44 g, calcium: 981 mg, iron: 20 mg, magnesium: 676 mg, phosphorus: 1,343 mg, potassium: 4,639 mg, sodium 1,012 mg, zinc: 11 mg, thiamin: 1.4 mg, riboflavin: 1.3 mg, niacin: 27 mg, vitamin B_6: 2.3 mg, folate: 503 mcg, pantothenic acid: 4.7 mg, vitamin B_{12}: 0 mcg, vitamin A: 746 mcg, vitamin C: 362 mg, vitamin E: 23 mg, omega-6 fatty acid: 221 g, omega-3 fatty acid: 3 g

Percentage of calories from: protein 12%, fat 30%, carbohydrates 58%

VARIATIONS

- For a 1,600-calorie menu with 52 grams of protein, have one slice of toast and almond butter and ½ cup (125 ml) of rice with dinner.
- For a 2,500-calorie menu with 70 grams of protein, add 2 ounces (60 g) of crackers at lunch, an additional ½ cup (125 ml) of rice at dinner, and two small oatmeal cookies.

④ Raw Menu

For a raw vegan diet to meet recommended calcium intakes, it is necessary to include greens throughout the day (or to include a calcium supplement, preferably one with vitamin D). Here, greens are featured ingredients in four items: the smoothie, salad, vegetable platter (broccoli), and juice. Oranges (in the smoothie) and tahini contribute additional calcium. Greens and tahini are sources of protein and other minerals. This is a powerfully protective menu.

BREAKFAST

2½ cups (625 ml) **Green Smoothie** (page 65)

LUNCH

6 cups (1.5 L) **Garden of Plenty Salad** (page 106)

¼ cup (60 ml) **Lemon-Tahini Dressing** (page 134)

2 cobs raw corn

DINNER

1 cup (250 ml) **Sprouted Lentils** (page 120)

2 tablespoons (30 ml) **Cucumber-Dill Dressing** (page 128)

1 cup (250 ml) **raw green peas**

2 cups (500 ml) **Raw Vegetable Platter** (page 86)

¼ cup (60 ml) **Pesto the Besto** (page 82) **or Limey Avocado Dip** (page 76)

SNACKS AND DESSERTS

12 ounces (340 g) **Green Giant Juice** (page 66)

1 slice **Mango-Strawberry Pie** (page 236)

Nutritional analysis of menu: calories 1,962, protein: 73 g, fat: 81 g, carbohydrates: 286 g (112 g from sugar), dietary fiber: 52 g, calcium: 967 mg, iron: 22 mg, magnesium: 741 mg, phosphorus: 1,752 mg, potassium: 6,764 mg, sodium: 1,602 mg, zinc: 12 mg, thiamin: 3.6 mg, riboflavin: 1.8 mg, niacin: 32 mg, vitamin B$_6$: 3.3 mg, folate: 917 mcg, pantothenic acid: 9 mg, vitamin B$_{12}$: 0.1 mcg, vitamin A: 2,276 mcg, vitamin C: 876 mg, vitamin E: 27 mg, omega-6 fatty acid: 33 g, omega-3 fatty acid: 4 g

Percentage of calories from: protein 13%, fat 34%, carbohydrates 53%

VARIATIONS

- For a 1,600-calorie menu with 65 grams of protein, eliminate either the pesto or the pie and decrease the portion of the other by half.

- For a 2,500-calorie menu with 80 grams of protein, have twice the amount of either the pesto or the pie and add 1½ cups (375 ml) of fruits or vegetables of your choice.

⑤ Asian Fusion Menu

Throughout Asia, people start the day with rice, miso soup, tofu, soymilk, fruit, or pancakes. Here we list pancakes, though for an instant version of this breakfast, you might try frozen vegan waffles with fruit or fruit syrup. This choice also can be gluten free. The lunch and dinner feature exotic flavors from China, Thailand, Vietnam, and other parts of Asia. Thai Pasta Salad (page 115) is another tasty lunch option. The calcium content of tofu varies from brand to brand, so compare labels and choose the brand with the greatest amount.

BREAKFAST

3 Whole Wheat Pancakes (page 71)

½ cup (125 ml) Blueberry-Orange Sauce (page 178)

1 tablespoon (15 ml) ground flaxseeds

LUNCH

2 cups (500 ml) Ginger, Carrot, and Yam Soup (page 94)

1 Vietnamese Salad Roll (page 110) with Spicy Peanut Sauce (page 182)

DINNER

1 cup (250 ml) Sweet-and-Sour Tofu (page 165), or ½ cup (125 ml) Marinated Tofu (page 160)

2 cups (500 ml) brown rice or millet

1 cup (250 ml) bok choy or Asian greens, steamed

SNACKS AND DESSERTS

1 Lemon-Sesame Cookie (page 226)

1 cup (250 ml) Green Smoothie (page 65)

Nutritional analysis of menu: calories: 2,037, protein: 52 g, fat: 64 g, carbohydrates: 333 g (86 g from sugar), dietary fiber: 42 g, calcium: 1,190 mg, iron: 16 mg, magnesium: 567 mg, phosphorus: 1,192 mg, potassium: 4,996 mg, sodium: 2,084 mg, zinc: 8.2 mg, thiamin: 3.2 mg, riboflavin: 1.2 mg, niacin: 27 mg, vitamin B_6: 2.9 mg, folate: 491 mcg, pantothenic acid: 6.2 mg, vitamin B_{12}: 0 mcg, vitamin A: 1,982 mcg, vitamin C: 507 mg, vitamin E: 13 mg, omega-6 fatty acid: 15 g, omega-3 fatty acid: 3 g

Percentage of calories from: protein 10%, fat 27%, carbohydrates 63%

VARIATIONS

- For a 1,600-calorie menu with 44 grams of protein, decrease the Blueberry-Orange Sauce to ¼ cup (60 ml) and the rice to 1 cup (250 ml).
- For a 2,500-calorie menu with 66 grams of protein, have two Vietnamese Salad Rolls with lunch and 2½ cups (625 ml) of the Green Smoothie as a snack or dessert. The cookie is optional.

⑥ French Menu

Enjoy this elegant menu on a special day. This menu features many calcium-rich foods, including carrots, leafy greens, parsnips, and pea soup. For dessert, alternative options include Lem-Un-Cheesecake with Crumb Crust (page 232) or Fresh Fruit as Dessert (page 215). The B vitamins in this menu, including vitamin B_{12}, are primarily from the nutritional yeast in the Gooda Cheez.

BREAKFAST

1½ cups (375 ml) Design-Your-Own Muesli (page 67) made with fortified juice

1 orange, or 2 fresh or dried figs

LUNCH

2 cups (500 ml) Classic Split Pea Soup (page 98)

½ cup (125 ml) Gooda Cheez (page 80)

5 slices whole-grain melba toast

DINNER

1 serving Watercress, Avocado, and Grapefruit Salad (page 109)

1 cup (250 ml) French Lentils with Fennel and Lemon (page 156)

½ cup (125 ml) Mashed Parsnips and Apple with Toasted Walnuts (page 195)

1 cup (250 ml) Carrots with Dijon Mustard and Tarragon (page 193)

1 cup (250 ml) Sautéed Garden Greens (page 190)

SNACKS AND DESSERTS

1 Baked Stuffed Apple (page 218)

1 tablespoon (15 ml) Cashew Cream Topping (page 212)

Nutritional analysis of menu: calories: 1,980, protein: 74 g, fat: 74 g, carbohydrates: 291 g (88 g from sugar), dietary fiber: 68 g, calcium: 998 mg, iron: 25 mg, magnesium: 614 mg, phosphorus: 1,566 mg, potassium: 6,020 mg, sodium: 2,294 mg, zinc: 13 mg, thiamin: 5.2 mg, riboflavin: 4 mg, niacin: 44 mg, vitamin B_6: 5 mg, folate: 921 mcg, pantothenic acid: 7.2 mg, vitamin B_{12}: 2 mcg, vitamin A: 3,840 mcg, vitamin C: 520 mg, vitamin E: 12 mg, omega-6 fatty acid: 21 g, omega-3 fatty acid: 3 g

Percentage of calories from: protein 14%, fat 31%, carbohydrates 55%

VARIATIONS

- For a 1,600-calorie menu with 59 grams of protein, have 1 cup (250 ml) of Classic Split Pea Soup and ¼ cup (60 ml) of Gooda Cheez at lunch and eliminate the parsnips at dinner. For omega-3 fatty acids, include 2 tablespoons (30 ml) of ground flaxseeds somewhere in the menu.

- For a 2,500-calorie menu with 87 grams of protein, have 8 slices of Melba toast at lunch, 1 cup (250 ml) of parsnips at dinner, and ¼ cup (60 ml) of Cashew Cream Topping with the baked apple for dessert. Add one piece of fruit.

7 Indian Menu

In India, from dawn to dusk, menus feature legumes, including varieties that are not well known in North America. It is common to include a lentil dish at breakfast. Another Indian breakfast delight is freshly squeezed orange juice. Here, we use fortified juice to increase the amount of calcium in this menu. Vitamin B_{12} is provided by the nutritional yeast in the Curried Sandwich Spread and the fortified nondairy milk.

BREAKFAST

1 cup (250 ml) **Hearty Whole-Grain Cereal** (page 69)

1 cup (250 ml) **fortified nondairy milk**

1 cup (250 ml) **calcium-fortified orange juice**

LUNCH

1 cup (250 ml) **Curried Kabocha Squash and Chickpea Soup** (page 99)

½ cup (125 ml) **Curried Sandwich Spread** (page 78)

1½ ounces (45 g) **chapatis, naan, or crackers**

1 **tomato**

DINNER

1 cup (250 ml) **Dahl-icious** (page 154)

½ cup (125 ml) **Coconut-Saffron Rice with Cardamom and Lime** (page 208)

1½ cups (375 ml) **Aloo Gobi** (page 202)

¼ cup (60 ml) **Apple-Plum Chutney** (page 180; optional)

SNACKS AND DESSERTS

2 **Almond Butter Balls** (page 224)

¼ cup (60 ml) **walnuts**

1½ cups (375 ml) **mango**

Nutritional analysis of menu: calories: 2,000, protein: 63 g, fat: 74 g, carbohydrates: 296 g (109 g from sugar), dietary fiber: 36 g, calcium: 1,195 mg, iron: 22 mg, magnesium: 512 mg, phosphorus: 1,312 mg, potassium: 4,326 mg, sodium: 1,813 mg, zinc: 8.6 mg, thiamin: 1.8 mg, riboflavin: 1.2 mg, niacin: 22 mg, vitamin B_6: 2.4 mg, folate: 599 mcg, pantothenic acid: 4.6 mg, vitamin B_{12}: 3.2 mcg, vitamin A: 953 mcg, vitamin C: 285 mg, vitamin E: 18 mg, omega-6 fatty acid: 18 g, omega-3 fatty acid: 3 g

Percentage of calories from: protein 12%, fat 31%, carbohydrates 57%

VARIATIONS

- For a 1,600-calorie menu with 54 grams of protein, decrease the chapati, naan, or crackers serving to 1 ounce (30 g), decrease the mango serving to 1 cup (250 ml), and eliminate the Almond Butter Balls.

- For a 2,500-calorie menu with 76 grams of protein, double the amount of chapatis, naan, or crackers to 3 ounces (90 g) at lunch. At dinner, increase the amounts of Dhal-icious and Coconut-Saffron Rice to 1½ cups (375 ml) of each.

Italian Menu

8 While you enjoy this menu, imagine yourself beside the blue of the Mediterranean or in the rolling hills of Tuscany. This menu's nutritional profile is as appealing as these images. The nutritional yeast in the pesto provides vitamin B_{12}, and many foods provide calcium: the bread, muffin, pesto, and soup, plus the tofu in the lasagne and cheesecake.

BREAKFAST

Good-quality Italian coffee

1 Blueberry-Cornmeal Muffin (page 227)

2 fresh or dried figs

2 cups (500 ml) grapes

LUNCH

1 cup (250 ml) Tuscan Minestrone (page 104)

¼ cup (60 ml) Pesto the Besto (page 82) or Walnut, Olive, and Sun-Dried Tomato Tapenade (page 77)

2 ounces (60 g) whole wheat bread or focaccia

DINNER

1 serving Cashew Cheese Lasagne (page 170)

3 cups (750 ml) Garden of Plenty Salad (page 106)

3 tablespoons (45 ml) Tomato-Herb Dressing (page 131)

SNACKS AND DESSERTS

1 slice Lem-Un-Cheesecake with Crumb Crust (page 232)

½ cup (125 ml) Blueberry-Orange Sauce (page 178)

1 cup (250 ml) calcium-fortified fruit juice

Nutritional analysis of menu: calories: 1,999, protein: 60 g, fat: 71 g, carbohydrates: 310 g (136 g from sugar), dietary fiber: 41 g, calcium: 1,076 mg, iron: 19 mg, magnesium: 564 mg, phosphorus: 1,190 mg, potassium: 5,391 mg, sodium: 2,396 mg, zinc: 9.4 mg, thiamin: 4 mg, riboflavin: 3.6 mg, niacin: 42 mg, vitamin B_6: 4.1 mg, folate: 648 mcg, pantothenic acid: 5 mg, vitamin B_{12}: 1.8 mcg, vitamin A: 1,660 mcg, vitamin C: 583 mg, vitamin E: 14 mg, omega-6 fatty acid: 16 g, omega-3 fatty acid: 4 g

Percentage of calories from: protein 12%, fat 30%, carbohydrates 58%

VARIATIONS

- For a 1,600-calorie menu with 50 grams of protein, decrease the amount of grapes to 1½ cups (375 ml), the pesto to 2 tablespoons (30 ml), the bread at lunch to 1 slice, and the pie and topping to a half serving.

- For a 2,500-calorie menu with 70 grams of protein, add another muffin and increase the amount of pesto to ½ cup (125 ml).

Japanese Menu (gluten-free)

9

Many recipes in this book are wheat-free and gluten-free; here is an example of a day's menu that can be used by those who are sensitive to wheat and gluten. If you are sensitive, be sure to choose wheat- and gluten-free ingredients, such as miso, rice syrup, and tamari. This menu can be enjoyed by anyone, not only those with food sensitivities.

BREAKFAST

1 serving Banana-Blueberry Power Drink (page 64)

LUNCH

½ cup (125 ml) **Adzuki Beans with Ginger and Lemon** (page 151)

½ cup (125 ml) **brown rice**

2 cups (500 ml) **Calcium-Rich Greens** (page 107)

8 cherry tomatoes

3 tablespoons (45 ml) **Asian Dressing** (page 125) or a dressing made with unrefined sesame oil, freshly squeezed lemon juice, or rice vinegar

DINNER

1 **Sushi Roll** (page 146)

½ cup (125 ml) **Teriyaki Tofu with Vegetables** (page 166)

1 cup (250 ml) **Shiitake Mushrooms, Kale, and Sesame** (page 201)

SNACK

1 cup (250 ml) **calcium-fortified orange juice**

Nutritional analysis of menu: calories: 1,991, protein: 58 g, fat: 58 g, carbohydrates: 327 g (112 g from sugar), dietary fiber: 53 g, calcium: 991 mg, iron: 18 mg, magnesium: 494 mg, phosphorus: 1,053 mg, potassium: 4822 mg, sodium: 1,650 mg, zinc: 9 mg, thiamin: 1.9 mg, riboflavin: 1 mg, niacin: 23 mg, vitamin B_6: 2.6 mg, folate: 521 mcg, pantothenic acid: 6.3 mg, vitamin B_{12}: 0 mcg, vitamin A: 2,727 mcg, vitamin C: 677 mg, vitamin E: 19 mg, omega-6 fatty acid: 22 g, omega-3 fatty acid: 3 g

Percentage of calories from: protein 12%, fat 25%, carbohydrates 63%

VARIATIONS

- For a 1,600-calorie menu with 49 grams of protein, have half of the Banana-Blueberry Power Drink and decrease the amount of rice at lunch to ½ cup (125 ml).

- For a 2,500-calorie menu with 71 grams of protein, increase the rice at lunch to 1 cup (250 ml). Add ¼ cup (60 ml) seeds or nuts. Add a serving of Apple-Pear Crumble (page 219). (For a gluten-free menu, use oats that are processed in a gluten-free facility.) Alternatively, have a second Sushi Roll instead of the crumble.

Mexican Menu

10

The flavorful lunch and dinner in this menu have a Mexican or Spanish theme. The foods highest in calcium include almonds, black beans, figs, fortified soymilk, and oranges. For a simple lunch alternative, choose a store-bought bean soup, crackers, a carrot, plus a handful of walnuts for omega-3 fatty acid.

BREAKFAST

1 cup (250 ml) **Hearty Whole-Grain Cereal** (page 69)

1 cup (250 ml) **fortified soymilk**

2 oranges

LUNCH

2 cups (500 ml) **Savory Black Bean Soup** (page 102)

1 cup (250 ml) **Fiesta Quinoa Salad with Lime Dressing** (page 113), **made with flaxseed oil**

1 carrot

DINNER

1 cup (250 ml) **Lima Beans, Corn, and Chipotle Chile** (page 157)

1 cup (250 ml) **Spanish Rice** (page 209)

SNACKS AND DESSERT

¼ cup (60 ml) **almonds**

¾ cup (185 ml) **Figgy Pudding** (page 239)

1 cup (250 ml) **papaya, or 1 Coconut Macaroon** (page 225)

Nutritional analysis of menu: calories: 1,993, protein: 73 g, fat: 54 g, carbohydrates: 328 g (96 g from sugar), dietary fiber: 63 g, calcium: 991 mg, iron: 22 mg, magnesium: 740 mg, phosphorus: 1,597 mg, potassium: 5,048 mg, sodium: 1,492 mg, zinc: 11 mg, thiamin: 2 mg, riboflavin: 1.8 mg, niacin: 29 mg, vitamin B_6: 2 mg, folate: 792 mcg, pantothenic acid: 6.8 mg, vitamin B_{12}: 3.1 mcg, vitamin A: 1,131 mcg, vitamin C: 341 mg, vitamin E: 18 mg, omega-6 fatty acid: 11 g, omega-3 fatty acid: 4 g

Percentage of calories from: protein 14%, fat 23%, carbohydrates 63%

VARIATIONS

- For a 1,600-calorie menu with 60 grams of protein, decrease the amount of grains served at each meal from 1 cup (250 ml) to ½ cup (125 ml). Use unsweetened soymilk. Have just 2 tablespoons (30 ml) of almonds.

- For a 2,500-calorie menu with 84 grams of protein, increase the amount of grains served at each meal from 1 cup (250 ml) to 1½ cups (375 ml) each. Add 3 Coconut Macaroons or other cookies, or increase portions as desired.

⑪ Middle Eastern Menu

This menu showcases the exotic flavors and ingredients typically found at Middle Eastern restaurants and take-out stands. Enjoy these tasty and healthful combinations, which are simple to prepare at home. You will find many flavorful variations of hummus at supermarkets or make your own.

BREAKFAST

1 cup (250 ml) soy yogurt, calcium-fortified

2 slices bread or toast

2 tablespoons (30 ml) tahini

LUNCH

1 Palate-Pleasing Pita Pockets (page 89) with ½ cup (125 ml) each of Heart-Healthy Hummus (page 81), lettuce, onion, and tomato

2 tablespoons (30 ml) Lemon-Tahini Dressing (page 134)

DINNER

1 cup (250 ml) Mediterranean Lentil Soup (page 100) or Spicy Eggplant Soup with Chickpeas and Olives (page 103)

1½ cups (375 ml) Kamut, Tomato, and Avocado Salad (page 114) or Brown Rice, Mushroom, and Walnut Pilaf (page 207)

SNACKS AND DESSERT

¼ cup (60 ml) walnuts

2 cups (500 ml) Fresh Fruit as Dessert (page 215)

1 cup (250 ml) fortified almond milk or other nondairy beverage

Nutritional analysis of menu: calories: 2,059, protein: 66 g, fat: 84 g, carbohydrates: 283 g (61 g from sugar), dietary fiber: 46 g, calcium: 982 mg, iron: 18 mg, magnesium: 379 mg, phosphorus: 1,643 mg, potassium: 3,648 mg, sodium: 2,114 mg, zinc: 9 mg, thiamin: 2 mg, riboflavin: 1 mg, niacin: 19 mg, vitamin B_6: 1.8 mg, folate: 534 mcg, pantothenic acid: 3.8 mg, vitamin B_{12}: 0 mcg, vitamin A: 366 mcg, vitamin C: 98 mg, vitamin E: 17 mg, omega-6 fatty acid: 27 g, omega-3 fatty acid: 3 g

Percentage of calories from: protein 12%, fat 35%, carbohydrates 53%

VARIATIONS

- For a 1,600-calorie menu with 52 grams of protein, have one slice of toast and tahini, a half cup (125 ml) of the Kamut salad, 1 tablespoon (15 ml) of walnuts, and add 1 tablespoon (15 ml) of ground flaxseeds.

- For a 2,500-calorie menu with 83 grams of protein, double the pita bread and fillings at lunch. At some point during the day, add one-third of an avocado, or a cookie.

12 Holiday Menu

For a lovely celebration lunch or dinner, select courses from this list:

Gooda Cheez (page 80) with crackers

Ginger, Carrot, and Yam Soup (page 94)

Kale and Red Bell Pepper Holly Ring (page 108)

Wild Rice, Walnut, and Cranberry Salad (page 116)

Holiday Stuffed Winter Squash (page 142)

Rosemary Gravy (page 188) or Light Mushroom Gravy (page 186)

Cranberry-Ginger Relish (page 179)

Blueberry Mince Tarts or Pies (page 233)

Pumpkin Spice Pie (page 237) with Cashew Cream Topping (page 212) or Holiday Pie Topping (page 213)

Introduction to the Recipes

Welcome to a collection of recipes that were developed for their outstanding flavor combinations and ease of preparation. Each was guided by sound nutritional information. The ingredients are simple to obtain in the marketplace, with just a few that are widely available in natural food or ethnic stores, or over the Internet. A comprehensive shopping list that includes all the food items used in recipes can be found on pages 30 to 32.

If you do not already have a good chef's knife, we recommend that this be your first investment. Visit a store that specializes in knives to get free instruction on what to look for and how to use a good quality knife. Also essential is a cutting board that is large enough to easily hold the food that you are working on. For other recipes, you may need a blender, a food processor, or a juicer. Continue to invest in your health by adding to your equipment one purchase at a time so that you are happy to spend time creating delicious, wholesome food in your kitchen. For a more detailed list of equipment see page 42.

HOW TO APPROACH THE RECIPES

✔ Read each recipe through before you start. This will help ensure that you understand the task at hand and will have a successful outcome.

✔ If possible, make the recipe exactly as it is written the first time you try it. After that, use your creativity to explore new taste possibilities.

✔ Look at the variations and ingredient options for the recipe, as you may find a version you prefer.

✔ At the beginning of each recipe you will find the yield, generally in cups (250 ml) or occasionally in servings. We recognize that appetites vary immensely, and what could be considered several servings in one group might be a single serving for one hungry, high-energy person.

✔ To increase your understanding of cooking and learn how to balance flavor, read chapter 3, Vegan Cooking.

HOW TO USE THE NUTRITIONAL ANALYSES

A special feature of these recipes is the nutritional analysis that accompanies each one. Following is some information on how to interpret the nutritional analyses.

- The nutritional analysis provided for each recipe does not include optional ingredients.

- Where two or more choices are given for an ingredient, the analysis is based on the first choice.

- Where there is a range in the amount of an ingredient, the smaller amount is used for the analysis.

- Metric measures were used for the analyses.

- Certain nutrients—such as choline, chromium, iodine, manganese, molybdenum, and selenium—are not included due to insufficient data. The databases used are those of the US Department of Agriculture online at nal.usda.gov/fnic/foodcomp/search/ and the professional nutritional analysis program ESHA/The Food Processor, esha.com.

- Although we list a specific amount of each nutrient per serving of a recipe, the actual amount can vary due to differences in plant varieties, growing conditions, and farming practices.

- Most of the values for sugar in the nutritional analyses reflect naturally occurring sugars in fruits and vegetables. Added sugars, such as those from maple syrup, also are included in this figure.

- For recipes calling for nutritional yeast, the analysis was done using Red Star Vegetarian Support Formula Nutritional Yeast, a source of vitamin B_{12}. For recipes calling for nondairy beverages, such as soymilk, fortified products were used.

PERCENTAGE OF CALORIES FROM PROTEIN, FAT, AND CARBOHYDRATE

The amounts of protein, carbohydrate, and fat are listed in grams in the nutritional analyses. Foods and beverages also can be described in terms of the percentage of calories that come from protein, fat, and carbohydrate. The bottom line of the analysis shows the percentage of calories that come from protein, fat, and carbohydrate. Note that 15 percent *calories from fat* is very different from 15 percent of the food's *weight* coming from fat.

By weight, 2 percent milk contains 2 grams of fat per 100 grams of milk (and 89 percent water). When our bodies convert fat, protein, and carbohydrate to calories, we derive 9 calories from each gram of fat and 4 calories from each gram of protein or carbohydrate. Therefore, in 2 percent milk, 35 percent of the calories are derived from fat, 27 percent from protein, and 38 percent from carbohydrate (the sugar lactose). So, from another perspective, it might be called 35 percent milk.

Food weight includes water, which is calorie-free, so when a food contains 15 percent of calories from fat by weight, depending on the water content, its calories from fat could be much higher. For example, an avocado is 15 percent fat by weight, with about 29.5 grams of fat in a 201-gram avocado. However, approximately 82 percent of the avocado's calories are from fat. In other words, 266 of the total 322 calories are from fat (29.5 grams fat x 9 calories per gram = 266 calories).

In chapter 1, table 1.1 (page 2), it is recommended that in our overall diet we get 10 to 20 percent of our calories from protein, 15 to 35 percent of our calories from fat, and 45 to 75 percent of our calories from carbohydrates. In a few recipes, such as African Chickpea Stew (page 153) and Black Beans with Coconut and Mango (page 152), the amounts of protein, fat, and carbohydrates in individual recipes will fit neatly into these ranges. In other recipes, the amounts will be quite different. For example, the tasty Marinated Tofu (page 160) and Dahl-icious (page 154) are relatively high in protein. These can be balanced at a meal and also over the course of the day by foods that are higher in carbohydrates and fat. Salad dressings tend to be relatively high in fat; this can be offset by choosing more fruits, vegetables, grains, and legumes.

Breakfast and Beverages

The fruit, hempseeds, and sunflower seeds in this smoothie provide abundant protein, minerals, vitamin E, and omega-3 fatty acid. As a single serving, this is a power-packed breakfast that will stave off hunger all morning. Although soaking the seeds and dates will increase their mineral availability and improve the smoothness of the final product, you can skip this step.

BANANA-BLUEBERRY Power Drink

MAKES ONE 2½-CUP (625-ML) SERVING

¼ cup (60 ml) **raw sunflower seeds**

3 **pitted dates**

1¼ cups (310 ml) **water**

1 **banana**

1 cup (250 ml) **fresh or frozen blueberries**

¼ cup (60 ml) **hempseeds**

Put the sunflower seeds and dates in a small bowl. Add water to cover and let soak at room temperature for 6 to 10 hours. Transfer the sunflower seeds, dates, and their soaking liquid to a blender. Add the banana, blueberries, and hempseeds and process on high speed until smooth, 30 to 60 seconds. For a thinner consistency, add a little more water.

Per 2½ cups (625 ml): calories: 584, protein: 18 g, fat: 28 g, carbohydrates: 74 g (44 g from sugar), dietary fiber: 21 g, calcium: 85 mg, iron: 5 mg, magnesium: 146 mg, phosphorus: 339 mg, potassium: 852 mg, sodium: 10 mg, zinc: 2 mg, thiamin: 1 mg, riboflavin: 0.1 mg, niacin: 4.3 mg, vitamin B_6: 0.4 mg, folate: 92 mcg, pantothenic acid: 2.7 mg, vitamin B_{12}: 0 mcg, vitamin A: 63 mcg, vitamin C: 17 mg, vitamin E: 13 mg, omega-6 fatty acid: 17 g, omega-3 fatty acid: 6 g

Percentage of calories from: protein 11%, fat 41%, carbohydrates 48%

This smoothie provides a satisfying breakfast for one or two people. It is rich in protein, calcium, iron, potassium, zinc, and folate and is a powerhouse of antioxidants, including selenium and vitamins A, C, and E. Soaking the seeds will increase their mineral availability, but the smoothie will taste just as good if you skip this step. If you use hempseeds, the protein and mineral content will be a little lower; however, the hempseeds will provide twice the daily supply of omega-3 fatty acid.

Green SMOOTHIE

MAKES ONE 2½-CUP (625-ML) SERVING

¼ **cup** (60 ml) **raw sunflower seeds or hempseeds**

1 **cup** (250 ml) **orange juice or a blend of orange and unsweetened apple juice**

2 **cups** (500 ml) **chopped kale leaves**

1 **orange, peeled and quartered**

1 **banana**

Soak the sunflower seeds in the juice for 15 minutes at room temperature or for 6 to 10 hours in the refrigerator. (This step can be skipped if you are using hempseeds.)

Transfer the seeds and juice to a blender. Add the kale, orange, and banana and process on high speed until smooth, about 1 minute.

Per 2½ cups (625 ml): calories: 552, protein: 17 g, fat: 20 g, carbohydrates: 88 g (49 g from sugar), dietary fiber: 13 g, calcium: 310 mg, iron: 6 mg, magnesium: 246 mg, phosphorus: 420 mg, potassium: 2,006 mg, sodium: 62 mg, zinc: 3 mg, thiamin: 1.4 mg, riboflavin: 0.5 mg, niacin: 8 mg, vitamin B_6: 1.2 mg, folate: 262 mcg, pantothenic acid: 4 mg, vitamin B_{12}: 0 mcg, vitamin A: 1,088 mcg, vitamin C: 371 mg, vitamin E: 14 mg, omega-6 fatty acid: 12 g, omega-3 fatty acid: 0.3 g

Percentage of calories from: protein 11%, fat 30%, carbohydrates 59%

A serving of this juice delivers 150 milligrams of calcium and 5 grams of protein, plus iron, magnesium, manganese, potassium, zinc, and vitamins A (beta-carotene), B_6, K, and folate, along with less than 0.5 gram of fat. As a bonus, the calcium in kale is about twice as available to the body as the calcium in cow's milk.

Green Giant JUICE

MAKES: TWO 1½-CUP (375-ML) SERVINGS

8 ounces (220 g) **kale, including stems**

½ **head romaine lettuce**

1 **cucumber, quartered lengthwise**

1 **apple**

4 **stalks celery**

1 **lemon, peeled**

1-inch (2.5-cm) **piece fresh ginger** (optional)

Juice the ingredients in the order listed. Serve immediately.

Per 1½ cups (375 ml): calories: 57, protein: 5 g, fat: 0.4 g, carbohydrates: 8 g, dietary fiber: 3 g, calcium: 155 mg, iron: 1.4 mg, magnesium: 48 mg, potassium: 835 mg, sodium: 110 mg, zinc: 0.6 mg, vitamin B_{12}: 0 mcg, vitamin C: 15 mg, vitamin E: 1.5 mg, omega-6 fatty acid: 0.1 g, omega-3 fatty acid: 0.2 g

Percent calories from: protein 35%, fat 7%, carbohydrates 58%

Reprinted by permission from *The Raw Food Revolution Diet* © Cherie Soria, Brenda Davis, and Vesanto Melina (Summertown, TN: Book Publishing Company, 2008).

Juicing Kale with Different Juicers

Champion juicer. If you use a Champion juicer, roll the kale leaves tightly and feed them through the chute in small quantities. To maximize the yield, put the pulp through the juicer a second time.

Green Power or Green Star juicer. If you use a Green Power or Green Star juicer, feed the stem end of the leaves in first and allow the twin gears to pull the leaves through the gears. Do not chop or roll the leaves.

Centrifugal juicer. Centrifugal juicers do not efficiently juice greens and are not recommended for that purpose.

The original muesli recipe, which included soaked raw oats, fruit, and ground nuts, was developed by Maximilian Bircher-Benner (1867–1939), a Swiss physician and pioneer in nutritional research, at his renowned healing clinic in Zurich as an easily digested, nourishing meal. This version takes less than three minutes to prepare, though preparation is best done the night before. Refrigerate any leftovers and enjoy them for breakfast another day or as a snack. See the variations that follow the recipe for a range of ways to adjust the ingredients to your tastes and needs.

Design-Your-Own MUESLI

MAKES ABOUT TWO 1½-CUP (375-ML) SERVINGS

1 cup (250 ml) **old-fashioned rolled oats**

¼ cup (60 ml) **raisins**

¼ cup (60 ml) **raw sunflower seeds**

pinch ground cinnamon

1¼ cups (310 ml) **unsweetened apple juice**

1 chopped banana

Put the oats, raisins, sunflower seeds, and cinnamon in a medium bowl. Stir in the juice, cover, and refrigerate for 6 to 10 hours. Top with the banana just before serving. For a thinner consistency, add a little more juice.

VARIATIONS

- Replace the oats with 1 cup (250 ml) of rolled barley, rye, or wheat.
- For gluten-free muesli, use certified gluten-free rolled oats; alternatively, use 1 cup (250 ml) of rice flakes and decrease the soaking time to 30 minutes.
- Replace the raisins with ¼ cup (60 ml) of dried blueberries, cranberries, or dates.
- Replace the sunflower seeds with ¼ cup (60 ml) of chopped raw almonds, raw pumpkin seeds, or chopped walnuts.
- Replace the cinnamon with a pinch of ground cardamom or fennel seeds.
- Replace the apple juice with 1¼ cups (310 ml) of almond milk, hempseed milk, rice milk, or soymilk.
- Replace the banana with 1 cup (250 ml) of blueberries, raspberries, sliced strawberries, or chopped apple.
- When serving, add a dollop of Cashew Cream Topping (page 212) or Holiday Pie Topping (page 213).

Per 1½ cups (375 ml): calories: 455, protein: 12 g, fat: 12 g, carbohydrates: 80 g (21 g from sugar), dietary fiber: 9 g, calcium: 67 mg, copper: 0.6 mcg, iron: 4 mg, magnesium: 158 mg, phosphorus: 374 mg, potassium: 839 mg, sodium: 16 mg, zinc: 2 mg, thiamin: 0.7 mg, riboflavin: 0.2 mg, niacin: 5 mg, vitamin B_6: 0.5 mg, folate: 62 mcg, pantothenic acid: 2 mg, vitamin B_{12}: 0 mcg, vitamin A: 4 mcg, vitamin C: 8 mg, vitamin E: 7 mg, vitamin K: 2 mcg, omega-6 fatty acid: 7 g, omega-3 fatty acid: 0.1 g

Percentage of calories from: protein 10%, fat 23%, carbohydrates 67%

This recipe makes a large quantity—enough for a quick, wholesome, delicious start to your day for a week or two.

GOOD MORNING Granola

MAKES TWELVE 1-CUP (250-ML) SERVINGS

½ cup (125 ml) **almond butter or tahini**

½ cup (125 ml) **frozen apple juice concentrate, thawed**

½ cup (125 ml) **maple syrup**

1 teaspoon (5 ml) **ground cinnamon**

1 teaspoon (5 ml) **vanilla extract or almond extract**

8 cups (2 L) **old-fashioned rolled oats**

1 cup (250 ml) **raw sunflower seeds or chopped raw almonds** (optional)

1 cup (250 ml) **dried currants, raisins, or chopped dates**

Preheat the oven to 350 degrees F (180 degrees C).

Put the almond butter, apple juice concentrate, maple syrup, cinnamon, and vanilla extract in a medium bowl and stir until well combined. Alternatively, process in a blender until smooth.

Combine the oats and optional sunflower seeds in a roasting pan or large bowl. Pour the almond butter mixture over the oats and toss well to distribute evenly.

Spread the oat mixture evenly in the roasting pan or on two baking sheets. Bake for 10 minutes, then stir to prevent burning. Bake for 10 minutes longer, or until golden brown.

Let cool thoroughly. Stir in the currants. Transfer to glass jars or heavy-duty ziplock storage bags. Stored in the refrigerator or freezer, Good Morning Granola will keep for 6 months.

VARIATIONS:

- Replace the maple syrup with an additional ½ cup (125 ml) of apple juice concentrate.
- Stir in 1½ cups (375 ml) of unsweetened shredded dried coconut 5 minutes before the granola is finished baking.

Per cup (250 ml): calories: 381, protein: 11 g, fat: 10 g, carbohydrates: 64 g (10 g from sugar), dietary fiber: 7 g, calcium: 84 mg, iron: 4 mg, magnesium: 126 mg, phosphorus: 344 mg, potassium: 480 mg, sodium: 57 mg, zinc: 3 mg, thiamin: 0.4 mg, riboflavin: 0.2 mg, niacin: 4 mg, vitamin B_6: 0.1 mg, folate: 17 mcg, pantothenic acid: 0.6 mg, vitamin B_{12}: 0 mcg, vitamin A: 67 mcg, vitamin C: 1 mg, vitamin E: 3 mg, omega-6 fatty acid: 2.6 g, omega-3 fatty acid: 0.1 g

Percentage of calories from: protein 12%, fat 23%, carbohydrates 65%

Having this hearty cereal for breakfast is a great way to add whole grains to your diet. Leftovers can be refrigerated and served as a cold pudding or reheated and served as a warm cereal. Begin by using a combination of three whole grains, then create your own mix with as many different grains as you like. Serve the cereal with your choice of fresh or dried fruit, nuts, seeds, and nondairy milk.

HEARTY Whole-Grain Cereal

1 cup (250 ml) **uncooked grain** (such as amaranth, barley, brown rice, buckwheat, Kamut berries, millet, oat groats, quinoa, spelt berries, wheat berries, or wild rice)

4 cups (1 L) **water**

Tasty and Nutritious Grain Combinations to Try

- ⅓ cup (85 ml) each of barley, Kamut berries, and oat groats

- ⅓ cup (85 ml) each of barley, brown rice, and wheat or spelt berries

- ⅓ cup (85 ml) each of brown rice, millet, and oat groats (this combination is gluten-free)

Stovetop method: Put the grains and water in a heavy pot and bring to a boil over high heat. Decrease the heat to low, cover, and cook for 2 to 3 hours, until the grains are tender. Add more water as needed during cooking.

Double-boiler method: Put the grains and water in the top portion of a double boiler, above plenty of simmering water in the lower pot. Cover and cook the grains for 2 to 3 hours. Check periodically to make sure there is sufficient water in the lower pot.

Slow-cooker method: Put the grains and water in a slow cooker and cook on low heat for 8 to 10 hours, until the water has been absorbed. Letting the cereal cook overnight is a great way to have a hot breakfast ready to go in the morning.

Per cup (250 ml): calories: 167, protein: 5 g, fat: 2 g, carbohydrates: 34 g (0 g from sugar), dietary fiber: 3 g, calcium: 7 mg, iron: 1 mg, magnesium: 71 mg, phosphorus: 142 mg, potassium: 111 mg, sodium: 3 mg, zinc: 1 mg, thiamin: 0.2 mg, riboflavin: 0.1 mg, niacin: 3 mg, vitamin B_6: 0.2 mg, folate: 23 mcg, pantothenic acid: 0.5 mg, vitamin B_{12}: 0 mcg, vitamin A: 0 mcg, vitamin C: 0 mg, vitamin E: 0.3 mg, omega-6 fatty acid: 0.6 g, omega-3 fatty acid: 0 g

Percentage of calories from: protein 11%, fat 8%, carbohydrates 81%

Note: Analysis was done using brown rice, millet, and oat groats.

Turmeric adds an appealing yellow color to this tasty, high-protein dish. Even though it resembles scrambled eggs, it is cholesterol-free. For breakfast, serve Scrambled Tofu with whole-grain toast and juice or a hot beverage. Later in the day, serve it as an easy-to-assemble lunch or dinner packed with vitamins and minerals. Add your favorite salsa for extra color and flavor.

Scrambled TOFU

MAKES TWO 1¼-CUP (310-ML) SERVINGS

1 pound (454 g) **firm tofu, pressed for 20 minutes** (see page 17)

2 teaspoons (10 ml) **coconut oil or extra-virgin olive oil**

1 cup (250 ml) **sliced mushrooms**

1 cup (250 ml) **sliced napa cabbage**

½ cup (125 ml) **diced red bell pepper**

1 clove garlic, minced

1 teaspoon (5 ml) **tamari**

¼ teaspoon (1 ml) **ground cumin**

⅛ teaspoon (0.5 ml) **ground turmeric**

2 tablespoons (30 ml) **chopped green onion**

1 tablespoon (15 ml) **chopped fresh cilantro or parsley**

1 tablespoon (15 ml) **nutritional yeast flakes** (optional)

¼ teaspoon (1 ml) **salt** (optional)

Put the tofu in a small bowl and mash with a fork. Heat the oil in a large skillet over medium heat. Add the mushrooms, napa cabbage, bell pepper, and garlic. Cook and stir for 5 minutes, or until the moisture has evaporated and the mushrooms start to brown. Stir in the tofu, tamari, cumin, and turmeric. Cook for 5 minutes, stirring occasionally. Stir in the green onion, cilantro, optional nutritional yeast, and optional salt. Serve immediately.

Per 1¼ cups (310 ml): calories: 243, protein: 23 g, fat: 14 g, carbohydrates: 12 g (5 g from sugar), dietary fiber: 4 g, calcium: 514 mg, iron: 5 mg, magnesium: 102 mg, phosphorus: 396 mg, potassium: 695 mg, sodium: 877 mg, zinc: 3 mg, thiamin: 0.2 mg, riboflavin: 0.4 mg, niacin: 9 mg, vitamin B_6: 0.4 mg, folate: 66 mcg, pantothenic acid: 1.1 mg, vitamin B_{12}: 0 mcg, vitamin A: 100 mcg, vitamin C: 92 mg, vitamin E: 1 mg, omega-6 fatty acid: 4 g, omega-3 fatty acid: 0.5 g

Percentage of calories from: protein 34%, fat 48%, carbohydrates 18%

Note: Analysis was done using calcium-set tofu; check tofu labels for calcium content. Adding the optional nutritional yeast significantly increases the amount of B vitamins in this dish.

These light pancakes are free of eggs, dairy, and (if you wish) soy. Serve them with your choice of toppings, such as Apple-Cinnamon Topping (page 72), fresh fruit, or maple syrup.

WHOLE WHEAT Pancakes

MAKES 8 OR 9 (4-INCH/10-CM) PANCAKES

1 cup (250 ml) **whole wheat pastry flour**

2 tablespoons (30 ml) **baking powder**

½ teaspoon (2 ml) **ground cinnamon**

⅛ teaspoon (0.5 ml) **salt**

1 cup (250 ml) **nondairy milk**

2½ tablespoons (37 ml) **coconut oil or extra-virgin olive oil**

1 tablespoon (15 ml) **sweetener** (optional)

Combine the flour, baking powder, cinnamon, and salt in a medium bowl. Combine the nondairy milk, oil, and optional sweetener in a small bowl or measuring cup.

Heat a large skillet over medium heat. Pour the nondairy milk mixture into the flour mixture and lightly whisk until just combined. (Overmixing will make the pancakes flat and less fluffy).

When the skillet is hot, add about 1 tablespoon (15 ml) of oil to coat the surface.

To make each pancake, pour about 3 tablespoons (45 ml) of the batter into the hot skillet. Cook for about 3 minutes, or until bubbles form on the surface and the bottom of the pancake is lightly browned. Turn the pancake over and cook until the other side is browned, about 2 minutes. Serve hot.

Per pancake: calories: 98, protein: 3 g, fat: 5 g, carbohydrates: 11 g (0 g from sugar), dietary fiber: 1 g, calcium: 137 mg, iron: 0.5 mg, magnesium: 1 mg, phosphorus: 37 mg, potassium: 80 mg, sodium: 244 mg, thiamin: 0.4 mg, riboflavin: 0.1 mg, niacin: 0.3 mg, vitamin B_6: 0 mg, vitamin B_{12}: 0.4 mcg, vitamin A: 13 mcg, vitamin C: 0 mg, omega-6 fatty acid: 0.1 g, omega-3 fatty acid: 0 g

Percentage of calories from: protein 10%, fat 45%, carbohydrates 45%

Note: Analysis was done using fortified soymilk.

Apples are one of the most widely cultivated tree fruits, with over 7,500 varieties grown worldwide. The classic combination of apples and cinnamon is fabulous in this warm topping. Only add the maple syrup if you are using tart apples. Serve this topping with Whole Wheat Pancakes (page 71), Hearty Whole-Grain Cereal (page 69), Lem-Un-Cheesecake with Crumb Crust (page 232), or Vegan Dazs Ice Cream (page 217).

APPLE-CINNAMON Topping

MAKES FOUR ½-CUP (125-ML) SERVINGS

3 apples, quartered, cored, and cut into ¼-inch (5-mm) slices

3 tablespoons (45 ml) chopped toasted almonds (optional)

1 tablespoon (15 ml) freshly squeezed lemon juice

1 tablespoon (15 ml) maple syrup (optional)

¼ teaspoon (1 ml) grated lemon zest

⅛ teaspoon (0.5 ml) ground cinnamon

Put the apples, optional almonds, lemon juice, optional maple syrup, zest, and cinnamon in a medium skillet over medium heat. Cover and cook, stirring occasionally, for 5 minutes, or until the apples are soft and moist.

Per ½ cup (125 ml): calories: 72, protein: 0.3 g, fat: 0.2 g, carbohydrates: 19 g (15 g from sugar), dietary fiber: 3 g, calcium: 11 mg, iron: 0.2 mg, magnesium: 7 mg, phosphorus: 13 mg, potassium: 135 mg, sodium: 2 mg, zinc: 0.3 mg, thiamin: 0 mg, riboflavin: 0 mg, niacin: 0.1 mg, vitamin B$_6$: 1 mg, folate: 4 mcg, pantothenic acid: 0.1 mg, vitamin B$_{12}$: 0 mcg, vitamin A: 3 mcg, vitamin C: 7 mg, vitamin E: 0.2 mg, omega-6 fatty acid: 0 g, omega-3 fatty acid: 0 g

Percentage of calories from: protein 2%, fat 2%, carbohydrates 96%

chapter 6

Dips, Spreads, Snacks, and Sandwiches

Black beans, which have a slightly earthy taste that is reminiscent of mushrooms, are often combined with assertive flavors, such as the chipotle chile in this recipe. Serve it as a quick dip or spread with bread, carrot sticks, or crackers. It's a great source of protein, trace minerals, and folate.

CHIPOTLE Black Bean Dip

MAKES FOUR ½-CUP (125-ML) SERVINGS

2 cups (500 ml) **cooked or canned black beans, rinsed**

¼ cup (60 ml) **freshly squeezed lime juice**

¼ cup (60 ml) **tahini**

¼ cup (60 ml) **water**

1 teaspoon (5 ml) **minced chipotle chile**

1 clove garlic, chopped

½ teaspoon (2 ml) **ground toasted cumin seeds** (see sidebar, page 100)

½ teaspoon (2 ml) **dried oregano**

¼ teaspoon (1 ml) **salt**

2 tablespoons (30 ml) **chopped fresh cilantro or parsley**

1 tablespoon (15 ml) **extra-virgin olive oil**

Put the black beans, lime juice, tahini, water, chile, garlic, cumin, oregano, and salt in a food processor and process until smooth. Add the cilantro and oil and process until evenly distributed, about 5 seconds. Stored in a sealed container in the refrigerator, Chipotle Black Bean Dip will keep for 4 to 5 days.

Per ½ cup (125 ml): calories: 247, protein: 11 g, fat: 12 g, carbohydrates: 27 g (0 g from sugar), dietary fiber: 9 g, calcium: 55 mg, iron: 3 mg, magnesium: 81 mg, phosphorus: 253 mg, potassium: 423 mg, sodium: 125 mg, zinc: 2 mg, thiamin: 0.5 mg, riboflavin: 0.1 mg, niacin: 3 mg, vitamin B_6: 0.1 mg, folate: 153 mcg, pantothenic acid: 0.2 mg, vitamin B_{12}: 0 mcg, vitamin A: 5 mcg, vitamin C: 7 mg, vitamin E: 1 mg, omega-6 fatty acid: 4 g, omega-3 fatty acid: 0.2 g

Percentage of calories from: protein 17%, fat 42%, carbohydrates 41%

Black beans are essential to the cuisines of the Caribbean, Central and South America, Cuba, and Mexico, where they are a daily staple. This hearty salsa has a Mexican influence; in Mexico, salsas are served as a condiment or side dish at every meal. Black Bean, Corn, and Avocado Salsa is rich in protein, dietary fiber, iron, potassium, zinc, and folate.

Black Bean, Corn, and Avocado SALSA

MAKES EIGHT TO NINE ½-CUP (125-ML) SERVINGS

2 cups (500 ml) **cooked or canned black beans, rinsed**

1 cup (250 ml) **fresh, canned, or frozen corn kernels, rinsed if canned**

1 cup (250 ml) **diced tomato**

¼ cup (60 ml) **chopped green onion**

2 tablespoons (30 ml) **chopped fresh cilantro or parsley**

2 tablespoons (30 ml) **freshly squeezed lime juice**

1 teaspoon (5 ml) **ground cumin**

¼ teaspoon (1 ml) **salt**

1 clove garlic, minced

1 ripe avocado, diced

½ fresh green chile, finely minced, or hot sauce

Put the black beans, corn, tomato, green onion, cilantro, lime juice, cumin, salt, and garlic in a medium bowl. Mix well to combine. Gently fold in the avocado. Season with the chile or hot sauce to taste. Serve immediately.

Per ½ cup (125 ml): calories: 114, protein: 5 g, fat: 4 g, carbohydrate: 17 g (1 g from sugar), dietary fiber: 6 g, calcium: 23 mg, iron: 2 mg, magnesium: 50 mg, phosphorus: 95 mg, potassium: 406 mg, sodium: 63 mg, zinc: 1 mg, thiamin: 0.2 mg, riboflavin: 0.1 mg, niacin: 1.3 mg, vitamin B6: 0.1 mg, folate: 91 mcg, pantothenic acid: 0.5 mg, vitamin B12: 0 mcg, vitamin A: 18 mcg, vitamin C: 14 mg, vitamin E: 0.5 mg, omega-6 fatty acids: 0.6 g, omega-3 fatty acids: 0.1 g

Percentage of calories from: protein 17%, fat 29%, carbohydrates 54%

Many Mexican foods, including black beans, chili beans, corn, tomato products, and tortilla shells, are low in fat. Avocados are an exception, but they are a source of healthful fats. They also add a creamy, soothing, and colorful touch to a festive meal. Nutritional yeast packs extra B vitamins into this dip, which can be served with crackers or rice cakes or spread on bread.

LIMEY Avocado Dip

MAKES FOUR ¼-CUP (60-ML) SERVINGS

2 ripe avocados

1 tablespoon (15 ml) freshly squeezed lime juice

2 teaspoons (10 ml) chopped fresh cilantro or parsley

2 teaspoons (10 ml) chopped green onion

1 teaspoon (5 ml) nutritional yeast flakes

1 clove garlic, minced

½ teaspoon (2 ml) tamari

¼ teaspoon (1 ml) chili powder

Scoop the avocado flesh into a medium bowl and mash with a fork until smooth. Stir in the lime juice, cilantro, green onion, nutritional yeast, garlic, tamari, and chili powder. Serve immediately.

Per ¼ cup (60 ml): calories: 167, protein: 2 g, fat: 15 g, carbohydrates: 8 g (0 g from sugar), dietary fiber: 5 g, calcium: 15 mg, iron: 1 mg, magnesium: 41 mg, phosphorus: 50 mg, potassium: 626 mg, sodium: 46 mg, zinc: 0.5 mg, thiamin: 0.4 mg, riboflavin: 0.4 mg, niacin: 4 mg, vitamin B_6: 0.6 mg, folate: 71 mcg, pantothenic acid: 1 mg, vitamin B_{12}: 0.2 mcg, vitamin A: 67 mcg, vitamin C: 10 mg, vitamin E: 1 mg, omega-6 fatty acid: 2 g, omega-3 fatty acid: 0.1 g

Percentage of calories from: protein 6%, fat 76%, carbohydrates 18%

Note: Analysis was done using Red Star Vegetarian Support Formula nutritional yeast flakes, a source of vitamin B_{12}.

Traditionally made with olives and capers, tapenade is a spread that originated in the French region of Provence. This version replaces the majority of the olives with walnuts, which provide less sodium and a significant amount of omega-3 fatty acid. This recipe tastes best when fresh basil is used, but it can also be made with the dried herb.

WALNUT, OLIVE & SUN-DRIED TOMATO Tapenade

MAKES EIGHT TO NINE ½-CUP (125 ML) SERVINGS

1 cup (250 ml) **walnuts**

½ cup (125 ml) **pitted kalamata olives**

½ cup (125 ml) **sun-dried tomatoes, soaked in water for 4 hours, then drained**

2 tablespoons (30 ml) **capers**

2 tablespoons (30 ml) **freshly squeezed lemon juice**

1 small clove **garlic, chopped**

1 tablespoon (15 ml) **chopped fresh parsley**

1½ teaspoons (7 ml) **chopped fresh basil, or ½ teaspoon** (2 ml) **dried**

Put the walnuts in a food processor and process into crumbs, about 15 seconds. Add the olives, tomatoes, capers, lemon juice, and garlic and process into a paste, stopping 2 or 3 times to scrape down the sides of the work bowl. Add the parsley and basil and process for 10 seconds. Stored in a sealed container in the refrigerator, Walnut, Olive, and Sun-Dried Tomato Tapenade will keep for 7 days.

Per ¼ cup (60 ml): calories: 74, protein: 2 g, fat: 6 g, carbohydrates: 6 g (2 g from sugar), dietary fiber: 2 g, calcium: 31 mg, iron: 1 mg, magnesium: 24 mg, phosphorus: 44 mg, potassium: 242 mg, sodium: 348 mg, zinc: 0.4 mg, thiamin: 0.1 mg, riboflavin: 0 mg, niacin: 1 mg, vitamin B_6: 0.1 mg, folate: 13 mcg, pantothenic acid: 0.2 mg, vitamin B_{12}: 0 mcg, vitamin A: 19 mcg, vitamin C: 7 mg, vitamin E: 0.3 mg, omega-6 fatty acid: 2.4 g, omega-3 fatty acid: 0.6 g

Percentage of calories from: protein 10%, fat 61%, carbohydrates 29%

This sandwich filling has a mild curry flavor and the look and texture of egg salad, but with a little more protein and none of the cholesterol. The recipe makes enough filling for four sandwiches. Alternatively, it can be served as an appetizer with raw vegetables, crackers, or bread.

Curried SANDWICH SPREAD

MAKES FOUR ½-CUP (125-ML) SERVINGS

1 pound (454 g) **medium-firm or firm tofu, pressed for 20 minutes** (see page 17)

¼ cup (60 ml) **vegan mayonnaise**

1 tablespoon (15 ml) **chopped green onion**

1 tablespoon (15 ml) **chopped fresh parsley**

2 teaspoons (10 ml) **tamari**

1 clove garlic, minced

½ teaspoon (2 ml) **chili powder**

½ teaspoon (2 ml) **curry powder**

½ teaspoon (2 ml) **nutritional yeast flakes**

salt

Drain the tofu. Transfer it to a medium bowl and mash it with a fork. Add the vegan mayonnaise, green onion, parsley, tamari, garlic, chili powder, curry powder, and nutritional yeast. Stir until well combined. Season with salt to taste. Stored in a sealed container in the refrigerator, Curried Sandwich Spread will keep for 4 to 5 days.

Per ½ cup (125 ml): calories: 119, protein: 10 g, fat: 8 g, carbohydrates: 4 g (1 g from sugar), dietary fiber: 1 g, calcium: 234 mg, iron: 2 mg, magnesium: 45 mg, phosphorus: 145 mg, potassium: 219 mg, sodium: 281 mg, zinc: 1 mg, thiamin: 0.2 mg, riboflavin: 0.2 mg, niacin: 4 mg, vitamin B_6: 0.3 mg, folate: 29 mcg, pantothenic acid: 0.2 mg, vitamin B_{12}: 0.1 mcg, vitamin A: 5 mcg, vitamin C: 2 mg, vitamin E: 0.1 mg, omega-6 fatty acid: 2 g, omega-3 fatty acid: 0.2 g

Percentage of calories from: protein 33%, fat 55%, carbohydrates 12%

Note: Analysis was done using Red Star Vegetarian Support Formula nutritional yeast flakes, a source of vitamin B_{12}.

Here's an easy-to-make and cheesy-tasting spread that has none of the saturated fat or cholesterol of cheese. Gee Whiz Spread is rich in protein, minerals, and B vitamins, and it's low in fat. Serve it on crackers, in sandwiches, or as a topping for vegan burgers. It also works great as a dairy-free cheese replacement in Mac Uncheese (page 169).

GEE WHIZ Spread

MAKES FOUR ½-CUP (125-ML) SERVINGS

1½ cups (375 ml) **cooked or canned white beans** (great northern, navy, or white kidney beans)**, rinsed**

½ cup (125 ml) **chopped pimiento**

6 to 8 tablespoons (90 to 125 ml) **nutritional yeast flakes**

3 tablespoons (45 ml) **freshly squeezed lemon juice**

2 to 3 tablespoons (30 to 45 ml) **tahini**

½ teaspoon (2 ml) **prepared yellow mustard**

½ teaspoon (2 ml) **onion powder**

½ teaspoon (2 ml) **salt**

Put all the ingredients in a food processor and process until smooth. Chill thoroughly before serving. Stored in a sealed container in the refrigerator, Gee Whiz Spread will keep for 4 to 5 days.

Per ½ cup (125 ml): calories: 173, protein: 12 g, fat: 5 g, carbohydrates: 23 g (1 g from sugar), dietary fiber: 6 g, calcium: 69 mg, iron: 3 mg, magnesium: 57 mg, phosphorus: 282 mg, potassium: 549 mg, sodium: 252 mg, zinc: 3 mg, thiamin: 6 mg, riboflavin: 6 mg, niacin: 36 mg, vitamin B_6: 6 mg, folate: 219 mcg, pantothenic acid: 0.8 mg, vitamin B_{12}: 4.6 mcg, vitamin A: 34 mcg, vitamin C: 28 mg, vitamin E: 0.6 mg, omega-6 fatty acid: 2 g, omega-3 fatty acid: 0.1 g

Percentage of calories from: protein 26%, fat 24%, carbohydrates 50%

Note: Analysis was done using Red Star Vegetarian Support Formula nutritional yeast flakes, a source of vitamin B_{12}.

Reprinted by permission from *The Ultimate Uncheese Cookbook* © Jo Stepaniak (Summertown, TN: Book Publishing Company, 2003).

This creamy, dome-shaped vegan cheese can be sliced or cut into wedges, making it a great addition to sandwiches or an appealing appetizer. The agar (see page 27) dissolves after simmering in water for a few minutes. When removed from the heat, the agar mixture begins to firm up quickly, so complete the procedure without interruption. Nutritional yeast makes this cheese alternative an excellent source of B vitamins and, along with the turmeric and paprika, gives it a golden color.

GOODA Cheez

MAKES SIX ½-CUP (125-ML) SERVINGS

1¾ cups (435 ml) **water**

½ cup (125 ml) **chopped carrot**

⅓ cup (85 ml) **agar flakes, or 2 teaspoons** (10 ml) **agar powder**

½ cup (125 ml) **raw cashew pieces**

¼ cup (60 ml) **nutritional yeast flakes**

3 tablespoons (45 ml) **freshly squeezed lemon juice**

3 tablespoons (45 ml) **tahini**

1 tablespoon (15 ml) **Dijon mustard**

2 teaspoons (10 ml) **onion powder**

1 teaspoon (5 ml) **salt**

½ teaspoon (2 ml) **dry mustard**

½ teaspoon (2 ml) **garlic powder**

¼ teaspoon (1 ml) **ground cumin**

¼ teaspoon (1 ml) **paprika**

¼ teaspoon (1 ml) **turmeric**

Lightly oil a 3-cup (750-ml) bowl or mold with a rounded bottom.

Put the water, carrot, and agar in a medium saucepan. Cover and bring to a boil. Decrease the heat and cook for 10 minutes. Pour the carrot mixture into a blender and add the cashews, nutritional yeast, lemon juice, tahini, Dijon mustard, onion powder, salt, dry mustard, garlic powder, cumin, paprika, and turmeric. Process until completely smooth. Pour immediately into the prepared bowl or mold. Cover and chill for at least 2 hours. To serve, turn out of the bowl or mold and slice into wedges. Stored in a sealed container in the refrigerator, Gooda Cheez will keep for 4 to 5 days.

Per ½ cup (125 ml): calories: 147, protein: 6 g, fat: 10 g, carbohydrates: 11 g (1 g from sugar), dietary fiber: 1 g, calcium: 38 mg, iron: 2 mg, magnesium: 55 mg, phosphorus: 178 mg, potassium: 259 mg, sodium: 471 mg, zinc: 2 mg, thiamin: 2.7 mg, riboflavin: 2.6 mg, niacin: 16 mg, vitamin B_6: 2.5 mg, folate: 86 mcg, pantothenic acid: 0.5 mg, vitamin B_{12}: 2 mcg, vitamin A: 185 mcg, vitamin C: 4.8 mg, vitamin E: 0.4 mg, omega-6 fatty acid: 2.7 g, omega-3 fatty acid: 0.1 g

Percentage of calories from: protein 15%, fat 57%, carbohydrates 28%

Note: Analysis was done using Red Star Vegetarian Support Formula nutritional yeast flakes, a source of vitamin B_{12}.

Reprinted by permission from *The Ultimate Uncheese Cookbook* © Jo Stepaniak (Summertown, TN: Book Publishing Company, 2003).

Originating in the Middle East, hummus is now popular worldwide thanks to its impressive nutritional profile and excellent taste. This nourishing spread is likely to become a staple in your household. Keep it stocked in the refrigerator and you'll always be able to create a quick snack or lunch to satisfy hungry children, teens, and adults.

Heart-Healthy HUMMUS

2 cups (500 ml) **cooked or canned chickpeas, rinsed**

⅓ cup (85 ml) **tahini**

¼ cup (60 ml) **freshly squeezed lemon juice**

¼ cup (60 ml) **water**

1 to 2 tablespoons (15 to 30 ml) **extra-virgin olive oil**

1½ teaspoons (7 ml) **ground cumin**

1 clove garlic, chopped

½ teaspoon (2 ml) **salt**

¼ cup (60 ml) **chopped fresh parsley**

Combine the chickpeas, tahini, lemon juice, water, oil, cumin, garlic, and salt in a food processor. Process until smooth, stopping occasionally to scrape down the sides of the work bowl. Add the parsley and process just until evenly distributed, about 5 seconds. Stored in a sealed container in the refrigerator, Heart-Healthy Hummus will keep for 4 to 5 days.

Per ½ cup (125 ml): calories: 223, protein: 9 g, fat: 11 g, carbohydrates: 24 g (4 g from sugar), dietary fiber: 4 g, calcium: 70 mg, iron: 3 mg, magnesium: 54 mg, phosphorus: 259 mg, potassium: 326 mg, sodium: 203 mg, zinc: 2 mg, thiamin: 0.4 mg, riboflavin: 0.1 mg, niacin: 1.4 mg, vitamin B_6: 0.1 mg, folate: 142 mcg, pantothenic acid: 0.2 mg, vitamin B_{12}: 0 mcg, vitamin A: 30 mcg, vitamin C: 12 mg, vitamin E: 0.7 mg, omega-6 fatty acid: 4.7 g, omega-3 fatty acid: 0.1 g

Percentage of calories from: protein 16%, fat 42%, carbohydrates 42%

This spread delivers the rich flavors of basil and garlic along with plenty of valuable omega-3 fatty acid. Enjoy it as a gourmet appetizer on fresh bread, as a pizza sauce (see page 173), or on pasta (see variation). Be sure to use fresh walnuts; rancid nuts will overpower the other ingredients. When basil is in season, make plenty of pesto and freeze it in small containers for use all winter.

PESTO the Besto

1 cup (250 ml) **walnuts**

4 cups (1 L) **fresh basil leaves and tender stems**

¼ cup (60 ml) **extra-virgin olive oil or hempseed oil**

2 tablespoons (30 ml) **freshly squeezed lemon juice**

2 tablespoons (30 ml) **tamari**

3 to 6 cloves **garlic**

⅛ teaspoon (0.5 ml) **ground pepper**

Put the walnuts in a food processor and process into fine crumbs, 15 to 30 seconds. Add the basil, oil, lemon juice, tamari, garlic, and pepper and process until smooth. Stored in a sealed container, Pesto the Besto will keep for 7 days in the refrigerator and 6 months in the freezer.

Pesto Pasta: To use the pesto as a pasta sauce, combine ½ cup (125 ml) of pesto with ⅓ cup (85 ml) of hot water or vegetable stock (for homemade, see page 92), and stir to make a sauce. Season with tamari to taste. Stir into 4 cups (1 L) of cooked pasta.

Per ¼ cup (60 ml): calories: 253, protein: 5 g, fat: 25 g, carbohydrates: 6g (1 g from sugar), dietary fiber: 3 g, calcium: 81 mg, iron: 2 mg, magnesium: 66 mg, phosphorus: 111 mg, potassium: 290 mg, sodium: 410 mg, zinc: 1 mg, thiamin: 0.1 mg, riboflavin: 0.1 mg, niacin: 2 mg, vitamin B_6: 0.2 mg, folate: 46 mcg, pantothenic acid: 0.2 mg, vitamin B_{12}: 0 mcg, vitamin A: 95 mcg, vitamin C: 10 mg, vitamin E: 2 mg, omega-6 fatty acid: 9 g, omega-3 fatty acid: 2 g

Percentage of calories from: protein 7%, fat 84%, carbohydrates 9%

Store-bought sunflower seed butter can be expensive. Here is an affordable and nutritious alternative—a homemade spread that combines sunflower seeds and tahini, which are both rich in protein, iron, zinc, and vitamin E. Sunflower-Sesame Spread can be used as a dip, in a sandwich, in raw celery sticks, or in Baked Stuffed Apples (page 218).

Sunflower-Sesame SPREAD

MAKES NINE ¼-CUP (60-ML) SERVINGS

1 cup (250 ml) **raw sunflower seeds, soaked in 1 cup** (250 ml) **water for 8 to 12 hours**

½ **cup** (125 ml) **tahini**

¼ **cup** (60 ml) **freshly squeezed lemon juice**

4 **teaspoons** (20 ml) **tamari**

1 **small clove garlic**

½ **teaspoon** (2 ml) **dried dill weed**

Drain the sunflower seeds and reserve the soaking liquid. Put the sunflower seeds, ½ cup (125 ml) of the soaking liquid, tahini, lemon juice, tamari, garlic, and dill weed in a food processor. Process until smooth. Stored in a sealed container in the refrigerator, Sunflower-Sesame Spread will keep for 2 to 3 weeks.

Per ¼ cup (60 ml): calories: 184, protein: 7 g, fat: 16 g, carbohydrates: 7 g (1 g from sugar), dietary fiber: 2 g, calcium: 42 mg, iron: 2 mg, magnesium: 75 mg, phosphorus: 235 mg, potassium: 198 mg, sodium: 157 mg, zinc: 2 mg, thiamin: 0.6 mg, riboflavin: 0.1 mg, niacin: 3 mg, vitamin B_6: 0.2 mg, folate: 53 mcg, pantothenic acid: 1 mg, vitamin B_{12}: 0 mcg, vitamin A: 2 mcg, vitamin C: 4 mg, vitamin E: 6 mg, omega-6 fatty acid: 9 g, omega-3 fatty acid: 0.1 g

Percentage of calories from: protein 14%, fat 14%, carbohydrates 72%

Common white beans, such as cannellini (white kidney), great northern, and navy beans, are used in casseroles and soups and are particularly tasty when baked with tomato sauce. Here, they are used to make a delectable spread that can be served with crackers, raw vegetables, or any of the grain products listed in the Satisfying Sandwiches chart (see page 88). The flavor of this mineral-rich spread will deepen if it is made a couple of hours before serving.

WHITE BEAN, OLIVE, AND THYME Spread

MAKES ABOUT FIVE ½-CUP (125-ML) SERVINGS

2½ cups (625 ml) **cooked or canned white beans, rinsed**

¼ cup (60 ml) **freshly squeezed lemon juice**

1 tablespoon (15 ml) **extra-virgin olive oil**

1 teaspoon (5 ml) **dried thyme**

1 clove garlic, chopped

½ teaspoon (2 ml) **salt**

¼ teaspoon (1 ml) **ground pepper**

¼ cup (60 ml) **chopped green or black olives**

2 tablespoons (30 ml) **chopped fresh parsley**

Put the beans, lemon juice, oil, thyme, garlic, salt, and pepper in a food processor and process until smooth. Add the olives and parsley and process until evenly distributed, about 5 seconds. Transfer the spread to a bowl or covered container and refrigerate for at least 2 hours before serving to allow the flavors to marry and deepen. Stored in a sealed container in the refrigerator, White Bean, Olive, and Thyme Spread will keep for 4 to 5 days.

Per ½ cup (125 ml): calories: 272, protein: 10 g, fat: 14 g, carbohydrates: 29 g (0 g from sugar), dietary fiber: 11 g, calcium: 95 mg, iron: 4 mg, magnesium: 75 mg, phosphorus: 182 mg, potassium: 520 mg, sodium: 281 mg, zinc: 1 mg, thiamin: 0.3 mg, riboflavin: 0.1 mg, niacin: 2 mg, vitamin B_6: 0.2 mg, folate: 149 mcg, pantothenic acid: 0.3 mg, vitamin B_{12}: 0 mcg, vitamin A: 19 mcg, vitamin C: 9 mg, vitamin E: 2 mg, omega-6 fatty acid: 1 g, omega-3 fatty acid: 0.2 g

Percentage of calories from: protein 14%, fat 44%, carbohydrates 42%

If you have tired of the margarine debate (is it healthful or isn't it?), opt for spreads that are clearly superior. For example, almond butter is a tasty source of calcium, cashew butter provides zinc, and the combination of tahini and blackstrap molasses is sweet and rich in calcium, iron, and other minerals. In addition, this book features several recipes for spreads that offer exceptional nutrition along with wonderfully satisfying flavor.

Tasty Spreads FOR BREAD, TOAST, AND CRACKERS

STORE-BOUGHT SPREADS

bean dips

fruit-sweetened jam

miso (spread thinly)

nut butters
(such as almond or cashew butter)

pesto

seed butters
(such as sunflower seed butter or tahini)

tapenade

tahini with a thin layer of blackstrap molasses

RECIPES

Chipotle Black Bean Dip (page 74)

Curried Sandwich Spread (page 78)

Gee Whiz Spread (page 79)

Gooda Cheez (page 80)

Heart-Healthy Hummus (page 81)

Limey Avocado Dip (page 76)

Sunflower-Sesame Spread (page 83)

Walnut, Olive, and Sun-Dried Tomato Tapenade (page 77)

White Bean, Olive, and Thyme Spread (page 84)

Vegetables deliver more vitamins and protective phytochemicals per calorie than any other food group. A snack of colorful veggies will balance the high fat content of many dips and thick salad dressings.

RAW VEGETABLE Platter

VEGETABLES

asparagus tips

bell peppers (orange, red, and yellow)

bok choy

broccoli

carrots

cauliflower

celery

cucumbers

green onions

jicama

parsnips

radishes (daikon, red, watermelon, or white)

snow peas

tomatoes

turnips (young)

yams

zucchini

Arrange the vegetables attractively on a platter, cutting them in similar shapes or creating a variety, such as cubes, diagonal slices, disks, matchsticks, spirals, or strips. Serve the vegetables with one of the dip, dressing, or spread recipes in this book, or use a store-bought version.

Per cup (250 ml) of assorted vegetables: calories: 38, protein: 1.5 g, fat: 0.3 g, carbohydrates: 8 g (3 from sugar), dietary fiber: 2 g, calcium: 31 mg, iron: 0.6 mg, magnesium: 16 mg, phosphorus: 38 mg, potassium: 292 mg, sodium: 25 mg, zinc: 0.3 mg, thiamin: 0.1 mg, riboflavin: 0.1 mg, niacin: 1 mg, pyridoxine: 0.1 mg, folate: 39 mcg, pantothenic acid: 0.3 mg, vitamin B_{12}: 0 mcg, vitamin A: 181 mcg, vitamin C: 41 mg, vitamin E: 0.6 mg, omega-6 fatty acid: 0.1 g, omega-3 fatty acid: 0 g

Percentage of calories from: protein 15%, fat 6%, carbohydrates 79%

These seeds are a savory alternative to deep-fried potato chips or corn chips. They are great for snacking at home or on the go. In addition, they can be used as a garnish for baked potatoes, cooked grains, and salads. Easy to make, these nutritious seeds provide protein, B vitamins, vitamin E, iron, and zinc.

TOASTED Sunflower or Pumpkin SEEDS

MAKES 2 CUPS (500 ML)

2 cups (500 ml) **raw sunflower or pumpkin seeds**

2 tablespoons (30 ml) **nutritional yeast flakes**

1 tablespoon (15 ml) **tamari**

Preheat the oven to 300 degrees F (150 degrees C).

Spread the seeds evenly on a baking sheet and bake for 7 to 9 minutes. Do not overcook; they burn easily.

Transfer to a bowl and stir in the nutritional yeast and tamari. Toss to coat the seeds evenly. Return the seeds to the baking sheet and bake for 1 minute to dry. Let cool before storing. Stored in a sealed container, Toasted Sunflower or Pumpkin Seeds will keep for 2 to 3 weeks in the refrigerator or 6 months in the freezer.

NOTE: The seeds will bake more quickly on dark baking sheets.

VARIATION: Toss the toasted sunflower seeds with 2 teaspoons (10 ml) of hot sauce, 2 teaspoons (10 ml) of tamari, and ½ teaspoon (2 ml) of garlic powder.

Per 2 tablespoons (30 ml): calories: 112, protein: 5 g, fat: 9 g, carbohydrates: 4 g (0.5 g from sugar), dietary fiber: 2 g, calcium: 23 mg, iron: 1 mg, magnesium: 69 mg, phosphorus: 144 mg, potassium: 149 mg, sodium: 65 mg, zinc: 1 mg, thiamin: 1 mg, riboflavin: 0.5 mg, niacin: 4 mg, vitamin B_6: 0.6 mg, folate: 55 mcg, pantothenic acid: 1 mg, vitamin B_{12}: 0.4 mcg, vitamin A: 1 mcg, vitamin C: 0 mg, vitamin E: 7 mg, omega-6 fatty acid: 6 g, omega-3 fatty acid: 0 g

Percentage of calories from: protein 16%, fat 71%, carbohydrates 13%

Note: Analysis was done using Red Star Vegetarian Support Formula nutritional yeast flakes, a source of vitamin B_{12}.

Read across each row to discover a tasty sandwich combination that includes a grain product, filling, and vegetables. If you like, mix and match the choices from different rows or add your own creative touches to your sandwiches along with buttery vegan spread, mustard, or vegan mayo.

SATISFYING Sandwiches

GRAIN PRODUCT	FILLING	VEGETABLES
Baguette or roll	Sunflower-Sesame Spread (page 83)	Cucumber slices, red onion slices, sprouts
Crusty roll	Vegan pepperoni slices and Walnut, Olive, and Sun-Dried Tomato Tapenade (page 77)	Bell pepper (green or red) slices, shredded lettuce, onion slices, tomato slices
Multigrain bread	Curried Sandwich Spread (page 78)	Lettuce, sprouts, tomato slices
Pita bread	Heart-Healthy Hummus (page 81), store-bought hummus, or Chipotle Black Bean Dip (page 74), Lemon-Tahini Dressing (page 134)	Olives, chopped onion, romaine lettuce, sprouts, diced tomato
Rice cakes or corn cakes	Gee Whiz Spread (page 79) or Gooda Cheez (page 80)	Cucumber slices, olive slices
Rice paper wrap	Marinated Tofu (page 160) strips or Crispy Tofu Slices (page 161), and rice, peanut sauce, and plum sauce	Shredded carrots, cucumber strips, lettuce, chopped peanuts, sprouts, sunflower seeds
Rye bread or roll	Vegan salami or deli slices	Lettuce, onion slices, pickles or sauerkraut
Sourdough or whole-grain roll	Vegan burger, ketchup, relish	Lettuce, onion slices, tomato slices
Toasted whole wheat bread	Vegan Canadian bacon and vegan cheese slices or shreds	Red onion slices, tomato slices
Tortilla (plain, spinach, or tomato)	Avocado slices, Limey Avocado Dip (page 76), or refried beans and salsa	Shredded carrots, green onions, sunflower sprouts
Whole wheat submarine roll	Vegan ham, vegan turkey, and vegan cheese slices or shreds	Cucumber slices, shredded lettuce, onion slices, sprouts, tomato slices

There is no end to delicious vegan sandwich options or alternatives. Here are some additional suggestions:

- Try the International Roll-Ups (page 144), Portobella Mushroom Burgers with Chickpea Topping (page 148), or Vietnamese Salad Roll (page 110).
- Make sandwiches with marinated or smoked tofu, seasoned tempeh or seitan, and other flavorful vegan meat alternatives that are available at supermarkets.
- Opt for nori rolls, Japan's contribution to the world of sandwiches, which use sheets of nori in place of bread. To make homemade Sushi Rolls, see page 146. Or look for vegan nori rolls at supermarkets, Japanese restaurants, and Japanese food outlets at airports.

Build a fantastic pita pocket by choosing one or two fillings from the first column, adding vegetables from the second column, and topping off these ingredients with a sauce from the third column. A couple of classic combinations include hummus, lettuce or sprouts, and Lemon-Tahini Dressing (page 134) or warmed refried beans, grated vegan cheese, avocado and tomato slices, sprouts, and salsa.

Palate-Pleasing PITA POCKETS

FILLING OR SPREAD	VEGETABLES	SAUCES
Chipotle Black Bean Dip (page 74)	Avocado slices	Lemon-Tahini
Crispy Tofu Slices (page 161)	Grated beets	Dressing (page 134)
Curried Sandwich Spread (page 78)	Chopped bell peppers (green, orange, red, or yellow)	Salsa
Gee Whiz Spread (page 79)	Cucumber slices	Spicy Peanut Sauce (page 182)
Gooda Cheez (page 80)	Grated carrot	Tabasco (or other hot sauce)
Heart-Healthy Hummus (page 81) or store-bought hummus	Grated jicama	Vegan mayonnaise
Lemon-Ginger Tempeh (page 167)	Chopped lettuce	
Limey Avocado Dip (page 76)	Olives	
Marinated Tofu (page 160)	Sliced onion (green, red, sweet, yellow, or white)	
Refried beans	Sprouts (alfalfa, broccoli, sunflower, or lentil)	
Sunflower-Sesame Spread (page 83)	Chopped tomato	
Vegan cheese		
Walnut, Olive, and Sun-Dried Tomato Tapenade (page 77)		

chapter 7

Soups

When making stock from scratch, try substituting different vegetables (such as fennel, leeks, mushrooms, and tomatoes) or herbs (such as basil, coriander, and rosemary). Do not use vegetables from the cabbage family in vegetable stock because their taste and odor are overpowering. If you use store-bought bouillon cubes or powders in place of homemade stock, avoid brands that contain hydrogenated fats, hydrolyzed protein, or MSG. Salt-free brands are available.

Vegetable STOCK

MAKES 6 CUPS (1.5 ML)

6 cups (1.5 L) **water**

2 carrots, diced

2 stalks celery, diced

1 large onion, chopped

½ fennel bulb, chopped (optional)

¼ cup (60 ml) chopped fresh parsley leaves and stems

2 large cloves garlic, chopped

½ teaspoon (2 ml) dried thyme

10 peppercorns, crushed

3 bay leaves

3 whole cloves

Put all the ingredients in a large soup pot. Bring to a boil over medium-high heat. Decrease the heat to medium, cover, and simmer, stirring occasionally, for 30 minutes. Strain the stock through a sieve or colander and discard the vegetables. Let the stock cool before refrigerating or freezing. Vegetable Stock will keep for 4 to 5 days in the refrigerator or 6 months in the freezer.

Native to India and Sri Lanka, lemongrass is a tropical grass that has a citrusy flavor but is not sour like lemons. The leafy, long-stemmed, aromatic stalks are popular in Thai cuisine and are typically combined with coconut milk, ginger, and vegetables to form a base for a wide variety of dishes. Here, these and other ingredients are used to make a creamy bright yellow-orange soup that is loaded with the antioxidant beta-carotene (vitamin A).

CARROT, LEMONGRASS, AND BASIL Soup

MAKES EIGHT 1-CUP (250-ML) SERVINGS

1 tablespoon (15 ml) **coconut oil or extra-virgin olive oil**

½ **onion, diced**

2 tablespoons (30 ml) **peeled and minced fresh ginger**

2 tablespoons (30 ml) **thinly sliced lemongrass**

3 cloves **garlic, minced**

4 cups (1 L) **sliced carrots**

3½ cups (875 ml) **water**

1¾ cups (435 ml) **coconut milk, or one 12-ounce (355-ml) can**

3 tablespoons (45 ml) **chopped fresh basil, or 1 tablespoon (15 ml) dried**

½ teaspoon (2 ml) **salt**

1 tablespoon (15 ml) **freshly squeezed lime juice**

Heat the oil in a large soup pot over medium heat. Add the onion and cook, stirring occasionally, for 3 to 5 minutes, or until soft. Add the ginger, lemongrass, and garlic and cook, stirring occasionally, for 2 minutes. Stir in the carrots, water, coconut milk, basil, and salt. Bring to a boil over medium-high heat. Decrease the heat to medium-low, cover, and simmer, stirring occasionally, for 15 minutes, or until the carrots are soft. Transfer the soup to a blender and process until smooth (it may be necessary to do this in two batches). Return the soup to the pot and reheat it over medium heat until steaming, 5 to 10 minutes. Stir in the lime juice. Serve hot.

Per cup (250 ml): calories: 159, protein: 2 g, fat: 14 g, carbohydrates: 10 g (3 g from sugar), dietary fiber: 2 g, calcium: 50 mg, iron: 2 mg, magnesium: 39 mg, phosphorus: 84 mg, potassium: 386 mg, sodium: 175 mg, zinc: 1 mg, thiamin: 0.1 mg, riboflavin: 0.1 mg, niacin: 2 mg, vitamin B_6: 0.2 mg, folate: 24 mcg, pantothenic acid: 0.3 mg, vitamin B_{12}: 0 mcg, vitamin A: 571 mcg, vitamin C: 6 mg, vitamin E: 0.5 mg, omega-6 fatty acid: 0.2 g, omega-3 fatty acid: 0 g

Percentage of calories from: protein 5%, fat 71%, carbohydrates 24%

The vitamins and phytochemicals in vegetables provide the splendid array of colors you see when you walk down the produce aisle. Three of these vitamins are bright yellow: folate, riboflavin, and vitamin A (also known as beta-carotene). This warming, golden soup is packed with all three.

Ginger, Carrot, and Yam SOUP

MAKES NINE 1-CUP (250-ML) SERVINGS

1 tablespoon (15 ml) **coconut oil or extra-virgin olive oil**

½ **small onion, chopped**

¼ **cup** (60 ml) **peeled and chopped fresh ginger**

4 **cups** (1 L) **chopped carrots**

4 **cups** (1 L) **water**

2 **cups** (500 ml) **peeled and chopped yams**

1 **orange, peeled, seeded, and chopped**

2 **teaspoons** (10 ml) **whole coriander seeds, or** 1 **teaspoon** (5 ml) **ground coriander**

½ **teaspoon** (2 ml) **salt**

¼ **teaspoon** (1 ml) **ground allspice**

¼ **teaspoon** (1 ml) **ground nutmeg**

½ **cup** (125 ml) **unsweetened apple juice**

Heat the oil in a large soup pot over medium heat. Add the onion and ginger and cook, stirring occasionally, for 3 to 5 minutes, or until soft. Stir in the carrots, water, yams, orange, coriander, salt, allspice, and nutmeg. Bring to a boil over medium-high heat. Decrease the heat to medium-low, cover, and simmer, stirring occasionally, for 15 to 20 minutes, or until the carrots and yams are soft. Transfer the soup to a blender and process until smooth (it may be necessary to do this in two batches). Return the soup to the pot, stir in the apple juice, and reheat the soup over medium heat until steaming, 5 to 10 minutes. Serve hot.

Per cup (250 ml): calories: 98, protein: 1 g, fat: 2 g, carbohydrates: 20 g (6 g from sugar), dietary fiber: 4 g, calcium: 38 mg, iron: 0.5 mg, magnesium: 20 mg, phosphorus: 46 mg, potassium: 543 mg, sodium: 153 mg, zinc: 0.3 mg, thiamin: 0.1 mg, riboflavin: 0.1 mg, niacin: 1 mg, vitamin B_6: 0.2 mg, folate: 25 mcg, pantothenic acid: 0.3 mg, vitamin B_{12}: 0 mcg, vitamin A: 508 mcg, vitamin C: 18 mg, vitamin E: 1 mg, omega-6 fatty acid: 0.1 g, omega-3 fatty acid: 0 g

Percentage of calories from: protein 6%, fat 16%, carbohydrates 78%

Many people believe that miso originated in Japan, but the history of miso can be traced back to China, as early as the fourth century. Different types of miso have distinctive aromas, colors, and flavors, so it is important to match each type with its best use. For example, light miso, which is sweeter and more subtle, is suitable for dishes that call for a delicate flavor. Dark miso, which is more robust and salty, is appropriate for recipes that need more assertive seasoning.

Shiitake Mushroom–Miso SOUP

MAKES SEVEN TO EIGHT 1-CUP (250-ML) SERVINGS

5 ounces (150 g) **shiitake mushrooms**

2 tablespoons (30 ml) **coconut oil or extra-virgin olive oil**

½ **onion, diced**

1 cup (250 ml) **diced carrots**

4 cloves garlic, chopped

6 cups (1.5 L) **water or vegetable stock** (for homemade, see page 92)

½ cup (125 ml) **brown rice**

2 teaspoons (10 ml) **dried marjoram**

2 teaspoons (10 ml) **dried thyme**

¼ cup (60 ml) **dark miso**

¼ cup (60 ml) **chopped fresh parsley**

Wash the mushrooms and remove and discard the tough stems. Thinly slice the caps.

Heat the oil in a large soup pot over medium heat. Add the mushrooms and onion and cook, stirring occasionally, until the onion is soft and starting to brown, about 3 minutes. Add the carrots and garlic and cook, stirring occasionally, for 2 minutes. Add the water, rice, marjoram, and thyme. Increase the heat to medium-high and bring to a boil. Decrease the heat to low, cover, and simmer, stirring occasionally, for 45 minutes, or until the rice is tender.

Put the miso in a small bowl or measuring cup and stir in about ½ cup (125 ml) of the soup broth to make a thin paste. Remove the soup from the heat and stir in the miso mixture and parsley. Serve immediately.

Per cup (250 ml): calories: 121, protein: 3 g, fat: 5 g, carbohydrates: 17 g (2 g from sugar), dietary fiber: 2 g, calcium: 37 mg, iron: 2 mg, magnesium: 31 mg, phosphorus: 63 mg, potassium: 144 mg, sodium: 369 mg, zinc: 1 mg, thiamin: 0.1 mg, riboflavin: 0.1 mg, niacin: 1 mg, vitamin B_6: 0.2 mg, folate: 14 mcg, pantothenic acid: 0.3 mg, vitamin B_{12}: 0 mcg, vitamin A: 155 mcg, vitamin C: 6 mg, vitamin E: 0.3 mg, omega-6 fatty acid: 0.5 g, omega-3 fatty acid: 0.1 g

Percentage of calories from: protein 10%, fat 34%, carbohydrates 56%

In one of the languages of southern India, mulligatawny means "pepper water." This light soup's spiciness varies according to how much pepper and ginger you add. If you like it hot, adjust the amounts; this version is moderately spicy. The sweetness of the apple and celery balances the spice. The crunch of uncooked apple as a garnish adds an appealing texture.

MULLIGATAWNY Soup

MAKES FOUR 1-CUP (250-ML) SERVINGS

1 tablespoon (15 ml) **coconut oil or extra-virgin olive oil**

1 cup (250 ml) **sliced celery**

½ **onion, diced**

1 tablespoon (15 ml) **peeled and minced fresh ginger**

2 cloves **garlic, minced**

1 tablespoon (15 ml) **tomato paste**

1½ teaspoons (7 ml) **curry powder**

¼ teaspoon (1 ml) **celery seeds**

¼ teaspoon (1 ml) **salt**

¼ teaspoon (1 ml) **ground pepper**

4 cups (1 L) **water**

¼ cup (60 ml) **white basmati rice**

1 **apple, diced, for garnish**

Heat the oil in a large soup pot over medium heat. Add the celery, onion, ginger, and garlic and cook, stirring occasionally, for about 5 minutes, or until the onion is soft and starts to brown. Stir in the tomato paste, curry powder, celery seeds, salt, and pepper. Cook for 3 minutes, stirring frequently to prevent sticking and scorching. Add the water and rice. Bring to a boil over medium-high heat. Decrease the heat to medium-low, cover, and simmer, stirring occasionally, for 30 minutes. Transfer to serving bowls and garnish each serving with one-quarter of the apple. Serve hot.

VARIATION: Replace the white basmati rice with brown basmati rice and simmer for 45 minutes.

Per cup (250 ml): calories: 118, protein: 2 g, fat: 4 g, carbohydrates: 22 g (6 g from sugar), dietary fiber: 3 g, calcium: 34 mg, iron: 1 mg, magnesium: 14 mg, phosphorus: 21 mg, potassium: 221 mg, sodium: 152 mg, zinc: 0.2 mg, thiamin: 0.1 mg, riboflavin: 0 mg, niacin: 1 mg, vitamin B_6: 0.1 mg, folate: 13 mcg, pantothenic acid: 0.1 mg, vitamin B_{12}: 0 mcg, vitamin A: 29 mcg, vitamin C: 7 mg, vitamin E: 1 mg, omega-6 fatty acid: 0.4 g, omega-3 fatty acid: 0 g

Percentage of calories from: protein 6%, fat 26%, carbohydrates 68%

This is the perfect soup for summertime, when fresh local produce and herbs are at their peak. To remove the corn from the cob, cut it in half and place the wider end on a cutting board. Use a sharp knife to slice the kernels away from the cob until all kernels have been removed.

Zucchini, Corn, and Amaranth SOUP

MAKES EIGHT 1-CUP (250-ML) SERVINGS

1 tablespoon (15 ml) **coconut oil or extra-virgin olive oil**

½ **onion, diced**

2 **cloves garlic, minced**

2 cups (500 ml) **diced tomatoes**

3 tablespoons (45 ml) **chopped fresh basil, or** 1 tablespoon (15 ml) **dried**

1 tablespoon (15 ml) **chopped fresh thyme, or** 1 teaspoon (5 ml) **dried**

1 **fresh red chile, chopped, or** ½ teaspoon (2 ml) **crushed red pepper flakes**

4 cups (1 L) **vegetable stock** (preferably homemade; see page 92)

⅓ cup (85 ml) **amaranth**

2 cups (500 ml) **fresh, canned, or frozen corn kernels, rinsed**

2 cups (500 ml) **diced zucchini**

salt

ground pepper

Heat the oil in a large soup pot over medium heat. Add the onion and garlic and cook, stirring occasionally, for 3 minutes, or until the onion is soft. Add the tomatoes, basil, thyme, and chile and cook, stirring occasionally, for 3 minutes. Stir in the stock and amaranth. Bring to a boil over medium-high heat. Decrease the heat to medium-low, cover, and simmer, stirring occasionally, for 20 minutes. Add the corn and zucchini. Return to a simmer and cook, stirring occasionally, for 5 minutes, or until the zucchini is tender-crisp. Season with salt and pepper to taste. Serve hot.

Per cup (250 ml): calories: 109, protein: 4 g, fat: 3 g, carbohydrates: 19 g (4 g from sugar), dietary fiber: 3 g, calcium: 34 mg, iron: 1 mg, magnesium: 53 mg, phosphorus: 108 mg, potassium: 394 mg, sodium: 159 mg, zinc: 1 mg, thiamin: 0.1 mg, riboflavin: 0.1 mg, niacin: 2 mg, vitamin B_6: 0.2 mg, folate: 43 mcg, pantothenic acid: 0.5 mg, vitamin B_{12}: 0 mcg, vitamin A: 101 mcg, vitamin C: 24 mg, vitamin E: 0.5 mg, omega-6 fatty acid: 0.6 g, omega-3 fatty acid: 0 g

Percentage of calories from: protein 13%, fat 25%, carbohydrates 62%

Note: Analysis was done without added salt.

Served with whole-grain bread and salad, this protein-rich soup satisfies the heartiest appetites. Each serving provides 12 grams of protein along with iron, other minerals, and folate. Freeze leftovers in individual portions for quick lunches and suppers.

CLASSIC Split Pea Soup

MAKES NINE 1-CUP (250-ML) SERVINGS

1 tablespoon (15 ml) **coconut oil or extra-virgin olive oil**

½ **onion, diced**

1 cup (250 ml) **diced carrots**

1 cup (250 ml) **diced celery**

2 cloves **garlic, minced**

8 cups (2 L) **water, plus more if needed**

2 cups (500 ml) **dried green split peas**

3 **bay leaves**

5 whole cloves, or ¼ teaspoon ground **cloves**

½ teaspoon **salt**

⅛ teaspoon (0.5 ml) **ground pepper**

1 tablespoon (15 ml) **chopped fresh parsley, for garnish**

Heat the oil in a large soup pot over medium heat. Add the onion and cook, stirring occasionally, for 3 to 5 minutes, or until the onion is soft. Add the carrots, celery, and garlic and cook, stirring occasionally, for 3 minutes. Stir in the water, split peas, bay leaves, and cloves. Bring to a boil over medium-high heat. Decrease the heat to medium-low, cover, and simmer, stirring occasionally, for 1 hour, or until the peas are soft. Add more water if the soup gets too thick. Stir in the salt and pepper. Transfer to serving bowls and garnish each serving with some of the parsley. Serve hot.

Per cup (250 ml): calories: 189, protein: 12 g, fat: 2 g, carbohydrates: 32 g (5 g from sugar), dietary fiber: 13 g, calcium: 56 mg, iron: 2.5 mg, magnesium: 63 mg, phosphorus: 183 mg, potassium: 575 mg, sodium: 146 mg, zinc: 1.5 mg, thiamin: 0.4 mg, riboflavin: 0.1 mg, niacin: 4 mg, vitamin B_6: 0.2 mg, folate: 136 mcg, pantothenic acid: 1 mg, vitamin B_{12}: 0 mcg, vitamin A: 169 mcg, vitamin C: 5 mg, vitamin E: 1 mg, omega-6 fatty acid: 0.4 g, omega-3 fatty acid: 0.1 g

Percentage of calories from: protein 24%, fat 11%, carbohydrates 65%

Kabocha squash is a Japanese variety of winter squash that has a hard shell and deep orange flesh. The shell is edible and the squash does not need to be peeled before cooking. Creamy and sweet, kabocha squash is exceptional when roasted or cooked in a soup. Butternut squash is a perfect substitute for kabocha; if you use butternut squash, be sure to peel it. Though this recipe may appear lengthy, many of the ingredients are ground spices. For convenience and speed, measure the spices into a small bowl and add them all at once when directed.

CURRIED Kabocha Squash and Chickpea SOUP

MAKES NINE TO TEN 1-CUP (250-ML) SERVINGS

2 tablespoons (30 ml) **coconut oil or extra-virgin olive oil**

1 onion, diced

1 tablespoon (15 ml) **peeled and minced fresh ginger**

4 cloves garlic, minced

2 tablespoons (30 ml) **ground coriander**

1½ tablespoons (30 ml) **ground toasted cumin seeds** (see sidebar, page 100)

½ teaspoon (2 ml) **cayenne**

½ teaspoon (2 ml) **salt**

½ teaspoon (2 ml) **ground turmeric**

¼ teaspoon (1 ml) **ground cardamom**

¼ teaspoon (1 ml) **ground cinnamon**

4 cups (1 L) **water**

4 cups (1 L) **diced, unpeeled kabocha squash**

2 cups (500 ml) **cooked or canned chickpeas, rinsed**

2 cups (500 ml) **chopped tomatoes**

Heat the oil in a large soup pot over medium heat. Add the onion, ginger, and garlic and cook, stirring occasionally, for 5 minutes, or until soft. Add the coriander, cumin, cayenne, salt, turmeric, cardamom, and cinnamon and cook for 2 minutes, stirring frequently to avoid scorching. Add ½ cup (125 ml) of the water and stir to loosen any spices that may have stuck to the bottom of the pot. Add the remaining 3½ cups (875 ml) of water, the squash, chickpeas, and tomatoes. Bring to a boil over medium-high heat. Decrease the heat to medium-low, cover, and simmer, stirring occasionally, for 20 minutes, or until the squash is soft. Serve hot.

Per cup (250 ml): calories: 135, protein: 5 g, fat: 5 g, carbohydrates: 22 g (5 g from sugar), dietary fiber: 4 g, calcium: 77 mg, iron: 3 mg, magnesium: 54 mg, phosphorus: 107 mg, potassium: 482 mg, sodium: 260 mg, zinc: 1 mg, thiamin: 0.1 mg, riboflavin: 0.1 mg, niacin: 2 mg, vitamin B$_6$: 0.2 mg, folate: 88 mcg, pantothenic acid: 0.4 mg, vitamin B$_{12}$: 0 mcg, vitamin A: 350 mcg, vitamin C: 20 mg, vitamin E: 1 mg, omega-6 fatty acid: 0.6 g, omega-3 fatty acid: 0.1 g

Percentage of calories from: protein 13%, fat 27%, carbohydrates 60%

Since antiquity, populations in many parts of the world have included lentils in their diets, and with good reason—these little gems contain 26 percent protein by weight. (For details about recommended protein intakes, see page 3.) This tasty protein- and mineral-rich lentil soup simmers for an hour, freeing you up to do other things around the house. The addition of molasses gives the soup a deep, rich flavor and a robust appearance.

MEDITERRANEAN Lentil Soup

MAKES SIX 1-CUP (250-ML) SERVINGS

1 tablespoon (15 ml) coconut oil or extra-virgin olive oil

½ onion, chopped

2 large cloves garlic, minced

5 cups (1.25 L) water

2 cups (500 ml) chopped fresh or canned tomatoes

1 cup (250 ml) dried lentils, rinsed

2 tablespoons (30 ml) chopped fresh basil, or 2 teaspoons (10 ml) dried

1 tablespoon (15 ml) chopped fresh oregano, or 1 teaspoon (5 ml) dried

2 bay leaves

1 tablespoon (15 ml) blackstrap molasses or brown sugar

1 tablespoon (15 ml) balsamic vinegar

1 teaspoon (5 ml) salt

⅛ teaspoon (0.5 ml) ground pepper

Heat the oil in a large soup pot over medium heat. Add the onion and cook, stirring occasionally, for 3 to 5 minutes, or until soft. Add the garlic and cook, stirring frequently, for 2 minutes. Stir in the water, tomatoes, lentils, basil, oregano, and bay leaves. Bring to a boil over medium-high heat. Decrease the heat to medium-low, cover, and simmer, stirring occasionally, for 1 hour. Stir in the molasses, vinegar, salt, and pepper. Serve hot.

Per cup (250 ml): calories: 164, protein: 10 g, fat: 3 g, carbohydrates: 26 g (6 g from sugar), dietary fiber: 5 g, calcium: 78 mg, iron: 4 mg, magnesium: 56 mg, phosphorus: 175 mg, potassium: 589 mg, sodium: 407 mg, zinc: 1.5 mg, thiamin: 0.2 mg, riboflavin: 0.1 mg, niacin: 3 mg, vitamin B_6: 0.3 mg, folate: 158 mcg, pantothenic acid: 0.7 mg, vitamin B_{12}: 0 mcg, vitamin A: 61 mcg, vitamin C: 12 mg, vitamin E: 1 mg, omega-6 fatty acid: 0.4 g, omega-3 fatty acid: 0.1 g

Percentage of calories from: protein 24%, fat 15%, carbohydrates 61%

Toasting Spices, Nuts, and Seeds

Stovetop method: Toasting spices (such as coriander, cumin, fenugreek, and mustard seeds) on the stovetop releases nonvolatile oils known as oleoresins that enhance and deepen flavors. Sesame seeds also can be toasted on the stovetop. Put the spices or seeds in a heavy skillet over medium heat. When the spices or seeds start to warm up, stir them continuously for several minutes with a wooden spoon. The amount of time needed to toast the spices or seeds will depend on the skillet and type of

A staple in Japanese cooking, miso is a fermented paste made from soybeans, salt, and a grain (most commonly rice or barley). A living culture initiates the fermentation process, which makes the nutrient-rich soybeans more digestible. Miso can be used to season many different savory dishes, such as dips, dressings, gravies, and soups.

Red Lentil Soup WITH MISO

MAKES SIX TO SEVEN 1-CUP (250-ML) SERVINGS

1 tablespoon (15 ml) **coconut oil or extra-virgin olive oil**

½ **onion, diced**

2 cups (500 ml) **diced carrots**

2 cloves garlic, **minced**

5 cups (1.25 L) **water**

1 cup (250 ml) **dried red lentils**

½ teaspoon (2 ml) **ground cumin**

2 tablespoons (30 ml) **dark miso**

½ teaspoon (2 ml) **salt**

Heat the oil in a large soup pot over medium heat. Add the onion and cook, stirring occasionally, for 3 to 5 minutes, or until soft. Add the carrots and garlic and cook, stirring occasionally, for 3 minutes. Stir in the water, lentils, and cumin. Bring to a boil over medium-high heat. Decrease the heat to medium-low, cover, and simmer, stirring occasionally, for 20 to 25 minutes, or until the lentils have disintegrated. Put the miso and salt in small bowl or measuring cup and stir in a small amount of the soup liquid to make a smooth paste. Stir the miso mixture into the soup. Serve hot.

Per cup (250 ml): calories: 160, protein: 9 g, fat: 3 g, carbohydrates: 25 g (3 g from sugar), dietary fiber: 5 g, calcium: 39 mg, iron: 3 mg, magnesium: 32 mg, phosphorus: 116 mg, potassium: 343 mg, sodium: 379 mg, zinc: 1.5 mg, thiamin: 0.2 mg, riboflavin: 0.1 mg, niacin: 2 mg, vitamin B_6: 0.2 mg, folate: 72 mcg, pantothenic acid: 0.2 mg, vitamin B_{12}: 0 mcg, vitamin A: 334 mcg, vitamin C: 4 mg, vitamin E: 0.5 mg, omega-6 fatty acid: 0.2 g, omega-3 fatty acid: 0 g

Percentage of calories from: protein 22%, fat 18%, carbohydrates 60%

spice or amount of seeds. For example, ¼ cup (60 ml) of sesame seeds should toast in 3 to 5 minutes.

Oven method: To accentuate their flavor, lightly toast nuts (such as almonds, cashews, hazelnuts, pecans, and walnuts) and seeds (such as pumpkin, sesame, and sunflower seeds) in the oven. Preheat the oven to 300 degrees F (150 degrees C). Spread the nuts or seeds on a baking sheet so that they heat evenly and don't burn. Pick through them and remove any foreign matter, such as pieces of husk, dirt, or pebbles. Put the baking sheet on the middle rack of the oven. For nuts, bake for up to 15 minutes, removing the baking sheet every 5 minutes to check for doneness and stirring them so they toast evenly. For seeds, bake for 7 to 9 minutes, removing the baking sheet every 3 to 4 minutes to check for doneness, stirring them so they toast evenly. Checking often is important because nuts and seeds can burn quickly.

Transfer toasted nuts or seeds to a plate and let cool. When completely cool, transfer to a jar, storage container, or ziplock bag. Toasted nuts and seeds will keep for 4 weeks at room temperature, 6 months in the refrigerator, or 1 year in the freezer.

Here is a tasty recipe that combines flavors from the Caribbean, Europe, and Mexico. This popular soup has an outstanding balance of protein, fat, and carbohydrates and is rich in fiber, iron, and potassium. Add freshly squeezed lime juice just before serving for a bright accent that would be lost if the juice were added while the soup is cooking.

SAVORY Black Bean Soup

1 tablespoon (15 ml) **coconut oil or extra-virgin olive oil**

½ **onion, diced**

1 cup (250 ml) **diced carrots**

1 cup (250 ml) **diced celery**

1 clove **garlic, minced**

4 cups (1 L) **water**

3 cups (750 ml) **cooked or canned black beans, rinsed**

¼ cup (60 ml) **tomato paste**

1½ teaspoons (7 ml) **ground cumin**

1 teaspoon (5 ml) **dried oregano**

1 teaspoon (5 ml) **dried thyme**

½ teaspoon (2 ml) **salt**

2 teaspoons (10 ml) **freshly squeezed lime juice**

Heat the oil in a large soup pot over medium heat. Add the onion and cook, stirring occasionally, for 3 to 5 minutes, or until soft. Add the carrots, celery, and garlic and cook, stirring occasionally, for 3 minutes. Stir in the water, beans, tomato paste, cumin, oregano, thyme, and salt. Bring to a boil over medium-high heat. Decrease the heat to medium-low, cover, and simmer, stirring occasionally, for 30 minutes. Just before serving, stir in the lime juice. Serve hot.

Per cup (250 ml): calories: 172, protein: 9 g, fat: 3 g, carbohydrates: 29 g (2 g from sugar), dietary fiber: 10 g, calcium: 65 mg, iron: 3 mg, magnesium: 82 mg, phosphorus: 158 mg, potassium: 618 mg, sodium: 205 mg, zinc: 1 mg, thiamin: 0.3 mg, riboflavin: 0.1 mg, niacin: 3 mg, vitamin B_6: 0.2 mg, folate: 153 mcg, pantothenic acid: 0.5 mg, vitamin B_{12}: 0 mcg, vitamin A: 187 mcg, vitamin C: 10 mg, vitamin E: 1 mg, omega-6 fatty acid: 0.4 g, omega-3 fatty acid: 0.2 g

Percentage of calories from: protein 21%, fat 15%, carbohydrates 64%

There are references to eggplant in ancient Sanskrit, and it is thought that this plant originated on the Indian subcontinent in prehistoric times and was introduced to Africa, Europe, and the Middle East as early as the sixth century. This soup has an excellent balance of protein, fat, and carbohydrates and provides iron and other minerals.

Spicy Eggplant Soup WITH CHICKPEAS AND OLIVES

MAKES NINE 1-CUP (250-ML) SERVINGS

1 tablespoon (15 ml) **coconut oil or extra-virgin olive oil**

½ **onion, diced**

3 cups (750 ml) **diced small eggplant**

1 cup (250 ml) **diced carrots**

1 cup (250 ml) **chopped red bell pepper**

2 cloves **garlic, minced**

5 cups (1.25 L) **water or vegetable stock** (for homemade, see page 92)

2 cups (500 ml) **cooked or canned chickpeas, rinsed**

1 cup (250 ml) **chopped fresh or canned tomatoes**

½ cup (125 ml) **chopped kalamata olives**

2 teaspoons (10 ml) **ground cumin**

1 teaspoon (5 ml) **salt** (use less if using salted vegetable stock)

¼ teaspoon (1 ml) **cayenne**

¼ cup (60 ml) **chopped fresh parsley**

Heat the oil in a large soup pot over medium heat. Add the onion and cook, stirring occasionally, for 3 to 5 minutes, or until soft. Add the eggplant, carrots, bell pepper, and garlic and cook, stirring occasionally, for 5 minutes. Stir in the water, chickpeas, tomatoes, olives, cumin, salt, and cayenne. Bring to a boil over medium-high heat. Decrease the heat to low, cover, and simmer, stirring occasionally, for 20 minutes. Stir in the parsley. Serve hot.

Per cup (250 ml): calories: 112, protein: 4 g, fat: 4 g, carbohydrates: 17 g (5 g from sugar), dietary fiber: 4 g, calcium: 47 mg, iron: 2 mg, magnesium: 33 mg, phosphorus: 92 mg, potassium: 338 mg, sodium: 350 mg, zinc: 1 mg, thiamin: 0.1 mg, riboflavin: 0.1 mg, niacin: 2 mg, vitamin B_6: 0.2 mg, folate: 85 mcg, pantothenic acid: 0.3 mg, vitamin B_{12}: 0 mcg, vitamin A: 167 mcg, vitamin C: 41 mg, vitamin E: 1 mg, omega-6 fatty acid: 0.6 g, omega-3 fatty acid: 0 g

Percentage of calories from: protein 15%, fat 28%, carbohydrates 57%

Tuscany, a region in central Italy, is a charmed land blessed with abundant sunshine. The cuisine from this famed tourist destination incorporates the garlic, herbs, olives, tomatoes, and white kidney beans that grow throughout the region. Although minestrones vary from one Italian kitchen to another, the ingredients in this version are typical. So that the vegetables cook evenly, it is best to cut them into equal-sized pieces, such as one-quarter-inch dice.

Tuscan MINESTRONE

2 tablespoons (30 ml) **extra-virgin olive oil**

½ **onion, diced**

1 cup (250 ml) **diced carrots**

1 cup (250 ml) **diced celery**

1 cup (250 ml) **scrubbed and diced russet, gold, or red-skinned potatoes**

½ cup (125 ml) **chopped green beans**

2 cloves garlic, **minced**

4 cups (1 L) **water**

1 cup (250 ml) **cooked or canned white beans, rinsed**

1 cup (250 ml) **tomato sauce**

2 tablespoons (30 ml) **chopped fresh basil, or 2 teaspoons** (10 ml) **dried**

1 tablespoon (15 ml) **minced fresh rosemary, or 1 teaspoon** (5 ml) **dried**

1 teaspoon (5 ml) **salt**

1 cup (250 ml) **diced zucchini**

Heat the oil in a large soup pot over medium heat. Add the onion and cook, stirring occasionally, for 3 to 5 minutes, or until soft. Add the carrots, celery, potato, green beans, and garlic and cook, stirring occasionally, for 3 minutes. Stir in the water, beans, tomato sauce, basil, rosemary, and salt. Bring to a boil over medium-high heat. Decrease the heat to medium-low, cover, and simmer, stirring occasionally, for 15 minutes, or until the potatoes are tender yet firm. Stir in the zucchini. Simmer for about 5 minutes, or until the vegetables are tender-crisp. Serve hot.

Per cup (250 ml): calories: 107, protein: 4 g, fat: 4 g, carbohydrates: 16 g (3 g from sugar), dietary fiber: 4 g, calcium: 50 mg, iron: 2 mg, magnesium: 35 mg, phosphorus: 66 mg, potassium: 512 mg, sodium: 494 mg, zinc: 1 mg, thiamin: 0.1 mg, riboflavin: 0.1 mg, niacin: 2 mg, vitamin B_6: 0.2 mg, folate: 42 mcg, pantothenic acid: 0.4 mg, vitamin B_{12}: 0 mcg, vitamin A: 157 mcg, vitamin C: 12 mg, vitamin E: 2 mg, omega-6 fatty acid: 0.4 g, omega-3 fatty acid: 0.1 g

Percentage of calories from: protein 14%, fat 30%, carbohydrates 56%

chapter 8

Salads

Spend half an hour cutting and slicing fresh vegetables, and you'll have an abundant salad for a big gathering. Alternatively, store most of the prepped ingredients in the refrigerator for use over five days—just add fresh romaine lettuce and red bell pepper immediately before serving. Serve this salad with Asian Dressing (page 125), Lemon-Tahini Dressing (page 134), Liquid Gold Dressing (page 126), or another favorite dressing.

Garden of Plenty SALAD

MAKES TEN 3-CUP (750-ML) SERVINGS

5 large kale leaves, stemmed and very thinly sliced

5 napa cabbage leaves, cut in half lengthwise, then into ¼-inch (5-mm) slices

5 large romaine lettuce leaves, torn into bite-sized pieces

¼ head red cabbage, thinly sliced

1 head broccoli, cut into bite-sized florets, stalk peeled and sliced

½ small head cauliflower, cut into bite-sized florets

3 to 4 carrots, cut into ¼-inch (5-mm) slices

1 red bell pepper, cut into ¼-inch (5-mm) slices

Put all ingredients in a large bowl and toss to combine.

Per 3 cups (750 ml): calories: 56, protein: 3 g, fat: 0.5 g, carbohydrates: 12 g (5 g from sugar), dietary fiber: 4 g, calcium: 90 mg, iron: 1 mg, magnesium: 29 mg, phosphorus: 75 mg, potassium: 523 mg, sodium: 56 mg, zinc: 0.5 mg, thiamin: 0.1 mg, riboflavin: 0.2 mg, niacin: 2 mg, vitamin B_6: 0.3 mg, folate: 84 mcg, pantothenic acid: 0.6 mg, vitamin B_{12}: 0 mcg, vitamin A: 461 mcg, vitamin C: 128 mg, vitamin E: 1 mg, omega-6 fatty acid: 0.1 g, omega-3 fatty acid: 0.1 g

Percentage of calories from: protein 21%, fat 7%, carbohydrates 72%

Kale can be eaten raw, as in this recipe, or steamed. Because it is very fibrous, kale must be sliced very thinly when eaten raw. Here, kale is combined with two other raw calcium-rich vegetables: napa cabbage and broccoli. Greens are potent providers of protein, vitamin A (beta-carotene), folate, and beneficial plant oils. Serve this salad with Asian Dressing (page 125) or Lemon-Tahini Dressing (page 134) if desired.

CALCIUM-RICH Greens

2 cups (500 ml) **very thinly sliced kale leaves, stemmed**

2 cups (500 ml) **thinly sliced napa cabbage**

2½ cups (625 ml) **broccoli florets and peeled, sliced stems**

1 cup (250 ml) **diced red bell pepper**

Put all the ingredients in a large bowl and toss to combine.

Per 2 cups (500 ml): calories: 52, protein: 4 g, fat: 0.6 g, carbohydrates: 11 g (2 g from sugar), dietary fiber: 4 g, calcium: 112 mg, iron: 1 mg, magnesium: 43 mg, phosphorus: 85 mg, potassium: 484 mg, sodium: 36 mg, zinc: 0.6 mg, thiamin: 0.1 mg, riboflavin: 0.1 mg, niacin: 2 mg, vitamin B_6: 0.4 mg, folate: 64 mcg, pantothenic acid: 0.4 mg, vitamin B_{12}: 0 mcg, vitamin A: 460 mcg, vitamin C: 185 mg, vitamin E: 1 mg, omega-6 fatty acid: 0.1 g, omega-3 fatty acid: 0.2 g

Percentage of calories from: protein 24%, fat 8%, carbohydrates 68%

When arranged in a ring on a round platter, deep green kale tossed with bright red bell pepper resembles a small holly wreath, making this simple yet elegant dish perfect for the holiday season. Any time of the year, it is a nutritional powerhouse packed with plenty of calcium, iron, omega-3 fatty acid, potassium, and antioxidant vitamins (A, C, and E). For small gatherings, halve the recipe.

Kale and Red Bell Pepper HOLLY RING

12 cups (3 L) **thinly sliced kale leaves, stemmed, packed**

3 tablespoons (45 ml) **flaxseed oil or extra-virgin olive oil**

4 teaspoons (20 ml) **tamari**

4 teaspoons (20 ml) **balsamic vinegar**

½ cup (125 ml) **diced red bell pepper**

Steam the kale until soft. Drain in a colander, cool, and squeeze out any excess water.

Put the oil, tamari, and vinegar in a large bowl and stir until well combined. Add the kale and toss to coat with the dressing.

Arrange the dressed kale on a platter. To create a wreath shape, push the kale toward the edges of the platter, leaving an open space in the center. Sprinkle with the bell pepper.

Per cup (250 ml): calories: 153, protein: 6 g, fat: 9 g, carbohydrates: 17g (1 g from sugar), dietary fiber: 3 g, calcium: 210 mg, iron: 3 mg, magnesium: 56 mg, phosphorus: 96 mg, potassium: 730 mg, sodium: 315 mg, zinc: 1 mg, thiamin: 0.2 mg, riboflavin: 0.2 mg, niacin: 3 mg, vitamin B_6: 0.5 mg, folate: 48 mcg, pantothenic acid: 0.2 mg, vitamin B_{12}: 0 mcg, vitamin A: 1,210 mcg, vitamin C: 212 mg, vitamin E: 3 mg, omega-6 fatty acid: 1.2 g, omega-3 fatty acid: 4.3 g

Percentage of calories from: protein 14%, fat 46%, carbohydrates 40%

This artistic arrangement is designed to be served as a side salad. Add more watercress if you want to serve it as a main dish. The dressing includes mirin, a Japanese rice wine that is subtle, delicious, and clean to the palate. The grapefruit juice for the dressing can be squeezed from the remaining skin and pulp after the segments are removed.

WATERCRESS, AVOCADO, AND GRAPEFRUIT Salad

MAKES 4 SERVINGS

16 stems watercress, washed and spun dry or patted dry

2 ripe avocados

1 grapefruit

2 tablespoons (30 ml) mirin

2 teaspoons (10 ml) rice vinegar

½ teaspoon (2 ml) tamari

1 teaspoon (5 ml) toasted sesame seeds (see sidebar, page 100)

Arrange four equal portions of the watercress on the top third of four plates. Set aside.

Cut the avocados in half lengthwise and remove the pits. Insert the edge of a soup spoon between the avocado flesh and skin. Carefully scoop out the flesh and put it on a cutting board. Starting ½ inch (1 cm) from the narrow end or top of the avocado, cut thin strips lengthwise to the bottom. Press the avocado lightly at a 45-degree angle to make the slices fan out. Arrange one avocado half on each bed of watercress so that the fanned slices are near the bottom of the plate.

Slice off the top and bottom of the grapefruit. Using a sharp knife, cut away the skin and the white part of the peel. Cut along both sides of each segment to loosen. Carefully remove all the segments. Reserve the skin and any pulp clinging to it. Garnish each plate with 4 grapefruit segments, forming an X on either side of the avocado.

After the grapefruit segments are removed, squeeze the juice from the grapefruit skin and pulp attached to it into a small bowl. It should be about 2 tablespoons (30 ml). Add the mirin, vinegar, and tamari and stir until well combined. Spoon 1 tablespoon (15 ml) of the dressing on each salad. Sprinkle each salad with a pinch of the sesame seeds.

Per serving: calories: 188, protein: 3 g, fat: 16 g, carbohydrates: 13 g (2 g from sugar), dietary fiber: 6 g, calcium: 39 mg, iron: 1 mg, magnesium: 49 mg, phosphorus: 57 mg, potassium: 728 mg, sodium: 14 mg, zinc: 1 mg, thiamin: 0.2 mg, riboflavin: 0.2 mg, niacin: 3 mg, vitamin B$_6$: 0.3 mg, folate: 70 mcg, pantothenic acid: 1 mg, vitamin B$_{12}$: 0 mcg, vitamin A: 1,164 mcg, vitamin C: 34 mg, vitamin E: 2 mg, omega-6 fatty acid: 2 g, omega-3 fatty acids: 0.1 g

Percentage of calories from: protein 5%, fat 61%, carbohydrates 30%, and alcohol 4%

After the ingredients are prepared and arranged on the counter, this salad roll can be assembled with ease. Choose from a variety of sauces to use inside the roll and for dipping. Aside from Spicy Peanut Sauce (page 182), Lemon-Tahini Dressing (page 134), Teriyaki Sauce (page 183), or plum sauce offer a range of flavor possibilities. Experiment with filling ingredients too. For example, replace the avocado with Crispy Tofu Slices (page 161).

Vietnamese SALAD ROLL

MAKES 1 ROLL

8 cups (2 L) **warm water**

1 (8½-inch/21-cm) **sheet of rice paper**

⅓ cup (85 ml) **cooked brown rice**

3 slices avocado

2 tablespoons (30 ml) **grated carrot**

1 teaspoon (5 ml) **Spicy Peanut Sauce** (page 182)

1 (6-inch/15-cm) **strip green onion**

½ teaspoon (2 ml) **chopped fresh cilantro or parsley**

½ teaspoon (2 ml) **thinly sliced pickled ginger** (optional)

Put the water in a large bowl. Dip the sheet of rice paper into the water for 5 seconds. Lay the rice paper on a cutting board and pat with a dry cloth to absorb any excess water. Spread the rice on the rice paper, forming a square and leaving a 1-inch (2.5-cm) border on all sides. On the bottom third of the rice, layer the avocado, carrot, sauce, green onion, cilantro, and optional pickled ginger. Fold the right and left sides and the bottom of the rice paper toward the center. Moisten the top border of the rice paper. Using both hands, tightly roll from the bottom. Apply a bit of pressure to seal the roll at the top.

Per roll: calories: 259, protein: 7 g, fat: 13 g, carbohydrates: 31 g (4 g from sugar), dietary fiber: 5 g, calcium: 33 mg, iron: 2 mg, magnesium: 73 mg, phosphorus: 129 mg, potassium: 522 mg, sodium: 596 mg, zinc: 1 mg, thiamin: 0.2 mg, riboflavin: 0.1 mg, niacin: 5 mg, vitamin B$_6$: 0.3 mg, folate: 57 mcg, pantothenic acid: 1 mg, vitamin B$_{12}$: 0 mcg, vitamin A: 118 mcg, vitamin C: 6 mg, vitamin E: 1 mg, omega-6 fatty acid: 3 g, omega-3 fatty acid: 0.1 g

Percentage of calories from: protein 10%, fat 44%, carbohydrates 46%

This marinated potato salad is ideal for a large family gathering, picnic, or potluck dinner. Use waxy, or boiling, potatoes rather than baking varieties, such as the russet, and pick red or yellow potatoes, which will hold their shape well when boiled. Fresh peppers add crispiness and contrast well with the soft texture of cooked potatoes.

FRENCH POTATO Salad

MAKES TEN 1-CUP (250-ML) SERVINGS

3.5 pounds (1.6 kg) **gold or red-skinned potatoes, scrubbed and cubed**
(11 cups/2.75 L)

⅓ cup (85 ml) **red wine vinegar**

¼ cup (60 ml) **extra-virgin olive oil**

2 tablespoons (30 ml) **Dijon mustard**

1 teaspoon (5 ml) **caraway seeds**

1 teaspoon (5 ml) **paprika**

1 teaspoon (5 ml) **salt**

½ teaspoon (2 ml) **ground pepper**

½ cup (125 ml) **diced green, orange, or yellow bell pepper**

½ cup (125 ml) **diced red bell pepper**

½ cup (125 ml) **sliced black or green olives**

¼ cup (60 ml) **diced green onion**

¼ cup (60 ml) **chopped fresh parsley**

Put the potatoes and water in a large pot and bring to a boil over medium-high heat. Decrease the heat to medium-low and cook for 8 to10 minutes, or until tender when pierced with a knife. Do not overcook. Drain the potatoes and put them in a large bowl.

Put the vinegar, oil, mustard, caraway seeds, paprika, salt, and pepper in a small bowl and stir until thoroughly combined. While the potatoes are still warm, pour the vinegar mixture over them. Cover and refrigerate for 1 hour to allow the potatoes to absorb the flavors.

Add the green and red bell peppers, olives, green onion, and parsley. Toss gently until evenly distributed. Stored in a sealed container in the refrigerator, French Potato Salad will keep for about 5 days.

Per cup (250 ml): calories: 194, protein: 4 g, fat: 9 g, carbohydrates: 31 g, (3 g from sugar), dietary fiber: 3 g, calcium: 29 mg, iron: 2 mg, magnesium: 38 mg, phosphorus: 88 mg, potassium: 933 mg, sodium: 383 mg, zinc: 1 mg, thiamin: 0.2 mg, riboflavin: 0.2 mg, niacin: 4 mg, vitamin B_6: 0.5 mg, folate: 28 mcg, pantothenic acid: 1 mg, vitamin B_{12}: 0 mcg, vitamin A: 28 mcg, vitamin C: 64 mg, vitamin E: 1.2 mg, omega-6 fatty acid: 0.6 g, omega-3 fatty acid: 0.1 g

Percentage of calories from: protein 8%, fat 30%, carbohydrates 62%

Basmati means "the fragrant one" in Sanskrit. This long-grain rice has been grown in the foothills of the Himalayan Mountains since ancient times. Either white or the slower-cooking brown basmati can be used in this salad (see variation). The aromatic rice's mild, nutty flavor combines well with the sweet currants. Both turmeric and coriander contain potent antioxidants. In addition, turmeric has cancer-protective qualities, and coriander seed has long been used to aid digestion.

Curried Basmati **RICE SALAD**

MAKES FOUR TO FIVE 1-CUP (250-ML) SERVINGS

1¾ cups (435 ml) **water**

1 cup (250 ml) **white basmati rice**

½ teaspoon (2 ml) **salt**

⅛ teaspoon (0.5 ml) **ground turmeric**

1 tablespoon (15 ml) **Indian curry paste**

¼ cup (60 ml) **dried currants, soaked in** ¼ cup (60 ml) **water for 20 minutes**

2 tablespoons (30 ml) **freshly squeezed lime juice**

1 cup (250 ml) **finely diced red bell pepper**

2 tablespoons (30 ml) **chopped fresh cilantro or parsley**

1 teaspoon (5 ml) **coriander seeds, crushed** (optional)

Put the water in a medium pot and bring to a boil over medium-high heat. Stir in the rice, salt, and turmeric. Decrease the heat to low, cover, and cook for 20 minutes. Remove from the heat and let cool.

Put the curry paste in a small bowl. Drain the currants and retain the soaking water. Gradually stir the soaking water into the curry paste until smooth. Stir in the lime juice. Add the curry paste mixture to the rice along with the currants, bell pepper, cilantro, and optional coriander seeds. Stir gently until evenly distributed. Stored in a sealed container in the refrigerator, Curried Basmati Rice Salad will keep for 4 to 5 days.

VARIATION: Replace the white basmati rice with brown basmati rice and increase the cooking water to 2 cups (500 ml). Cook the rice for 45 minutes.

Per cup (250 ml): calories: 220, protein: 3 g, fat: 2 g, carbohydrates: 52 g (7 g from sugar), dietary fiber: 3 g, calcium: 22 mg, iron: 2 mg, magnesium: 13 mg, phosphorus: 26 mg, potassium: 181 mg, sodium: 215 mg, zinc: 0.2 mg, thiamin: 0.2 mg, riboflavin: 0.1 mg, niacin: 2 mg, vitamin B_6: 0.1 mg, folate: 12 mcg, pantothenic acid: 0.1 mg, vitamin B_{12}: 0 mcg, vitamin A: 63 mcg, vitamin C: 71 mg, vitamin E: 1 mg, omega-6 fatty acid: 0.2 g, omega-3 fatty acid: 0 g

Percentage of calories from: protein 6%, fat 6%, carbohydrates 88%

Quinoa (pronounced keen-wa), an ancient grain native to the Andean region of South America, was introduced to North America in the 1980s. It is often called a "supergrain" because of its excellent protein content and nutritional profile. In nature, quinoa is coated with a slightly bitter resin that repels birds and insects. To remove any bitterness, always wash quinoa using a fine sieve until the rinse water is no longer foamy.

FIESTA QUINOA SALAD with Lime Dressing

MAKES FOUR TO FIVE 1-CUP (250-ML) SERVINGS

1½ cups (375 ml) **water**

1 cup (250 ml) **quinoa, rinsed and drained**

½ teaspoon (2 ml) **salt**

¼ cup (60 ml) **freshly squeezed lime juice**

2 tablespoons (30 ml) **extra-virgin olive oil or flaxseed oil**

1 teaspoon (5 ml) **toasted sesame oil**

pinch **ground pepper**

½ cup (125 ml) **fresh or thawed frozen corn kernels**

½ cup (125 ml) **diced cucumber**

¼ cup (60 ml) **diced red bell pepper**

2 tablespoons (30 ml) **finely chopped green onion**

4 teaspoon (20 ml) **finely chopped fresh cilantro**

Put the water in a medium saucepan and bring to a boil over high heat. Stir in the quinoa and salt. Decrease the heat to low, cover, and cook for 15 minutes, or until all the water is absorbed. Remove from the heat and let cool.

Put the lime juice, olive oil, sesame oil, and pepper in a small bowl and stir until thoroughly combined. Pour over the cooled quinoa and toss gently with a fork. Add the corn, cucumber, bell pepper, green onion, and cilantro and stir until evenly distributed. Stored in a sealed container in the refrigerator, Fiesta Quinoa Salad with Lime Dressing will keep for 4 to 5 days.

Per cup (250 ml): calories: 249, protein: 7 g, fat: 10 g, carbohydrates: 35 g (3 g from sugar), dietary fiber: 4 g, calcium: 32 mg, iron: 4 mg, magnesium: 89 mg, phosphorus: 171 mg, potassium: 437 mg, sodium: 221 mg, zinc: 1 mg, thiamin: 0.1 mg, riboflavin: 0.2 mg, niacin: 2 mg, vitamin B_6: 0.1 mg, folate: 26 mcg, pantothenic acid: 0.5 mg, vitamin B_{12}: 0 mcg, vitamin A: 36 mcg, vitamin C: 23 mg, vitamin E: 1 mg, omega-6 fatty acid: 2 g, omega-3 fatty acid: 0.1 g

Percentage of calories from: protein 11%, fat 35%, carbohydrates 54%

Kamut is a trademark name for an ancient grain that is a close relative to durum wheat (the wheat used for making pasta). Some people with sensitivities to common wheat find that they can tolerate Kamut or spelt (see variation). Kamut has a sweet taste and soft, chewy texture. It blends well with the other flavors in this simple, nutritious, and refreshing salad.

KAMUT, TOMATO, AND AVOCADO Salad

MAKES FOUR TO FIVE 1-CUP (250-ML) SERVINGS

3 cups (750 ml) **water**

1 cup (250 ml) **Kamut berries**

½ teaspoon (2 ml) **salt**

2 tomatoes, diced

1 ripe avocado, diced

½ cup (125 ml) **diced cucumber**

3 tablespoons (45 ml) **freshly squeezed lemon juice**

2 tablespoons (30 ml) **extra-virgin olive oil or hempseed oil**

½ teaspoon (2 ml) **ground toasted cumin seeds** (see sidebar, page 100)

¼ cup (60 ml) **chopped fresh parsley**

Put the water in a medium saucepan and bring to a boil over high heat. Stir in the Kamut and salt. Decrease the heat to low, cover, and cook for 45 minutes, or until tender. Drain any excess water and set aside to cool.

Put the tomatoes, avocado, cucumber, lemon juice, oil, cumin, and parsley in a medium bowl and toss to combine. Gently stir in the cooled Kamut until evenly distributed. Serve immediately.

Variation: Replace the Kamut berries with whole spelt berries.

Per cup (304 ml): calories: 304, protein: 7 g, fat: 14 g, carbohydrates: 40 g (3 g from sugar), dietary fiber: 12 g, calcium: 29 mg, iron: 2 mg, magnesium: 86 mg, phosphorus: 167 mg, potassium: 614 mg, sodium: 224 mg, zinc: 2 mg, thiamin: 0.2 mg, riboflavin: 0.1 mg, niacin: 2 mg, vitamin B_6: 0.2 mg, folate: 44 mcg, pantothenic acid: 0.5 mg, vitamin B_{12}: 0 mcg, vitamin A: 105 mcg, vitamin C: 20 mg, vitamin E: 2 mg, omega-6 fatty acid: 2 g, omega-3 fatty acid: 0.1 g

Percentage of calories from: protein 9%, fat 40%, carbohydrates 51%

The appetizing sauce for this pasta salad is inspired by the rich flavors of Thai cuisine. Whole wheat or refined wheat pasta may be used. If you are sensitive to wheat or gluten, replace the wheat pasta with rice pasta or noodles. Other fresh vegetables that work well in this salad include broccoli, carrots, celery, mung bean sprouts, napa cabbage, shelled peas, snap peas, yellow beans, and zucchini.

Thai Pasta Salad **WITH SPICY PEANUT SAUCE**

MAKES EIGHT 1-CUP (250-ML) SERVINGS

2 quarts (2 L) **water**

½ teaspoon (2 ml) **salt**

2½ cups (625 ml) **uncooked whole wheat pasta spirals**

¾ cup (185 ml) **Spicy Peanut Sauce** (page 182)

1 cup (250 ml) **diced cucumber**

1 cup (250 ml) **sliced green beans**

1 cup (250 ml) **trimmed and sliced snow peas**

1 cup (250 ml) **diced tomatoes**

½ cup (125 ml) **roasted peanuts** (optional)

¼ cup (60 ml) **chopped green onion**

2 tablespoons (30 ml) **finely chopped fresh cilantro or parsley**

2 tablespoons (30 ml) **freshly squeezed lime juice**

Put the water and salt in a large pot and bring to a boil over high heat. Stir in the pasta and cook until tender yet firm, 9 to 10 minutes.

Fill a large bowl with cold water. Drain the pasta and plunge it into the cold water. Drain well and transfer to a large bowl. Add the sauce, cucumber, green beans, snow peas, tomatoes, optional peanuts, green onion, cilantro, and lime juice. Stir until thoroughly combined. Stored in a sealed container in the refrigerator, Thai Pasta Salad with Spicy Peanut Sauce will keep for 4 to 5 days.

Per cup (250 ml): calories: 196, protein: 7 g, fat: 6 g, carbohydrates: 30 g (5 g from sugar), dietary fiber: 3 g, calcium: 39 mg, iron: 2.4 mg, magnesium: 44 mg, phosphorus: 95 mg, potassium: 332 mg, sodium: 355 mg, zinc: 1 mg, thiamin: 0.4 mg, riboflavin: 0.2 mg, niacin: 4 mg, vitamin B_6: 0.2 mg, folate: 94 mcg, pantothenic acid: 0.6 mg, vitamin B_{12}: 0 mcg, vitamin A: 17 mcg, vitamin C: 21 mg, vitamin E: 1 mg, omega-6 fatty acid: 1.4 g, omega-3 fatty acid: 0 g

Percentage of calories from: protein 14%, fat 27%, carbohydrates 59%

Wild rice is not true rice but rather a grain harvested from species of grasses that grow in shallow freshwater streams and lakes. Once harvested only in the wild, this rice is now available world-wide thanks to large commercial operations. Wild rice has a nutty flavor that goes very well with oranges and cranberries. Here, the addition of walnuts enhances the taste and provides a good measure of omega-3 fatty acid. If you make this salad in the summer, consider adding a cup of fresh blueberries for their protective antioxidant content.

WILD RICE, WALNUT, AND CRANBERRY Salad

MAKES SIX 1-CUP (250-ML) SERVINGS

4 cups (1 L) **water**

1 cup (250 ml) **wild rice**

¾ teaspoon (4 ml) **salt**

¼ cup (60 ml) **frozen orange juice concentrate, thawed**

1 tablespoon (15 ml) **extra-virgin olive oil**

1 teaspoon (5 ml) **peeled and minced fresh ginger**

pinch **ground pepper**

1 cup (250 ml) **chopped walnuts**

½ cup (125 ml) **diced red bell pepper**

½ cup (125 ml) **dried cranberries**

Put the water in a medium saucepan and bring to a boil over high heat. Stir in the rice and ½ teaspoon (2 ml) of the salt. Decrease the heat to low, cover, and cook for 45 minutes or until all the kernels of rice have fully opened. Drain any excess water. Transfer the rice to a medium bowl and set aside to cool.

Put the orange juice concentrate, oil, ginger, remaining ¼ teaspoon (1 ml) of salt, and pepper in a small bowl and whisk until combined. Stir into the rice. Add the walnuts, bell pepper, and cranberries and stir until thoroughly combined. Stored in a sealed container in the refrigerator, Wild Rice, Walnut, and Cranberry Salad will keep for 4 to 5 days.

Per cup (250 ml): calories: 310, protein: 8 g, fat: 16 g, carbohydrates: 37 g (9 g from sugar), dietary fiber: 4 g, calcium: 34 mg, iron: 1 mg, magnesium: 90 mg, phosphorus: 204 mg, potassium: 321 mg, sodium: 321 mg, zinc: 2 mg, thiamin: 0.1 mg, riboflavin: 0.1 mg, niacin: 4 mg, vitamin B$_6$: 0.3 mg, folate: 68 mcg, pantothenic acid: 0.5 mg, vitamin B$_{12}$: 0 mcg, vitamin A: 21 mcg, vitamin C: 44 mg, vitamin E: 1 mg, omega-6 fatty acid: 8 g, omega-3 fatty acid: 2 g

Percentage of calories from: protein 9%, fat 45%, carbohydrates 46%

Enjoy different colored beans, including varieties not listed here, in this salad. Adding various vegetables will further expand the range of possibilities. If you use green vegetables, such as green bell pepper or broccoli as suggested in the variation, add them to the marinade just before serving. When green vegetables are immersed in an acid, such as the lemon juice in the marinade, their lovely color becomes dull. To retain a bright green color, it is best to put green peppers, broccoli, and other greens in the marinade, which contains vinegar, just before serving.

Multicolored BEAN AND VEGETABLE SALAD

MAKES SIX 1-CUP (250-ML) SERVINGS

3 cups (750 ml) **cooked or canned beans** (such as black, pinto, red, or white beans or chickpeas)**, rinsed**

¼ cup (60 ml) **freshly squeezed lemon juice or cider vinegar**

2 tablespoons (30 ml) **extra-virgin olive oil**

1 teaspoon (5 ml) **dried dill weed**

1 teaspoon (5 ml) **garlic powder**

1 teaspoon (5 ml) **Dijon mustard**

½ teaspoon (2 ml) **ground pepper**

½ teaspoon (2 ml) **salt**

1 cup (250 ml) **diced yellow bell pepper**

1 cup (250 ml) **chopped celery**

1 cup (250 ml) **halved cherry tomatoes**

Put the beans in a large bowl. Put the lemon juice, oil, dill weed, garlic powder, mustard, pepper, and salt in a jar and shake well. Alternatively, put them in a bowl and whisk until thoroughly combined. Pour over the beans and stir gently until evenly distributed. Cover and refrigerate for 6 hours, stirring occasionally, so the beans absorb the flavors. Stir in the bell pepper, celery, and cherry tomatoes just before serving. Stored in a sealed container in the refrigerator, Multicolored Bean and Vegetable Salad will keep for 4 to 5 days.

VARIATION: Replace the bell pepper, celery, and cherry tomatoes with 3 cups (750 ml) of any combination of the following sliced or chopped vegetables: asparagus, bell pepper (green, orange, or red), broccoli, cauliflower, green beans, napa cabbage, olives, snow peas, yellow cherry tomatoes, or zucchini.

Per cup (250 ml): calories: 197, protein: 9 g, fat: 6 g, carbohydrates: 29 g (3 g from sugar), dietary fiber: 10 g, calcium: 50 mg, iron: 2 mg, magnesium: 66 mg, phosphorus: 171 mg, potassium: 470 mg, sodium: 426 mg, zinc: 1 mg, thiamin: 0.2 mg, riboflavin: 0.1 mg, niacin: 3 mg, vitamin B_6: 0.2 mg, folate: 147 mcg, pantothenic acid: 0.4 mg, vitamin B_{12}: 0 mcg, vitamin A: 18 mcg, vitamin C: 58 mg, vitamin E: 1 mg, omega-6 fatty acid: 0.2 g, omega-3 fatty acid: 0.1 g

Percentage of calories from: protein 19%, fat 24%, carbohydrates 57%

This colorful salad is rich in protein and iron. After straining the tofu, reserve the flavorful marinade. It will keep for three to four days in the refrigerator or six months in the freezer. Thicken it with arrowroot starch to make a sauce for Stir-Fry 101 (page 138), or reuse it to make another batch of marinated tofu.

SPICY MARINATED Tofu Salad

MAKES SEVEN 1-CUP (250-ML) SERVINGS

1 recipe Marinated Tofu (page 160), cubed

1 tablespoon (15 ml) extra-virgin olive oil

1 teaspoon (5 ml) chili paste

1 teaspoon (5 ml) toasted sesame oil

1 teaspoon (5 ml) tamari

1 teaspoon (5 ml) rice vinegar

1 cup (250 ml) diced red bell pepper

1 cup (250 ml) thinly sliced carrots

1 cup (250 ml) thinly sliced celery

1 cup (250 ml) sliced cucumber

1 cup (250 ml) trimmed, quartered, and diagonally sliced snow peas

¼ cup (60 ml) chopped fresh cilantro or parsley

¼ cup (60 ml) sliced green onion

1 tablespoon (15 ml) toasted sesame seeds, for garnish (see sidebar, page 100)

Strain the tofu (and reserve the marinade if desired). To make the dressing, put the olive oil, chili paste, sesame oil, tamari, and vinegar in a small bowl and stir to combine.

Put the bell pepper, carrots, celery, cucumber, snow peas, cilantro, and green onion in a large bowl. Add the dressing and toss until the vegetables are well coated. Stir in the tofu until evenly distributed. Sprinkle with the sesame seeds. Stored in a sealed container in the refrigerator, Spicy Marinated Tofu Salad will keep for 4 to 5 days.

Per cup (250 ml): calories: 132, protein: 10 g, fat: 8 g, carbohydrates: 9 g (3 g from sugar), dietary fiber: 3 g, calcium: 371 mg, iron: 6 mg, magnesium: 45 mg, phosphorus: 133 mg, potassium: 362 mg, sodium: 246 mg, zinc: 1 mg, thiamin: 0.2 mg, riboflavin: 0.1 mg, niacin: 0.2 mg, vitamin B_6: 0.2 mg, folate: 42 mcg, pantothenic acid: 0.4 mg, vitamin B_{12}: 0 mcg, vitamin A: 204 mcg, vitamin C: 60 mg, vitamin E: 1 mg, omega-6 fatty acid: 3 g, omega-3 fatty acid: 0.3 g

Percentage of calories from: protein 27%, fat 49%, carbohydrates 24%

Fresh sprout salads can provide wholesome nutrition when access to other produce is limited. During winter months, sprouts can provide fresh food and an excellent source of vitamin C. In this recipe, sprouts occupy the center of the salad plate, with avocado, olives, tomatoes, and walnuts arranged attractively around them. This nourishing and protein-rich meal can showcase a variety of fresh ingredients. See Salad Bar (page 137) for inspiration. If you like, add Coconut-Almond Dressing (page 132), Cucumber-Dill Dressing (page 128), or another favorite dressing.

Sprouted Lentil SALAD PLATE

MAKES 1 SERVING

1 cup (250 ml) **sprouted lentils** (see page 120)

5 tomato wedges

5 kalamata olives

5 walnut halves

½ ripe avocado

Place the sprouts in the center of a plate. Arrange the tomato wedges just above the sprouts. Arrange the olives on one side of the tomatoes and the walnuts on the other.

Insert the edge of a soup spoon between the avocado flesh and skin. Carefully scoop out the flesh and put it on a cutting board. Starting ½ inch (1 cm) from the narrow end, or top, of the avocado, cut thin strips lengthwise to the bottom. Press the avocado lightly at a 45-degree angle to make the slices fan out. Arrange the narrow end of the avocado near the bottom edge of the plate and spread out the fanned slices over the top of the sprouts.

Per serving: calories: 448, protein: 13 g, fat: 34 g, carbohydrates: 34 g (4 g from sugar), dietary fiber: 11 g, calcium: 61 mg, iron: 5 mg, magnesium: 109 mg, phosphorus: 270 mg, potassium: 1,123 mg, sodium: 332 mg, zinc: 2 mg, thiamin: 0.4 mg, riboflavin: 0.3 mg, niacin: 5 mg, vitamin B_6: 0.6 mg, folate: 175 mcg, pantothenic acid: 2 mg, vitamin B_{12}: 0 mcg, vitamin A: 114 mcg, vitamin C: 36 mg, vitamin E: 2 mg, omega-6 fatty acid: 10 g, omega-3 fatty acid: 2 g

Percentage of calories from: protein 11%, fat 62%, carbohydrates 27%

The equipment needed to grow sprouts is basic and affordable. Use a widemouthed 1-quart (1-L) mason jar covered with a sprouting lid or mesh screen that will allow the rinse water to flow in and out while keeping the sprouts in the jar. Plastic sprouting lids can be purchased at natural food stores. Alternatively, cover the jar with a piece of mesh screen or cotton cheesecloth held in place with a rubber band. A dish rack is helpful, though not essential, for holding the jar at an angle so that the water drains completely after rinsing.

SPROUTED Mung Beans or Lentils

MAKES 3 TO 4 CUPS (750 ML TO 1 L) SPROUTS

¼ cup (60 ml) **dried mung beans, or**
½ cup (125 ml) **dried lentils**

2 cups (500 ml) **water**

Put the mung beans or lentils in a 1-quart (1-L) mason jar and add the water. Cover the jar with a sprouting lid or mesh screen secured with a rubber band. Let the jar stand at room temperature for 12 hours.

Drain the beans or lentils, rinse thoroughly with cool water, and drain again. Repeat 2 to 3 times per day. After draining, put the covered jar upside down at a 45-degree angle over a saucer or in a bowl (to collect the water that drains off) or in a dish rack. Cover the jar with a tea towel or keep it away from sunlight so the sprouts can grow in the dark.

Rinse and drain the beans as directed for 2 to 4 days, until a 1-inch (2.5-cm) tail is visible on the mung beans or a ¼-inch (5-mm) tail is visible on the lentils. Stored in a sealed container in the refrigerator, the sprouts will keep for 1 week. Rinse every 3 days.

NOTE: Homegrown mung bean sprouts will have much shorter tails than commercially grown sprouts. In commercial operations, mung beans are grown under weights that exert pressure on them, so the tails become longer.

Sprouted Mung Beans and Lentils Promote Health

Mung beans and lentils contain a rich store of vitamins, minerals, proteins, fats, and carbohydrates. When sprouted, these legumes are easier to digest and provide us with a variety of health benefits. Following are some of the chemical changes that occur when mung beans and lentils are sprouted:

- Protein is created, and protein quality improves because the amount of essential amino acids increases.
- Trypsin inhibitors, substances that make the protein in legumes hard to digest, are destroyed, making these sprouted legumes easier to digest.
- Starch is converted to simple sugars, which are easier to digest. Glucose and fructose amounts in sprouted mung beans increase tenfold.
- The number of enzymes, including those that break down or begin the digestion of protein and starch, increases significantly.
- The carbohydrates in mung beans that can produce intestinal gas largely disappear.
- Antioxidant production is stimulated, helping to protect us against disease.
- The vitamin C content becomes seventeen times greater in lentils and eight times greater in mung beans.
- The riboflavin content of mung beans triples; in lentils, it increases by 50 percent. The content of other B vitamins also increases.
- Phytate-mineral complexes are broken down, greatly increasing mineral availability.
- The small amounts of hemagglutinins that are present in raw mung beans and lentils are destroyed, making these raw sprouts safe. Most legumes, however, contain too many of these illness-producing proteins to be eaten raw. Hemagglutinins are completely destroyed by cooking, so legumes other than mung beans and lentils should be eaten only if cooked.

Salad Dressings

Simple Dressings for Greens

French vinaigrette is a classic dressing that enhances the fresh taste of salad greens. The ingredients are oil, vinegar, mustard, minced garlic, salt, and pepper. Making this dressing at home is simple. Use three parts oil to one part vinegar. Put the vinegar, mustard, garlic, salt, and pepper in a small bowl and stir with a fork or whisk. Pour in the oil in a thin, steady stream and stir until it is thoroughly incorporated. If you prefer less vinegar, use four parts oil to one part vinegar.

Even more basic than making French vinaigrette is dressing greens with a sprinkle of oil right out of the bottle, followed by a squirt of freshly squeezed lemon juice and a dash of salty seasoning. Use one of three premium oils for this purpose: extra-virgin olive oil, flaxseed oil, or hempseed oil. You might want to have all three oils on hand for variety. Each has distinctive flavors and nutritional benefits.

Arrange the greens on a plate. Sprinkle a little bit of oil evenly over the greens. Squeeze the juice directly from half of a lemon (remove any visible seeds after cutting the lemon in half). Sprinkle a few drops of Bragg Liquid Aminos or tamari over the greens and serve. To dress 3 cups (750 ml) of greens, use 1 tablespoon (15 ml) of oil and 1 teaspoon (5 ml) of freshly squeezed lemon juice. If you prefer, replace the lemon juice with lime juice, cider vinegar, balsamic vinegar, or another vinegar.

The intriguing flavors in this low-fat dressing come from Chinese 5-spice powder, which is composed of anise, cinnamon, fennel, pepper, and star anise. Rice vinegar lends a delicate flavor, as it has about half the acidity of other vinegars. Allow the dressing to stand for one hour for flavors to develop. Serve Asian Dressing with Calcium-Rich Greens (page 107) or Sprouted Lentil Salad Plate (page 119) or use it as a sauce for Easy Tofu Entrées (page 162).

Asian DRESSING

MAKES 1¼ CUPS (310 ML)

½ cup (125 ml) **rice syrup or agave nectar**

½ cup (125 ml) **rice vinegar**

2 tablespoons (30 ml) **unrefined sesame oil**

2 tablespoons (30 ml) **water**

2 teaspoons (10 ml) **peeled and minced fresh ginger**

1 clove garlic, minced

½ teaspoon (2 ml) **toasted sesame oil**

¼ teaspoon (1 ml) **Chinese 5-spice powder**

Put all the ingredients in a blender and process for 15 seconds. Alternatively, put all the ingredients in a jar, cover with a lid, and shake for 15 seconds, or until the rice syrup is dissolved. (It dissolves more easily at room temperature.) Stored in a sealed container in the refrigerator, Asian Dressing will keep for 3 weeks.

Per 2 tablespoons (30 ml): calories: 88, protein: 0.2 g, fat: 3 g, carbohydrates: 15 g (9 g from sugar), dietary fiber: 0.1 g, calcium: 6 mg, iron: 0 mg, magnesium: 0 mg, phosphorus: 1 mg, potassium: 46 mg, sodium: 30 mg, zinc: 0 mg, thiamin: 0 mg, riboflavin: 0 mg, niacin: 0 mg, vitamin B$_6$: 0 mg, folate: 0 mcg, pantothenic acid: 0 mg, vitamin B$_{12}$: 0 mcg, vitamin A: 0 mcg, vitamin C: 0 mg, vitamin E: 0 mg, omega-6 fatty acid: 1 g, omega-3 fatty acid: 0 g

Percentage of calories from: protein 1%, fat 30%, carbohydrates 69%

The name suits this dressing, and not just because of its beautiful golden color. This creamy dressing is a rich source of omega-3 fatty acid and vitamin B$_{12}$ (when made with Red Star Vegetarian Support Formula nutritional yeast flakes). It is also packed with riboflavin and other B vitamins. The ground flaxseeds not only provide omega-3 fatty acid but also make the dressing smooth, add body, and provide a nutty flavor. Use Liquid Gold Dressing on salads, baked potatoes, rice, and steamed broccoli and other veggies.

Liquid Gold **DRESSING**

MAKES 1¾ CUPS (435 ML)

½ **cup** (125 ml) **flaxseed oil**

½ **cup** (125 ml) **water**

⅓ **cup** (85 ml) **freshly squeezed lemon juice**

¼ **cup** (60 ml) **nutritional yeast flakes**

¼ **cup** (60 ml) **tamari or Bragg Liquid Aminos**

2 **tablespoons** (30 ml) **ground flaxseeds**

2 **tablespoons** (30 ml) **cider vinegar or balsamic vinegar**

2 **teaspoons** (10 ml) **Dijon mustard**

1 **teaspoon** (5 ml) **ground cumin**

Put all the ingredients in a blender and process for about 30 seconds, or until smooth. Stored in a sealed container in the refrigerator, Liquid Gold Dressing will keep for 2 to 3 weeks.

Per 2 tablespoons (30 ml): calories: 99, protein: 2 g, fat: 9 g, carbohydrates: 2 g (0 g from sugar), dietary fiber: 1 g, calcium: 11 mg, iron: 0.5 mg, magnesium: 15 mg, phosphorus: 45 mg, potassium: 80 mg, sodium: 311 mg, zinc: 0.5 mg, thiamin: 1.2 mg, riboflavin: 1.2 mg, niacin: 7 mg, vitamin B$_6$: 1 mg, folate: 31 mcg, pantothenic acid: 0.2 mg, vitamin B$_{12}$: 1 mcg, vitamin A: 0 mcg, vitamin C: 3 mg, vitamin E: 1.5 mg, omega-6 fatty acid: 5 g, omega-3 fatty acid: 1.2 g

Percentage of calories from: protein 8%, fat 82%, carbohydrates 10%

Avocados are high in fiber (soluble and insoluble) and have more potassium than bananas. Though naturally abundant in fat, avocados contain mainly monounsaturated fats, which raise HDL, or "good" cholesterol, levels. Add more grapefruit juice or lime juice if the dressing is too thick. The acidity in these juices prevents the avocado from turning brown.

AVOCADO, GRAPEFRUIT, AND CHIPOTLE Dressing

MAKES 1¾ CUPS (435 ML)

1 ripe avocado, cut into chunks

¾ cup (185 ml) freshly squeezed grapefruit juice

¼ cup (60 ml) freshly squeezed lime juice

2 tablespoons (30 ml) chopped green onion, including white part

2 tablespoons (30 ml) maple syrup

1 small clove garlic, chopped

½ teaspoon (2 ml) chopped chipotle chile

¼ teaspoon (1 ml) salt

Put all the ingredients in a blender and process for 30 seconds, or until smooth. Stored in a sealed container in the refrigerator, Avocado, Grapefruit, and Chipotle Dressing will keep for 3 to 4 days.

Per ¼ cup (60 ml): calories: 106, protein: 1 g, fat: 6 g, carbohydrates: 13 g (5 g from sugar), dietary fiber: 2 g, calcium: 18 mg, iron: 1 mg, magnesium: 23 mg, phosphorus: 26 mg, potassium: 346 mg, sodium: 100 mg, zinc: 1 mg, thiamin: 0.1 mg, riboflavin: 0.1 mg, niacin: 1 mg, vitamin B_6: 0.1 mg, folate: 32 mcg, pantothenic acid: 0.5 mg, vitamin B_{12}: 0 mcg, vitamin A: 23 mcg, vitamin C: 22 mg, vitamin E: 1 mg, omega-6 fatty acid: 0.8 g, omega-3 fatty acid: 0.1 g

Percentage of calories from: protein 4%, fat 49%, carbohydrates 47%

This simple-to-prepare salad dressing is refreshing and cool, making it ideal for summer salads, although it can be a delicious staple all year round. Made with hempseed oil, Cucumber-Dill Dressing is an excellent source of omega-3 fatty acid and has an ideal balance of omega-6 and omega-3 fatty acid.

CUCUMBER-DILL Dressing

MAKES 1½ CUPS (375 ML)

1 cup (250 ml) **peeled and chopped or grated cucumber**

1 cup (250 ml) **chopped or grated zucchini**

¼ cup (60 ml) **hempseed oil or extra-virgin olive oil**

¼ cup (60 ml) **freshly squeezed lemon juice**

1 tablespoon (15 ml) **fresh dill, or**
1 teaspoon (5 ml) **dried dill weed**

2 teaspoons (10 ml) **Dijon mustard**

1 teaspoon (5 ml) **nutritional yeast flakes**

1 teaspoon (5 ml) **maple syrup or agave nectar**

1 clove garlic, chopped

½ teaspoon (2 ml) **salt**

½ teaspoon (2 ml) **hot sauce**

Put all the ingredients in a blender and process for 20 seconds. Scrape down the sides of the blender jar and process for 10 seconds longer, or until all the ingredients are well combined. Stored in a sealed container in the refrigerator, Cucumber-Dill Dressing will keep for 4 to 5 days.

Per 2 tablespoons (30 ml): calories: 41, protein: 0.5 g, fat: 5 g, carbohydrates: 2 g (1 g from sugar), dietary fiber: 0.4 g, calcium: 6 mg, iron: 0.1 mg, magnesium: 5 mg, phosphorus: 9 mg, potassium: 61 mg, sodium: 104 mg, zinc: 0.1 mg, thiamin: 0.1 mg, riboflavin: 0.1 mg, niacin: 1 mg, vitamin B_6: 0.1 mg, folate: 8 mcg, pantothenic acid: 0.1 mg, vitamin B_{12}: 0.1 mcg, vitamin A: 1 mcg, vitamin C: 4 mg, vitamin E: 0 mg, omega-6 fatty acid: 3 g, omega-3 fatty acid: 1 g

Percentage of calories from: protein 4%, fat 82%, carbohydrates 14%

With its combination of orange and lemon juices, fresh ginger, miso, and tamari, this dressing features five tastes that are fundamental to our enjoyment of food: sweet, sour, salty, astringent, and pungent. For a superb blend of all six tastes, serve this dressing on bitter greens, such as raw or cooked kale. (See pages 36 to 37.)

Orange-Ginger DRESSING

4 pitted dates, soaked in 1 cup (250 ml) **freshly squeezed orange juice for 6 to 10 hours**

2 tablespoons (30 ml) **almond butter**

2 tablespoons (30 ml) **peeled and grated fresh ginger**

2 tablespoons (30 ml) **freshly squeezed lemon juice**

2 tablespoons (30 ml) **miso**

2 tablespoons (30 ml) **tamari**

pinch cayenne

Put the dates and orange juice in a blender along with the almond butter, ginger, lemon juice, miso, tamari, and cayenne. Process for 30 seconds, or until smooth. Stored in a sealed container in the refrigerator, Orange-Ginger Dressing will keep for 1 to 2 weeks.

Per ¼ cup (60 ml): calories: 73, protein: 2 g, fat: 3 g, carbohydrates: 10 g (6 g from sugar), dietary fiber: 1 g, calcium: 22 mg, iron: 0.5 mg, magnesium: 25 mg, phosphorus: 48 mg, potassium: 170 mg, sodium: 498 mg, zinc: 0.3 mg, thiamin: 0.1 mg, riboflavin: 0.1 mg, niacin: 1 mg, vitamin B_6: 0.1 mg, folate: 18 mcg, pantothenic acid: 0.2 mg, vitamin B_{12}: 0 mcg, vitamin A: 4 mcg, vitamin C: 21 mg, vitamin E: 1 mg, omega-6 fatty acid: 0.7 g, omega-3 fatty acid: 0.1 g

Percentage of calories from: protein 11%, fat 36%, carbohydrates 53%

This versatile recipe can be used as a salad dressing or served with the Baked Potato Bar (page 136), International Roll-Ups (page 144), Timesaving Tacos (page 159), or Vietnamese Salad Roll (page 110). It also makes an excellent sauce for Easy Tofu Entrées (page 162).

Serrano Chile and Cilantro DRESSING

MAKES ¾ CUP (185 ML)

2 cups (500 ml) **cilantro leaves, loosely packed**

⅓ cup (85 ml) **freshly squeezed lemon juice**

2 whole serrano chiles, chopped

2 tablespoons (30 ml) **hempseed oil or extra-virgin olive oil**

1 tablespoon (15 ml) **tamari**

1 clove garlic, chopped

Put all the ingredients in a blender and process for 20 seconds. Scrape down the sides of the blender jar and process for 10 seconds longer, or until smooth. Stored in a sealed container in the refrigerator, Serrano Chile and Cilantro Dressing will keep for 1 to 2 weeks.

Per 2 tablespoons (30 ml): calories: 40, protein: 0.5 g, fat: 5 g, carbohydrates: 2 g (0.4 g from sugar), dietary fiber: 0.2 g, calcium: 3 mg, iron: 0.1 mg, magnesium: 3 mg, phosphorus: 7 mg, potassium: 36 mg, sodium: 171 mg, zinc: 0 mg, thiamin: 0 mg, riboflavin: 0 mg, niacin: 0.3 mg, vitamin B$_6$: 0 mg, folate: 3 mcg, pantothenic acid: 0 mg, vitamin B$_{12}$: 0 mcg, vitamin A: 2 mcg, vitamin C: 8 mg, vitamin E: 0 mg, omega-6 fatty acid: 3 g, omega-3 fatty acid: 1 g

Percentage of calories from: protein 4%, fat 82%, carbohydrates 14%

Vary this healthful, low-oil dressing by adding different herbs, such as dill, marjoram, oregano, or a combination. The tomato juice provides body and considerably reduces the amount of oil required.

TOMATO-HERB Dressing

MAKES 1¼ CUPS (310 ML)

1 cup (250 ml) **tomato juice**

2 tablespoons (30 ml) **freshly squeezed lemon juice**

2 tablespoons (30 ml) **extra-virgin olive oil**

2 tablespoons (30 ml) **cider vinegar**

1½ teaspoons (7 ml) **chopped fresh basil, or ½ teaspoon dried**

1 teaspoon (5 ml) **Dijon mustard**

½ teaspoon (2 ml) **dried tarragon**

pinch ground pepper

Put all the ingredients in a jar, cover with a lid, and shake for 30 seconds. Stored in a sealed container in the refrigerator, Tomato-Herb Dressing will keep for 2 to 3 weeks.

Per 2 tablespoons (30 ml): calories: 30, protein: 0.3 g, fat: 3 g, carbohydrates: 1 g (1 g from sugar), dietary fiber: 0.2 g, calcium: 4 mg, iron: 0.2 mg, magnesium: 3 mg, phosphorus: 7 mg, potassium: 64 mg, sodium: 106 mg, zinc: 0 mg, thiamin: 0 mg, riboflavin: 0 mg, niacin: 0 mg, vitamin B_6: 0 mg, folate: 6 mcg, pantothenic acid: 0.1 mg, vitamin B_{12}: 0 mcg, vitamin A:15 mcg, vitamin C: 4 mg, vitamin E: 0.2 mg, omega-6 fatty acid: 0 g, omega-3 fatty acid: 0 g

Percentage of calories from: protein 3%, fat 79 %, carbohydrates 18%

The exotic flavors in this dressing are borrowed from Thai cuisine. Allow Coconut-Almond Dressing to slightly thicken in the refrigerator for one hour before using it to dress a crisp, leafy green salad or as a sauce for Easy Tofu Entrées (page 162). Alternatively, serve this dressing over cooked brown rice or steamed broccoli or cauliflower.

Coconut-Almond DRESSING

½ **cup** (125 ml) **coconut milk**

½ **cup** (125 ml) **water**

¼ **cup** (60 ml) **almond butter**

2 **tablespoons** (30 ml) **peeled and minced fresh ginger**

2 **tablespoons** (30 ml) **freshly squeezed lime juice**

1 **tablespoon** (15 ml) **maple syrup or other sweetener**

1 **teaspoon** (5 ml) **curry powder**

1 **small clove garlic, chopped**

pinch salt

Put the coconut milk, water, almond butter, ginger, lime juice, maple syrup, curry powder, and garlic in a blender and process for 30 seconds, or until smooth. Season with salt to taste and process for 5 seconds. Stored in a sealed container in the refrigerator, Coconut-Almond Dressing will keep for 1 to 2 weeks if using canned coconut milk and 2 to 3 days if using freshly made coconut milk.

Per 2 tablespoons (30 ml): calories: 60, protein: 1 g, fat: 5 g, carbohydrates: 3 g (1 g from sugar), dietary fiber: 0.4 g, calcium: 19 mg, iron: 1 mg, magnesium: 22 mg, phosphorus: 40 mg, potassium: 76 mg, sodium: 31 mg, zinc: 0.3 mg, thiamin: 0 mg, riboflavin: 0 mg, niacin: 0.5 mg, vitamin B_6: 0 mg, folate: 5 mcg, pantothenic acid: 0 mg, vitamin B_{12}: 0 mcg, vitamin A: 0 mcg, vitamin C: 1 mg, vitamin E: 1.5 mg, omega-6 fatty acid: 1 g, omega-3 fatty acid: 0 g

Percentage of calories from: protein 7%, fat 74%, carbohydrates 19%

Making Coconut Milk

Making fresh coconut milk is easy, and the reward is worth the effort. One average coconut will make 2 to 3 cups (500 to 750 ml) of coconut milk.

Hold the coconut over the sink and strike it with a hammer to crack open the shell. Retain and use the thin coconut water inside if you like, but it is not necessary. Split the shell into three or four pieces. Remove the tender white coconut meat using a dull knife. Before digging out the meat, score it in a number of places by pressing the knife all the way through to the shell. This step will make it easier to pry the meat away from the shell. It is not necessary to remove the brown skin that may adhere to the meat.

Wash the coconut chunks and cut them into 1- to 2-inch (2.5- to 5-cm) pieces. Put 1 cup (250 ml) of water in a blender. Take out the removable cap in the blender lid and secure the lid on the blender. Turn the blender on low speed and drop 1 or 2 pieces of coconut at a time into the blender. Add just enough water to keep the milk moving. It shouldn't be too thick or too thin, but about the consistency of lightly puréed soup. Increase the speed to high and process until the milk is smooth, about 1 minute.

Rest a fine-mesh strainer over a medium bowl and pour the milk through it. Press down with a spoon to extract as much liquid as possible. Discard the pulp. Stored in a sealed container in the refrigerator, coconut milk will keep for 2 to 3 days. Frozen coconut milk is likely to curdle when thawed, so use it while it is fresh.

Tahini is a delicious sesame seed butter that is used in Heart-Healthy Hummus (page 81). Tahini can also be used to flavor sauces and soups or to provide a creamy texture in a dressing like this one. Tahini is not hydrogenated, so oil may rise to the surface during storage, and you may need to stir it before using. Try Lemon-Tahini Dressing on salads, baked potatoes, steamed greens, and other vegetables.

LEMON-TAHINI Dressing

MAKES 1½ CUPS (375 ML)

½ cup (125 ml) **tahini**

½ cup (125 ml) **water**

¼ cup (60 ml) **freshly squeezed lemon juice**

¼ cup (60 ml) **tamari**

2 cloves garlic, chopped

1 teaspoon (5 ml) ground cumin

½ teaspoon (2 ml) toasted sesame oil

pinch cayenne

Put all the ingredients in a blender and process for 30 seconds, or until smooth. Stored in a sealed container in the refrigerator, Lemon-Tahini Dressing will keep for about 3 weeks.

Per 2 tablespoons (30 ml): calories: 70, protein: 3 g, fat: 6 g, carbohydrates: 3 g (0 g from sugar), dietary fiber: 1 g, calcium: 19 mg, iron: 1 mg, magnesium: 14 mg, phosphorus: 93 mg, potassium: 73 mg, sodium: 344 mg, zinc: 0.5 mg, thiamin: 0.2 mg, riboflavin: 0 mg, niacin: 1 mg, vitamin B_6: 0 mg, folate: 12 mcg, pantothenic acid: 0 mg, vitamin B_{12}: 0 mcg, vitamin A: 1 mcg, vitamin C: 3 mg, vitamin E: 0.3 mg, omega-6 fatty acid: 2 g, omega-3 fatty acid: 0 g

Percentage of calories from: protein 14%, fat 69%, carbohydrates 17%

chapter 10

Entrées

Forget butter and sour cream. There are many more delicious and healthful ways to top a baked potato. For example, try Crispy Tofu Slices (page 161), Lemon-Tahini Dressing (page 134), or some of the listed toppings. Pair a creatively topped baked potato with soup or salad for a simple and nutritious meal. Potatoes bake very well without oil; however, a light coating will soften the potato skin, which some people prefer.

Baked Potato BAR

MAKES 1 POTATO WITH TOPPINGS

1 russet potato, scrubbed

extra-virgin olive oil (optional)

Preheat the oven to 375 degrees F (190 degrees C).

Pierce the potato 3 or 4 times with a knife or fork. Lightly coat the potato with olive oil if desired. Bake for about 45 minutes, or until fork-tender. Add the toppings of your choice.

LOW-CALORIE TOPPINGS

- diced red bell pepper, cucumber, or tomato
- dulse or kelp powder or flakes
- chopped fresh herbs (such as basil or parsley)
- gomasio
- low-fat salad dressing
- miso, thinned with a little water
- nutritional yeast flakes
- salsa or hot sauce
- salt and ground pepper
- sliced green onion or diced red onion
- vegan bacon bits

CREAMY TOPPINGS

- grated vegan cheese
- Lemon-Tahini Dressing (page 134)
- Light Mushroom Gravy (page 186)
- Limey Avocado Dip (page 76)
- Liquid Gold Dressing (page 126)
- Pesto the Besto (page 82)
- Rosemary Gravy (page 188)
- Sunflower-Sesame Spread (page 83)
- vegan buttery spread
- Walnut, Olive, and Sun-Dried Tomato Tapenade (page 84)

OTHER

- Toasted Sunflower or Pumpkin Seeds (page 100)

A salad buffet can be simple or gourmet. Choose from the following lists to build a colorful and appealing assortment of ingredients. Prepare them using a single technique, such as slicing them into matchsticks, or get creative and give some ingredients a unique treatment or shape. If you like, include one or more prepared salads from the Salads chapter (pages 105 to 121) for additional variety and nutrition, and serve one or more dressings from the Salad Dressings chapter (pages 123 to 134).

SALAD Bar

GREENS AND LETTUCES

- arugula, endive, radicchio, or watercress
- butterhead, leaf, or romaine lettuce, chopped
- collard greens or kale, thinly sliced
- napa cabbage, sliced
- red or green cabbage, chopped
- spinach
- spring mix

SPROUTS

- alfalfa sprouts
- broccoli sprouts
- lentil sprouts
- mung bean sprouts
- mustard sprouts
- radish sprouts
- red clover sprouts
- sunflower sprouts

VEGETABLES

- asparagus tips
- avocado slices
- beets, sliced or grated
- bell pepper slices (green, orange, red, or yellow)
- broccoli, broccoflower, or broccolini florets
- carrots, sliced or grated
- cauliflower florets
- celeriac, grated
- celery, sliced
- cherry tomatoes
- corn kernels (young raw)
- daikon radishes, sliced or grated
- fennel, sliced
- green onions, sliced
- green peas, raw or steamed
- jerusalem artichokes
- jicama, sliced or grated
- olives, whole or sliced
- radishes, whole or grated
- snow peas
- sugar snap peas
- red or sweet white onions, thinly sliced
- rutabagas, sliced
- turnips, sliced or grated
- tomato wedges
- zucchini slices

LEGUMES, NUTS, AND SEEDS

- almonds or cashews
- black, lima, white, or other cooked beans
- chickpeas
- sunflower or pumpkin seeds (raw or toasted; see sidebar, page 100)

FRESH HERBS

- basil
- chives
- cilantro
- dill
- fennel leaves
- mint
- oregano
- parsley
- sage
- tarragon
- thyme

If you try only one recipe from this book, this should be it! Whether you make it by yourself or with company, creating a stir-fry is fun and the combinations are unlimited (see variations). A traditional stir-fry is cooked over high heat in a round-bottomed cooking vessel known as a wok. Alternatively, use a large skillet. Serve the stir-fry with cooked rice or noodles if desired.

Stir-Fry 101

MAKES FOUR TO FIVE 1-CUP (250-ML) SERVINGS

1 tablespoon (15 ml) **coconut oil or olive oil**

½ **onion, diced**

1 cup (250 ml) **broccoli florets**

1 cup (250 ml) **diagonally sliced carrots**

1 cup (250 ml) **cooked or canned chickpeas, rinsed**

1 cup (250 ml) **sliced red bell peppers**

1 cup (250 ml) **sliced bok choy**

1 cup (250 ml) **trimmed snow peas**

¼ cup (60 ml) **store-bought stir-fry sauce**

Heat the oil in a wok or large skillet over medium-high heat. (If using an electric skillet or wok, heat to 375 degrees F/190 degrees C). Add the onion and cook for 3 to 5 minutes or until soft. Add the broccoli, carrots, and chickpeas and cook and stir until the carrots and broccoli are almost tender-crisp, 5 to 7 minutes. Add the bell pepper, bok choy, snow peas, and sauce and cook and stir for 1 to 2 minutes, or until the vegetables are warm and wilted.

VARIATIONS

- Replace 1 teaspoon (5 ml) of the oil with toasted sesame oil.
- Add 2 cloves garlic, minced.
- Add 1 tablespoon (15 ml) of peeled and minced fresh ginger.
- Replace any of the vegetables with others, such as sliced celery, green or yellow beans, green or yellow bell peppers, green onions, mung bean sprouts, mushrooms, napa cabbage, okra, or sugar snap peas.
- Replace the chickpeas with cubed firm tofu, Marinated Tofu (page 160) cut into ½-inch (1 cm) cubes, cubed vegan chicken, or sliced seitan.
- Omit the stir-fry sauce. Instead, add 2 tablespoons (30 ml) of peeled and finely chopped fresh ginger with the onion and add 1 tablespoon (15 ml) of tamari plus ¼ cup (60 ml) of orange juice concentrate with the bell peppers, bok choy, and snow peas.
- Replace the stir-fry sauce with Teriyaki Sauce (page 183) or Tofu Marinade (page 184).
- Top the stir-fry with ½ cup (125 ml) of cashews.

Per cup (250 ml): calories: 168, protein: 7 g, fat: 4 g, carbohydrates: 27 g (7 g from sugar), dietary fiber: 5 g, calcium: 80 mg, iron: 3 mg, magnesium: 51 mg, phosphorus: 138 mg, potassium: 591 mg, sodium: 269 mg, zinc: 1 mg, thiamin: 0.2 mg, riboflavin: 0.2 mg, niacin: 3 mg, vitamin B_6: 0.4 mg, folate: 143 mcg, pantothenic acid: 1 mg, vitamin B_{12}: 0 mcg, vitamin A: 333 mcg, vitamin C: 137 mg, vitamin E: 2 mg, omega-6 fatty acid: 0.8 g, omega-3 fatty acid: 0.1 g

Percentage of calories from: protein 15%, fat 23%, carbohydrates 62%

Note: Analysis was done with the addition of ¼ cup (60 ml) of orange juice concentrate and 2 tablespoons (30 ml) of fresh ginger, and using 2 tablespoons (30 ml) of tamari in place of the stir-fry sauce.

Stir-Frying

Stir-frying is an Asian technique whereby food is rapidly cooked in a large bowl-shaped pan called a wok or in a large skillet. The ingredients are cooked over high heat and constantly stirred (hence the name). There are three keys to making a good stir-fry:

- Cut each vegetable into uniform pieces so they cook at the same rate.
- Add vegetables in batches. Start with onions, then add dense vegetables (such as carrots) that take the longest to cook, and finish with light vegetables (such as greens) that take the least time to cook.
- Do not overcrowd the wok or skillet. Putting too much food in the wok will decrease the cooking temperature, and the vegetables will steam rather than remain crisp.

PREPARATION

Wash and assemble the vegetables on the counter near a cutting board. As you cut each vegetable, group them in piles or rows on a baking sheet, platter, or flat serving dish in the order that you will add them to the wok. It can be a pleasure to see the colorful chopped vegetables lined up in preparation for a stir-fry.

COOKING

Heat the oil until it is hot but not smoking (see page 23). Add the onion and cook and stir until soft. This develops an underlying sweetness to the dish. If using garlic, add whole crushed garlic with the onion. Wait until the onion is soft before adding chopped or minced garlic to avoid burning the garlic. Ginger may be added along with the garlic.

The sequence of adding the vegetables to the wok is important. After the onion, garlic, and ginger are soft, add the vegetables that are most dense, such as broccoli, carrots, and cauliflower, and cook and stir for a few minutes, until tender-crisp. Progressively add softer vegetables, such as bell peppers, daikon radish, and zucchini, and cook and stir until tender-crisp. Kale and Swiss chard stems also can be added at this stage. Next add leafy greens, such as boy choy, mung bean sprouts, napa cabbage, and spinach and cook and stir until warm and wilted.

A final addition is a liquid, such as a stir-fry sauce, lemon juice, or tamari. If liquids are added to a stir-fry too early, the texture of the vegetables will change from tender-crisp to soggy.

Skewered tofu and vegetables make a colorful addition to a barbecue or picnic. The kabobs can be grilled, baked, or broiled. The Marinated Tofu (page 160) provides a burst of flavor that is bound to make this dish a favorite. As a bonus, the kabobs are excellent sources of protein, calcium, iron, zinc, vitamin C, and many B vitamins.

VEGETABLE Kabobs

(See photo on back cover)

MAKES 6 LARGE KABOBS

2 cups (500 ml) **Marinated Tofu** (page 160), covered and refrigerated for 6 to 10 hours

24 cremini or white button mushrooms

12 pieces red bell pepper, each about 1½ inches (4 cm)

12 cherry tomatoes

12 cubes zucchini, each about 1½ inches (4 cm)

Thread the vegetables and tofu onto six 10-inch (25-cm) bamboo or metal skewers (see note). A good sequence is mushroom, bell pepper, tofu, mushroom, zucchini, tomato, tofu, tomato, zucchini, mushroom, tofu, bell pepper, and mushroom. Thread the food snugly so that the barbecue fire doesn't burn the bamboo skewers.

Grill the kabobs on high heat. Alternatively, put the kabobs on a baking sheet 6 inches (15 cm) under the broiler and broil for 10 minutes or bake at 350 degrees F (180 degrees C) for 20 minutes.

NOTE: If using bamboo skewers, soak them in warm water for at least 20 minutes to keep them from igniting on the grill. Metal skewers don't need to be soaked, of course, but they do get (and stay) very hot.

Per kabob: calories: 125, protein: 13 g, fat: 6 g, carbohydrates: 9 g (4 g from sugar), dietary fiber: 3 g, calcium: 411 mg, iron: 7 mg, magnesium: 54 mg, phosphorus: 204 mg, potassium: 589 mg, sodium: 206 mg, zinc: 2 mg, thiamin: 0.2 mg, riboflavin: 0.4 mg, niacin: 7 mg, vitamin B$_6$: 0.4 mg, folate: 51 mcg, pantothenic acid: 1 mg, vitamin B$_{12}$: 0 mcg, vitamin A: 89 mcg, vitamin C: 89 mg, vitamin E: 1 mg, omega-6 fatty acid: 3 g, omega-3 fatty acid: 0.4 g

Percentage of calories from: protein 36%, fat 39%, carbohydrates 25%

Note: Calcium content depends on brand of tofu used.

This classic comfort food has a rich, meaty-tasting bottom layer, a middle layer of yellow corn, and a smooth top layer of mashed potatoes that bakes to a golden brown. The nutritional profile is superb. Each serving provides abundant protein, iron, zinc, potassium, and B vitamins. Alongside a colorful salad, this is the perfect entrée to serve to nonvegans.

Shepherd's PIE

MAKES 8 HEARTY SERVINGS (EACH ABOUT 3 X 4 INCHES/8 X 10 CM)

5 large russet potatoes, peeled (about 4 pounds)

½ cup (125 ml) **soymilk or other nondairy milk**

3 tablespoons (45 ml) **extra-virgin olive oil**

½ teaspoon (2 ml) **salt, plus more if needed**

¾ teaspoon (3 ml) **ground pepper**

1 tablespoon (15 ml) **coconut oil or extra-virgin olive oil**

2 cups (500 ml) **chopped celery**

2 cups (500 ml) **diced onion**

6 cloves garlic, minced

24 ounces (680 g) **vegan ground round or crumbles**

2 tablespoons (30 ml) **tamari**

2 tablespoons (30 ml) **vegan Worcestershire sauce**

2 teaspoons (10 ml) **dried tarragon**

1½ cups (375 ml) **fresh, canned, or frozen corn kernels, rinsed if canned**

¼ teaspoon (1 ml) **paprika**

Preheat the oven to 350 degrees F (180 degrees C). Lightly oil a 13 x 9-inch (33 x 23-cm) casserole.

Cut each potato into thirds and put the pieces in a medium saucepan. Cover with water. Bring to a boil over medium-high heat and cook until tender yet firm, 10 to 15 minutes. Drain the potatoes and put them in a medium bowl. Add the soymilk, olive oil, salt, and ¼ teaspoon of the pepper and mash until fluffy.

While the potatoes are cooking, heat the coconut oil in a skillet over medium heat. Add the celery, onion, and garlic and cook for 3 minutes, or until soft. Remove from the heat. Add the vegan ground round, tamari, vegan Worcestershire sauce, tarragon, and remaining ½ teaspoon of pepper and stir until well combined. Taste and add additional salt if desired. Transfer the vegan ground round mixture to the prepared casserole. Spoon the corn evenly over the vegan ground round mixture.

Spoon the mashed potatoes evenly over the corn and sprinkle with the paprika. Bake for 20 minutes, or until heated through and the potatoes start to turn golden brown.

Per serving: calories: 399, protein: 26 g, fat: 8 g, carbohydrates: 60 g (5 g from sugar), dietary fiber: 5 g, calcium: 89 mg, iron: 9 mg, magnesium: 78 mg, phosphorus: 198 mg, potassium: 1,588 mg, sodium: 855 mg, zinc: 10 mg, thiamin: 0.7 mg, riboflavin: 0.4 mg, niacin: 5 mg, vitamin B_6: 1.3 mg, folate: 67 mcg, pantothenic acid: 2 mg, vitamin B_{12}: 6 mcg, vitamin A: 9 mcg, vitamin C: 52 mg, vitamin E: 1 mg, omega-6 fatty acid: 1 g, omega-3 fatty acid: 0.1 g

Percentage of calories from: protein 25%, fat 17%, carbohydrates 58%

Note: Analysis was done using Yves Veggie Cuisine Meatless Ground Round and fortified soymilk, both sources of vitamin B_{12}.

For some people, getting together to cook during the holidays is one of the best parts of a celebration. Assembling this stuffed, baked squash can be a wonderful group effort. If you can't find a single large squash, use a few smaller ones instead. If you like, serve Holiday Stuffed Winter Squash with Light Mushroom Gravy (page 186), Miso Gravy (page 187), or Rosemary Gravy (page 188).

HOLIDAY STUFFED Winter Squash

MAKES 8 SERVINGS

1 winter squash, such as hubbard, butternut, or acorn (about 5 pounds/2.25 kg)

6 cups Quinoa Stuffing for Vegetables (page 143)

Preheat the oven to 350 degrees F (180 degrees C).

Remove a cone-shaped piece from the top of the squash by inserting a sharp knife at a 45-degree angle about 2 inches (5 cm) from the stem. Pushing the knife blade away from your body, cut around the stem and remove the top. Remove any fibrous material from the top and set it aside. Remove the seeds and pulp from the cavity of the squash with a spoon. Put the top back on the squash, put the squash on a baking sheet, and bake for 30 minutes. Remove from the oven and let cool for 15 minutes.

Remove the top from the squash and spoon the stuffing into the squash cavity. Leave space to allow the stuffing to expand while baking. Put the top on the squash. Bake for 45 to 60 minutes, or until a toothpick can be easily inserted into the side of the squash. To serve, slice into wedges.

NOTE: Any extra stuffing can be put in a loaf pan, sprinkled with 2 to 3 tablespoons (30 to 45 ml) of water, covered, and heated in the oven during the last 20 minutes of the baking time for the squash.

Per serving: calories: 293, protein: 12 g, fat: 9 g, carbohydrates: 48 g (2 g from sugar), dietary fiber: 10 g, calcium: 82 mg, iron: 4 mg, magnesium: 148 mg, phosphorus: 247 mg, potassium: 1,264 mg, sodium: 156 mg, zinc: 2 mg, thiamin: 0.5 mg, riboflavin: 0.3 mg, niacin: 6 mg, vitamin B_6: 0.6 mg, folate: 96 mcg, pantothenic acid: 2 mg, vitamin B_{12}: 0 mcg, vitamin A: 781 mcg, vitamin C: 53 mg, vitamin E: 4 mg, omega-6 fatty acid: 4 g, omega-3 fatty acid: 0.4 g

Percentage of calories from: protein 15%, fat 26%, carbohydrates 59%

Quinoa is not a true cereal grain but a seed from a plant family known as goosefoot. Other members of this family include beets, lamb's-quarters, and spinach. In its natural state, quinoa has a bitter, resinous coating that foams up like soap when the seeds are rinsed in water. Even though most of this resin is removed after harvest, quinoa should always be rinsed before cooking. This nutrition-packed mixture can be used in Holiday Stuffed Winter Squash (page 142) or to stuff a variety of vegetables, including bell peppers (see variation), tomatoes, and zucchini.

Quinoa Stuffing FOR VEGETABLES

MAKES SIX 1-CUP (250-ML) SERVINGS

1½ (375 ml) **cups water**

1 cup (250 ml) **quinoa**

½ teaspoon (2 ml) **salt**

1 tablespoon (15 ml) **coconut oil or extra-virgin olive oil**

½ **onion, diced**

2 stalks **celery, diced**

2 cloves **garlic, minced**

1 cup (250 ml) **fresh, canned, or frozen corn kernels, rinsed**

½ cup (125 ml) **diced red bell pepper**

½ cup (125 ml) **raw sunflower seeds**

¼ cup chopped **fresh parsley** (optional)

1 tablespoon (15 ml) **freshly squeezed lime juice**

1½ teaspoons (7 ml) **dried basil**

1½ teaspoons (7 ml) **dried dill weed**

½ teaspoon (2 ml) **dried thyme**

⅛ teaspoon (0.5 ml) **ground pepper**

Put the water in a small saucepan and bring to a boil over high heat. Stir in the quinoa and salt. Decrease the heat to low, cover, and cook for 20 minutes, or until the water is absorbed. Transfer to a large bowl and let cool.

Heat the oil in a large skillet over medium heat. Add the onion and cook, stirring occasionally, for 3 to 5 minutes, or until soft. Add the celery and garlic and cook, stirring occasionally, for 3 minutes. Stir into the cooled quinoa. Add the corn, bell pepper, sunflower seeds, optional parsley, lime juice, basil, dill weed, thyme, and pepper and stir until well combined.

Stuffed Bell Peppers: Preheat the oven to 350 degrees F (180 degrees C). Slice the top off 6 red, yellow, orange, or green bell peppers and remove the seeds and membranes to create a cavity. Spoon about 1 cup (250 ml) of Quinoa Stuffing into each bell pepper. Put the peppers in a baking dish, cover, and bake for 30 minutes, or until a knife easily pierces the pepper skin. Remove the lid and bake for an additional 10 minutes.

Per cup (250 ml): calories: 240, protein: 8 g, fat: 11 g, carbohydrates: 31 g (2 g from sugar), dietary fiber: 5 g, calcium: 57 mg, iron: 4 mg, magnesium: 125 mg, phosphorus: 250 mg, potassium: 485 mg, sodium: 181 mg, zinc: 2 mg, thiamin: 0.4 mg, riboflavin: 0.2 mg, niacin: 4 mg, vitamin B_6: 0.3 mg, folate: 66 mcg, pantothenic acid: 1 mg, vitamin B_{12}: 0 mcg, vitamin A: 29 mcg, vitamin C: 29 mg, vitamin E: 5 mg, omega-6 fatty acid: 5 g, omega-3 fatty acid: 0.1 g

Percentage of calories from: protein 13%, fat 38%, carbohydrates 49%

Get on a roll with the variety of choices that comes from this recipe. Start with a soft whole wheat flour tortilla and pick a country you want to visit. Here are lists of six possible types of fillings based on different national cuisines.

INTERNATIONAL Roll-Ups

1 9-inch tortilla

filling of choice (see options that follow)

To assemble each roll, arrange the rice or spread in a strip on the tortilla, leaving a 2-inch (5-cm) margin on the bottom and along the right edge free of ingredients. Spread the sauce evenly along the rice, then layer the other ingredients on top of the rice or spread. Lift the right edge of the tortilla and fold it toward the center. Starting with the bottom, roll up the tortilla tightly to keep the contents snuggly inside.

Per 1 International Roll-Up with African-Style Filling: calories: 247, protein: 8 g, fat: 7 g, carbohydrates: 41 g (9 g from sugar), dietary fiber: 6 g, calcium: 77 mg, iron: 2 mg, magnesium: 80 mg, phosphorus: 152 mg, potassium: 499 mg, sodium: 709 mg, zinc: 1 mg, thiamin: 0.2 mg, riboflavin: 0.1 mg, niacin: 5 mg, vitamin B$_6$: 0.4 mg, folate: 29 mcg, pantothenic acid: 1 mg, vitamin B$_{12}$: 0 mcg, vitamin A: 2 mcg, vitamin C: 33 mg, vitamin E: 2 mg, omega-6 fatty acid: 2 g, omega-3 fatty acid: 0.1 g

Percentage of calories from: protein 12%, fat 24%, carbohydrates 64%

AFRICAN-STYLE FILLING

⅓ cup (85 ml) cooked brown rice

2 tablespoons (30 ml) Spicy Peanut Sauce (page 182)

⅓ cup (85 ml) lightly steamed sliced kale

⅓ cup (85 ml) cooked mashed yam

¼ cup (60 ml) alfalfa sprouts

Dash hot sauce

INDONESIAN-STYLE FILLING

½ cup (125 ml) cooked brown rice

2 tablespoons (30 ml) Tamarind-Date Sauce (page 181)

2 ounces (55 g) Lemon-Ginger Tempeh (page 167)

¼ cup (60 ml) sliced napa cabbage

2 tablespoons (30 ml) sliced water chestnuts

1 teaspoon (5 ml) sliced pickled ginger

ITALIAN-STYLE FILLING

½ cup (125 ml) cooked brown rice

2 tablespoons (30 ml) tomato sauce

½ cup (125 ml) raw spinach, chopped

2 artichoke hearts, sliced

1 lettuce leaf, cut into strips

1 teaspoon (5 ml) chopped fresh basil

JAPANESE-STYLE FILLING

½ cup (125 ml) cooked brown rice

2 teaspoons (10 ml) vegan mayonnaise

¼ cup (60 ml) grated carrot

¼ cup (60 ml) grated daikon radish

2 tablespoons (30 ml) Teriyaki Sauce (page 183)

1 tablespoon (15 ml) thinly sliced green onion

2 teaspoons (10 ml) sliced pickled ginger

½ teaspoon (2 ml) toasted sesame seeds
(see sidebar, page 100)

MEXICAN-STYLE FILLING

½ cup (125 ml) cooked brown rice

2 teaspoons (10 ml) vegan mayonnaise

¼ cup (60 ml) grated carrot

¼ cup (60 ml) shredded vegan cheese

1 lettuce leaf, cut into strips

2 tablespoons (30 ml) salsa

1 teaspoon (5 ml) chopped fresh cilantro

MIDDLE EASTERN–STYLE FILLING

½ cup (125 ml) Heart-Healthy Hummus (page 81)

2 tablespoons (30 ml) Lemon-Tahini Dressing
(page 134)

¼ cup (60 ml) grated carrot

¼ cup (60 ml) chopped fresh tomato

1 lettuce leaf, cut into strips

1 tablespoon (15 ml) chopped fresh parsley

Sushi Rolls are made using a bamboo sushi mat, which can be purchased at an Asian specialty food store. The rolls are filled with sticky white rice, vegetables, and condiments, all held together by sheets of nori, a type of sea vegetable. If you prefer, brown rice can be used instead of the white rice (see variation). Countless filling combinations are possible. Try the ingredients listed in the recipe or use your own ideas.

Sushi ROLLS

MAKES 3 ROLLS

1½ cups (375 ml) **water**

1 cup (250 ml) **white sushi rice**

¼ teaspoon (1 ml) **salt**

2 tablespoons (30 ml) **rice vinegar**

1 tablespoon (15 ml) **sugar or other granulated sweetener**

3 sheets **nori**

3 tablespoons (45 ml) **vegan mayonnaise**

½ ripe **avocado, cut into 6 slices**

1½ cups (375 ml) **grated carrot**

6 **cucumber sticks, ¼ inch x 2 inches** (5 mm x 5 cm)

2 **lettuce leaves, cut into ½-inch** (1-cm) **strips**

3 tablespoons (45 ml) **thinly sliced pickled ginger**

1 teaspoon (5 ml) **wasabi powder, for garnish**

2 tablespoons (30 ml) **tamari, for garnish**

Put the water and salt in a medium saucepan and bring to a boil over high heat. Stir in the rice. Decrease the heat to low, cover, and cook for 20 minutes, or until the water is absorbed.

Put the rice vinegar and sugar in a small bowl and stir until the sugar is dissolved. Drizzle the vinegar mixture over the hot cooked rice and fluff with a fork. Set aside and let cool completely before assembling the rolls.

Arrange the ingredients and a small bowl filled with water on the counter. Position the sushi mat so that the bamboo strips are horizontal. Put a sheet of nori on the mat. Spoon ¾ cup (185 ml) of the rice on the nori sheet and spread it evenly to the edges, leaving a 1-inch (2.5-cm) border at the bottom and top of the sheet. Spread 1 tablespoon (5 ml) of the vegan mayonnaise in a single strip from left to right on the rice. Layer one-third of the avocado, carrots, cucumber, and lettuce and 1 teaspoon of the ginger over the vegan mayonnaise. Dip your index finger into the bowl of water and moisten the top edge of the nori sheet (this will help to provide a good seal). Fold the bottom edge of the nori sheet over the filling. Using both hands and firm, even pressure, lift the mat and roll the nori and filling forward, jelly-roll style, into a log. Gently press the top end of the nori against the roll to seal it. Repeat until all three rolls have been assembled.

Place a roll seam-side down on a cutting board. Trim the ends to remove any ingredients that may have squeezed out during the rolling process. Use a serrated knife to cut each roll in half crosswise. Cut each piece in half crosswise again, and then cut each of those pieces in half crosswise to make 8 equal slices. Trim and cut the remaining rolls the same way and arrange all the slices on a serving platter, with the filling-side up.

Put the wasabi powder in a small bowl and stir in a few drops of water. Gradually add more water, a few drops at a time, to make a smooth paste. Put the remaining 2 tablespoons of pickled ginger in a small bowl. Put the tamari in a small bowl. Pass the wasabi, pickled ginger, and tamari at the table.

VARIATION: Brown rice may be used in place of the white sushi rice, although it is less sticky. Cook 1 cup (250 ml) of brown rice in 2 cups (500 ml) of water for 45 minutes.

Per roll (250 ml): calories: 402, protein: 7 g, fat: 9 g, carbohydrates: 73 g (10 g from sugar), dietary fiber: 6 g, calcium: 54 mg, iron: 2 mg, magnesium: 51 mg, phosphorus: 98 mg, potassium: 604 mg, sodium: 455 mg, zinc: 1 mg, thiamin: 0.2 mg, riboflavin: 0.2 mg, niacin: 4 mg, vitamin B_6: 0.6 mg, folate: 44 mcg, pantothenic acid: 1 mg, vitamin B_{12}: 0 mcg, vitamin A: 504 mcg, vitamin C: 7 mg, vitamin E: 1 mg, omega-6 fatty acid: 1 g, omega-3 fatty acid: 0.1 g

Percentage of calories from: protein 7%, fat 20%, carbohydrates 73%

Note: Analysis was done without tamari.

Portobello mushrooms are large, mature cremini mushrooms. They have a meaty texture, making the mushroom caps the ideal alternatives to burgers. Serve with or without the bun, adding condiments and toppings of your choice (see note). Portobello Mushroom Burgers with Chickpea Topping are excellent sources of protein, iron, zinc, and B vitamins.

Portobello Mushroom Burgers WITH CHICKPEA TOPPING

(See photo on front cover)

MAKES 4 BURGERS

4 portobello mushrooms

1 tablespoon (15 ml) **extra-virgin olive oil**

1 teaspoon (5 ml) **tamari**

1 teaspoon (5 ml) **balsamic vinegar**

2 cups (500 ml) **cooked or canned chickpeas, rinsed**

1 cup (250 ml) **diced zucchini**

¼ cup (60 ml) **dried sun-dried tomatoes, soaked in water for 15 minutes, drained, and chopped**

2 to 4 tablespoons (30 to 60 ml) **chopped walnuts or pine nuts** (optional)

2 teaspoons (10 ml) **freshly squeezed lemon juice**

2 cloves garlic, minced

½ teaspoon (2 ml) **dried basil**

½ teaspoon (2 ml) **salt**

4 whole wheat buns (optional)

Preheat the oven to 375 degrees F (190 degrees C).

Remove and chop the mushroom stems. Using a spoon, scoop out and discard the gills from the mushroom caps.

Put the oil, tamari, and vinegar in a small bowl and stir until combined. Put the mushroom stems in a medium bowl. Put the mushroom caps on a baking pan, top-side down, and drizzle with the oil mixture.

Put the chickpeas in a food processor and pulse until pulverized but not smooth. Add to the mushroom stems and stir until combined. Add the zucchini, sun-dried tomatoes, optional walnuts, lemon juice, garlic, basil, and salt and stir until well combined. Pack each mushroom cap with one-quarter of the chickpea mixture. Bake for 15 minutes, or until the mushrooms and filling are heated through.

NOTE: If you serve the stuffed mushroom on a bun, possible condiments and garnishes include mustard (Dijon, grainy, or prepared yellow mustard) or vegan mayonnaise, a lettuce leaf, and sliced cucumber, pickle, red onion, and tomato.

Per burger: calories: 333, protein: 15 g, fat: 8 g, carbohydrates: 54 g (11 g from sugar), dietary fiber: 9 g, calcium: 110 mg, iron: 5 mg, magnesium: 92 mg, phosphorus: 272 mg, potassium: 1,001 mg, sodium: 614 mg, zinc: 3 mg, thiamin: 0.3 mg, riboflavin: 0.6 mg, niacin: 8 mg, vitamin B_6: 0.4 mg, folate: 194 mcg, pantothenic acid: 2 mg, vitamin B_{12}: 0 mcg, vitamin A: 5 mcg, vitamin C: 11 mg, vitamin E: 1 mg, omega-6 fatty acid: 2 g, omega-3 fatty acid: 0.1 g

Percentage of calories from: protein 17%, fat 21%, carbohydrates 62%

Note: Analysis includes the bun but does not include condiments or garnishes.

Supermarkets stock an array of frozen vegan burgers, but it's easy and affordable to make your own from scratch. This rendition, made with lentils and rice, is full of flavor, protein, B vitamins, iron, and zinc. Vary the seasoning by adding a cajun spice blend, celery seeds, or cumin. Serve these patties with Light Mushroom Gravy (page 186) or your favorite tomato sauce if desired.

MUSHROOM-LENTIL Patties

MAKES 5 PATTIES

2 cups (500 ml) **water**

½ cup (125 ml) **dried lentils**

½ cup (125 ml) **brown rice**

2 tablespoons (30 ml) **coconut oil or extra-virgin olive oil**

2 cups (500 ml) **sliced mushrooms**

½ onion, diced

¼ cup (60 ml) **dry breadcrumbs**

3 tablespoons (45 ml) **chopped fresh parsley**

2 tablespoons (30 ml) **nutritional yeast flakes**

½ teaspoon (2 ml) **salt**

¼ teaspoon (1 ml) **dried basil**

¼ teaspoon (1 ml) **paprika**

¼ teaspoon (1 ml) **dried thyme**

pinch ground pepper

Bring the water to a boil in a medium saucepan over high heat. Stir in the lentils and rice. Decrease the heat to low, cover, and cook for 50 minutes. Transfer to a bowl and mash with the back of a spoon until the lentils and rice bind together.

Meanwhile, heat the oil in a skillet over medium heat. Add the mushrooms and onion and cook, stirring occasionally, for 5 minutes, or until the moisture from the mushrooms has evaporated. Add the breadcrumbs, parsley, nutritional yeast, salt, basil, paprika, thyme, and pepper and stir until combined. Add to the lentil mixture and stir until well combined. Form into five 4-inch patties (see note).

Heat the remaining tablespoon of oil in a large skillet over medium heat. Cook the patties for 2 to 3 minutes on each side, or until golden brown and crispy.

NOTE: To easily form each patty, line a 4-inch-wide jar lid with plastic wrap, tightly fill the lid with one-fifth of the patty mix, and turn the patty out onto a plate.

Per patty: calories: 222, protein: 11 g, fat: 5 g, carbohydrates: 35 g (3 g from sugar), dietary fiber: 4 g, calcium: 41 mg, iron: 3 mg, magnesium: 64 mg, phosphorus: 222 mg, potassium: 466 mg, sodium: 239 mg, zinc: 2 mg, thiamin: 2 mg, riboflavin: 2 mg, niacin: 14 mg, vitamin B$_6$: 2 mg, folate: 149 mcg, pantothenic acid: 2 mg, vitamin B$_{12}$: 1.3 mcg, vitamin A: 16 mcg, vitamin C: 7 mg, vitamin E: 0.3 mg, omega-6 fatty acid: 0.5 g, omega-3 fatty acid: 0 g

Percentage of calories from: protein 18%, fat 21%, carbohydrates 61%

Note: Analysis was done using Red Star Vegetarian Support Formula nutritional yeast flakes, a source of vitamin B$_{12}$.

A relative of kidney and black beans, pinto beans have a mottled appearance like the "painted" horse of the same name. Here, pinto beans are featured in a quick-to-make stovetop version of baked beans. If you like, bake these beans in the oven instead (see variation). Just one low-fat serving provides abundant protein, dietary fiber, calcium, iron, potassium, zinc, and B vitamins.

STOVETOP "Baked" Beans

MAKES FIVE 1-CUP (250-ML) SERVINGS

1 tablespoon (15 ml) **coconut oil or extra-virgin olive oil**

1 onion, **diced**

5 cups (1.25 L) **cooked or canned pinto beans, rinsed**

1½ cups (375 ml) **water**

¼ cup (60 ml) **maple syrup or brown sugar**

¼ cup (60 ml) **cider vinegar**

2 teaspoons (10 ml) **dried dill weed**

2 teaspoons (10 ml) **Dijon mustard**

1 teaspoon (5 ml) **salt**

½ teaspoon (2 ml) **ground pepper**

¼ teaspoon (1 ml) **ground cloves**

Heat the oil in a large skillet over medium heat. Add the onion and cook, stirring occasionally, for 5 minutes, or until soft. Add the beans, water, maple syrup, vinegar, dill weed, mustard, salt, pepper, and cloves and stir until well combined. Bring to a boil. Decrease the heat to low, cover, and cook, stirring occasionally, for 1 hour, or until the liquid turns into a thick sauce.

VARIATIONS

- Replace the maple syrup with organic black-strap molasses. This simple substitution increases the calcium content to 253 milligrams per serving, or one-quarter of the daily recommended intake.

- To bake the beans, preheat the oven to 350 degrees F (180 degrees C). After bringing the beans to a boil in the skillet, pour into a 1½-quart (1.5-L) casserole, cover, and bake for 45 minutes.

Per cup (250 ml): calories: 367, protein: 20 g, fat: 6 g, carbohydrates: 60 g (11 g from sugar), dietary fiber: 17 g, calcium: 112 mg, iron: 5 mg, magnesium: 101 mg, phosphorus: 306 mg, potassium: 913 mg, sodium: 537 mg, zinc: 3 mg, thiamin: 0.4 mg, riboflavin: 0.1 mg, niacin: 5 mg, vitamin B$_6$: 0.5 mg, folate: 314 mcg, pantothenic acid: 0.5 mg, vitamin B$_{12}$: 0.4 mcg, vitamin A: 1 mcg, vitamin C: 2 mg, vitamin E: 2 mg, omega-6 fatty acid: 0.3 g, omega-3 fatty acid: 0.2 g

Percentage of calories from: protein 22%, fat 14%, carbohydrates 64%

Adzuki beans are reddish beans that are believed to have originated in the Himalayas. A low-fat source of protein, iron, zinc, potassium, B vitamins, and fiber, they have been used for thousands of years in Chinese, Japanese, and Korean cuisines. Nutty and sweet, the cooked beans are sometimes ground into a paste and used as a filling in buns and cakes. Here, adzuki beans are seasoned and served as a hot, savory dish. Try pairing them with Coconut-Saffron Rice with Cardamom and Lime (page 208).

Adzuki Beans WITH GINGER AND LEMON

MAKES FIVE 1-CUP (250-ML) SERVINGS

1 tablespoon (15 ml) coconut oil or extra-virgin olive oil

2 teaspoons (10 ml) toasted sesame oil

½ onion, diced

2 tablespoons (30 ml) peeled and minced fresh ginger

3 large cloves garlic, minced

6 cups (750 ml) cooked or canned adzuki beans, rinsed

2 cups (500 ml) water

2 tablespoons (30 ml) tamari

½ teaspoon (2ml) salt

2 tablespoons (30 ml) freshly squeezed lemon juice

Heat the coconut oil and toasted sesame oil in a large pot over medium heat. Add the onion and cook, stirring occasionally, for 3 to 5 minutes, until soft. Add the ginger and garlic and cook, stirring occasionally, for 1 minute. Add the adzuki beans, water, tamari, and salt and stir until combined. Decrease the heat to low and cook, stirring occasionally, for 10 minutes. Stir in the lemon juice.

Per cup (250 ml): calories: 439, protein: 23 g, fat: 6 g, carbohydrates: 75 g (1 g from sugar), dietary fiber: 22 g, calcium: 92 mg, iron: 6 mg, magnesium: 159 mg, phosphorus: 506 mg, potassium: 1,608 mg, sodium: 623 mg, zinc: 5 mg, thiamin: 0.4 mg, riboflavin: 0.2 mg, niacin: 6 mg, vitamin B_6: 0.3 mg, folate: 357 mcg, pantothenic acid: 1.3 mg, vitamin B_{12}: 0 mcg, vitamin A: 1 mcg, vitamin C: 4 mg, vitamin E: 0 mg, omega-6 fatty acid: 1 g, omega-3 fatty acid: 0 g

Percentage of calories from: protein 20%, fat 12%, carbohydrates 68%

African Chickpea Stew has a good balance of protein, fat, and carbohydrates and is well loved by adults and children. One reason is the peanut butter, which provides a creamy base for this nutrition-packed stew. Lemon juice adds liveliness. If you like, add a dash of hot sauce, fiery chipotle sauce, or chili sauce for some extra heat.

AFRICAN Chickpea Stew

MAKES SIX 1-CUP (250-ML) SERVINGS

1 tablespoon (15 ml) **coconut oil or extra-virgin olive oil**

1 **onion, diced**

2 **cloves garlic, minced**

4 **cups** (1 L) **vegetable stock** (for homemade, see page 92) **or water**

2 **cups** (500 ml) **peeled and diced sweet potatoes or yams**

1 **cup** (250 ml) **cooked or canned chickpeas, rinsed**

½ **cup** (125 ml) **brown rice**

¼ **teaspoon** (1 ml) **salt**

¼ **cup** (60 ml) **peanut butter**

2 **cups** (500 ml) **thinly sliced kale leaves or collard greens**

2 **tablespoons** (30 ml) **freshly squeezed lemon juice**

½ **teaspoon** (2 ml) **ground pepper**

tamari

hot sauce (optional)

Heat the oil in a large soup pot over medium heat. Add the onion and cook, stirring occasionally, for 3 to 5 minutes, or until soft. Add the garlic and cook, stirring occasionally, for 3 minutes. Add the stock, sweet potatoes, chickpeas, rice, and salt and stir until combined. Bring to a boil. Decrease the heat to low, cover, and simmer for 45 minutes.

Put the peanut butter in a small bowl. Stir in enough liquid from the stew to make a smooth paste. Stir into the stew. Add the kale, lemon juice, and pepper. Season with the tamari to taste and hot sauce if desired and stir until combined. Cover and cook for 5 minutes, or until the kale is tender.

Per cup (250 ml): calories: 383, protein: 12 g, fat: 14 g, carbohydrates: 55 g (8 g from sugar), dietary fiber: 7 g, calcium: 102 mg, iron: 3 mg, magnesium: 106 mg, phosphorus: 247 mg, potassium: 661 mg, sodium: 530 mg, zinc: 2 mg, thiamin: 0.3 mg, riboflavin: 0.1 mg, niacin: 7.6 mg, vitamin B$_6$: 0.6 mg, folate: 142 mcg, pantothenic acid: 1.7 mg, vitamin B$_{12}$: 0 mcg, vitamin A: 498 mcg, vitamin C: 15 mg, vitamin E: 3 mg, omega-6 fatty acid: 3.2 g, omega-3 fatty acid: 0.1 g

Percentage of calories from: protein 13%, fat 32%, carbohydrates 55%

When you stock a few staples, such as canned black beans and frozen mango pieces, you can make this simple entrée in a matter of minutes. Experiment by replacing the chili powder with allspice, fresh chile peppers (such as ancho, chipotle, or jalapeño), cilantro, ground coriander, ground cumin (regular or toasted), curry powder, garlic, minced fresh ginger, minced lemongrass, or a combination of seasonings. For a complete meal, serve it with rice and salsa.

Black Beans WITH COCONUT AND MANGO

MAKES ABOUT TWO 1-CUP (250-ML) SERVINGS

1¾ cups (435 ml) **cooked or canned black beans, rinsed**

¼ cup (60 ml) **coconut milk**

1 tablespoon (15 ml) **freshly squeezed lime juice**

1 teaspoon (5 ml) **chili powder**

¼ teaspoon (1 ml) **salt**

2 cups (500 ml) **fresh or frozen mango pieces**

Put the black beans, coconut milk, lime juice, chili powder, and salt in a medium saucepan and stir until combined. Cook over medium-high heat until the coconut milk comes to a boil. Decrease the heat to medium-low, cover, and cook, stirring occasionally, for 10 minutes. Stir in the mango, cover, and cook, stirring occasionally, for 3 minutes, or until heated through.

VARIATIONS:

- Omit the mango. Slice or cube 1 avocado. Garnish each portion with half of the avocado before serving.
- Replace the mango with 1 small papaya, peeled, seeded, and cubed.

Per cup (250 ml): calories: 396, protein: 16 g, fat: 8 g, carbohydrates: 71 g (26 g from sugar), dietary fiber: 16 g, calcium: 78 mg, iron: 5 mg, magnesium: 148 mg, phosphorus: 283 mg, potassium: 985 mg, sodium: 285 mg, zinc: 2 mg, thiamin: 1 mg, riboflavin: 0.2 mg, niacin: 5 mg, vitamin B_6: 0.5 mg, folate: 269 mcg, pantothenic acid: 1 mg, vitamin B_{12}: 0 mcg, vitamin A: 125 mcg, vitamin C: 53 mg, vitamin E: 3 mg, omega-6 fatty acid: 0.6 g, omega-3 fatty acid: 0.3 g

Percentage of calories from: protein 15%, fat 18%, carbohydrates 67%

Dahl is an Indian dish made of beans, lentils, or peas. In this version, mustard seeds and the other spices release their fragrant oils and acids during cooking, creating appetizing aromas and flavors. Although the dahl is ready to eat when the lentils are soft, the best flavor is achieved by simmering on very low heat for two hours, adding water if necessary.

Dahl-ICIOUS

MAKES THREE 1-CUP (250-ML) SERVINGS

2 tablespoons (30 ml) **coconut oil or extra-virgin olive oil**

1 teaspoon (5 ml) **brown mustard seeds**

½ **onion, diced**

1 tablespoon (15 ml) **peeled and minced fresh ginger**

1 **clove garlic, minced**

1 teaspoon (5 ml) **curry powder**

1 teaspoon (5 ml) **garam masala**

1 cup (250 ml) **dried lentils or mung beans**

3 cups (750 ml) **water**

1 tablespoon (15 ml) **freshly squeezed lemon juice**

½ **teaspoon** (2 ml) **salt**

¼ **teaspoon** (1 ml) **ground pepper**

Heat the oil in a large pot over medium heat. Add the mustard seeds, cover, and cook for 1 to 2 minutes, or until the seeds have stopped popping. Add the onion, ginger, and garlic and cook, stirring occasionally, until the onion is soft. Add the curry powder and garam masala and cook for 1 to 2 minutes, stirring frequently to avoid scorching. Stir in the lentils and water and bring to a boil. Decrease the heat to low, cover, and simmer, stirring occasionally, for 60 minutes. Just before serving, stir in the lemon juice, salt, and pepper.

Per cup (250 ml): calories: 341, protein: 20 g, fat: 11 g, carbohydrates: 45 g (5 g from sugar), dietary fiber: 9 g, calcium: 73 mg, iron: 8 mg, magnesium: 92 mg, phosphorus: 340 mg, potassium: 732 mg, sodium: 330 mg, zinc: 3 mg, thiamin: 0.4 mg, riboflavin: 0.2 mg, niacin: 5 mg, vitamin B$_6$: 0.5 mg, folate: 304 mcg, pantothenic acid: 1.3 mg, vitamin B$_{12}$: 0 mcg, vitamin A: 2 mcg, vitamin C: 9 mg, vitamin E: 2 mg, omega-6 fatty acid: 1 g, omega-3 fatty acid: 0.2 g

Percentage of calories from: protein 23%, fat 27%, carbohydrates 50%

Once you've discovered commercial curry pastes, you'll be able to put together a vegetable or bean curry with ease. Even the mild pastes are hot enough for most people. Patak's is our favorite brand. Use a little or a lot, depending on your preference. Chickpeas are rich in protein, minerals, and folate.

CHICKPEAS WITH Indian Spices

MAKES FOUR 1-CUP (250-ML) SERVINGS

1 tablespoon (15 ml) **coconut oil or extra-virgin olive oil**

½ **onion, diced**

2 cloves **garlic, minced**

2 cups (500 ml) **chopped fresh or canned tomatoes**

1 tablespoon (15 ml) **mild Indian curry paste**

3 cups (750 ml) **cooked or canned chickpeas, rinsed**

1 tablespoon (15 ml) **freshly squeezed lemon juice**

1 teaspoon (5 ml) **tamari**

¼ teaspoon (1 ml) **salt** (optional)

Heat the oil in a medium saucepan over medium heat. Add the onion and cook, stirring occasionally, for 3 to 5 minutes, or until soft. Add the garlic, tomatoes, and curry paste and cook, stirring occasionally, for 3 minutes. Add the chickpeas, lemon juice, tamari, and optional salt and cook, stirring occasionally, for 15 minutes.

Per cup (250 ml): calories: 288, protein: 13 g, fat: 9 g, carbohydrates: 42 g (9 g from sugar), dietary fiber: 8 g, calcium: 83 mg, iron: 4 mg, magnesium: 77 mg, phosphorus: 252 mg, potassium: 649 mg, sodium: 100 mg, zinc: 2 mg, thiamin: 0.2 mg, riboflavin: 0.1 mg, niacin: 3 mg, vitamin B_6: 0.3 mg, folate: 242 mcg, pantothenic acid: 0.5 mg, vitamin B_{12}: 0 mcg, vitamin A: 40 mcg, vitamin C: 17 mg, vitamin E: 2 mg, omega-6 fatty acid: 2 g, omega-3 fatty acid: 0.1 g

Percentage of calories from: protein 17%, fat 27%, carbohydrates 56%

Lentils have a mild, earthy flavor and are rich in protein, iron, and many of the B vitamins, while being very low in fat. The best lentils for this recipe are small French green lentils, considered to be the Rolls-Royce of the lentil world. Some French lentils are known as Puy lentils, a name given only to those lentils grown near Le Puy-en-Velay in Auvergne, a rugged mountainous region with volcanic soil in the south of France.

French Lentils WITH FENNEL AND LEMON

MAKES SIX 1-CUP (250-ML) SERVINGS

1 tablespoon (15 ml) **coconut oil or extra-virgin olive oil**

1 **bulb fennel, chopped** (about 2 cups/500 ml)

½ **onion, chopped**

2 **cloves garlic, minced**

5 cups (1.25 L) **water**

1 cup (250 ml) **dried French lentils**

2 cups (500 ml) **diced tomatoes**

1 teaspoon (5 ml) **dried basil**

1 teaspoon (5 ml) **dried thyme**

½ teaspoon (2 ml) **grated lemon zest**

1 teaspoon (5 ml) **salt**

¼ teaspoon (1 ml) **ground pepper**

Heat the oil in a large pan over medium heat. Add the fennel, onion, and garlic and cook, stirring occasionally, for 5 minutes, or until soft. Stir in the water, lentils, tomatoes, basil, thyme, and zest. Bring to a boil. Decrease the heat to low, cover, and cook, stirring occasionally, for 45 to 60 minutes, or until the lentils are tender. Stir in the salt and pepper.

Per cup (250 ml): calories: 157, protein: 10 g, fat: 3 g, carbohydrates: 24 g (4 g from sugar), dietary fiber: 5 g, calcium: 45 mg, iron: 4 mg, magnesium: 49 mg, phosphorus: 181 mg, potassium: 539 mg, sodium: 407 mg, zinc: 1 mg, thiamin: 0.2 mg, riboflavin: 0.1mg, niacin: 3 mg, vitamin B_6: 0.3 mg, folate: 162 mcg, pantothenic acid: 0.7 mg, vitamin B_{12}: 0 mcg, vitamin A: 29 mcg, vitamin C: 13 mg, vitamin E: 0.5 mg, omega-6 fatty acid: 0.1 g, omega-3 fatty acid: 0 g

Percentage of calories from: protein 26%, fat 15%, carbohydrates 59%

Lima beans originated in South America and are named after the capital of Peru. They have a flat, oblong shape; a creamy, starchy texture; and a sweet flavor. This recipe is similar to succotash but has a Mexican twist thanks to the addition of cilantro, chipotle chile, and lime juice.

LIMA BEANS, CORN, AND CHIPOTLE Chile

MAKES FOUR 1-CUP (250-ML) SERVINGS

1 tablespoon (15 ml) **coconut oil or extra-virgin olive oil**

½ onion, diced

2 cloves garlic, minced

2½ cups (625 ml) **cooked, canned, or frozen baby lima beans, rinsed**

1 cup (250 ml) **fresh, canned, or frozen corn kernels, rinsed if canned**

½ cup (125 ml) **diced red bell pepper**

½ cup (125 ml) **water**

¼ cup (60 ml) **freshly squeezed lime juice**

1 to 2 teaspoons (5 to 10 ml) **minced chipotle chile**

½ teaspoon (2 ml) **salt**

¼ cup (60 ml) **chopped fresh cilantro or parsley**

Heat the oil in a large skillet over medium heat. Add the onion and cook, stirring occasionally, for 3 to 5 minutes, or until soft. Add the garlic and cook, stirring occasionally, for 2 minutes. Stir in the lima beans, corn, bell pepper, water, lime juice, chile, and salt. Cook, stirring occasionally, for 10 minutes, adding more water if the mixture becomes too dry. Stir in the cilantro just before serving.

Per cup (250 ml): calories: 233, protein: 11 g, fat: 4 g, carbohydrates: 40 g (3 g from sugar), dietary fiber: 11 g, calcium: 46 mg, iron: 3 mg, magnesium: 85 mg, phosphorus: 203 mg, potassium: 680 mg, sodium: 248 mg, zinc: 2 mg, thiamin: 0.3 mg, riboflavin: 0.1 mg, niacin: 4 mg, vitamin B$_6$: 0.2 mg, folate: 207 mcg, pantothenic acid: 1 mg, vitamin B$_{12}$: 0 mcg, vitamin A: 36 mcg, vitamin C: 48 mg, vitamin E: 1 mg, omega-6 fatty acid: 0.4 g, omega-3 fatty acid: 0.1 g

Percentage of calories from: protein 19%, fat 16%, carbohydrates 65%

This spicy bean dish is low in fat and rich in protein, minerals (calcium, iron, magnesium, phosphorus, potassium, and zinc), and folate and other B vitamins. If you prefer a milder dish, use only one chile. Try this recipe with Fiesta Quinoa Salad with Lime Dressing (page 113) for a hearty, tasty meal.

MOROCCAN BLACK BEANS with Yams and Currants

MAKES FOUR 1-CUP (250-ML) SERVINGS

1 tablespoon (15 ml) **coconut oil or extra-virgin olive oil**

½ **onion, diced**

2 **red chiles, minced**

2 **cloves garlic, minced**

3 cups (750 ml) **cooked or canned black beans, rinsed**

2½ cups (625 ml) **water**

2 cups (500 ml) **peeled and diced yams**

½ cup (125 ml) **dried currants**

1 tablespoon (15 ml) **ground coriander**

1 tablespoon (15 ml) **ground toasted cumin seeds** (see sidebar, page 100)

½ teaspoon (2 ml) **cinnamon**

½ teaspoon (2 ml) **salt**

¼ cup (60 ml) **chopped fresh cilantro or parsley** (optional)

1 tablespoon (15 ml) **freshly squeezed lemon juice**

Heat the oil in a large pot over medium heat. Add the onion and cook, stirring occasionally, for 3 to 5 minutes, until soft. Add the chiles and garlic and cook, stirring occasionally, for 1 minute. Stir in the black beans, water, yams, currants, coriander, cumin, cinnamon, and salt and bring to a boil. Decrease the heat to low, cover, and cook, stirring occasionally, for 20 to 30 minutes, or until the yams are tender. Just before serving, stir in the optional cilantro and lemon juice.

Per cup (250 ml): calories: 359, protein: 14 g, fat: 5 g, carbohydrates: 69 g (14 g from sugar), dietary fiber: 16 g, calcium: 92 mg, iron: 5 mg, magnesium: 127 mg, phosphorus: 266 mg, potassium: 1,349 mg, sodium: 240 mg, zinc: 2 mg, thiamin: 0.5 mg, riboflavin: 0.2 mg, niacin: 4 mg, vitamin B_6: 0.5 mg, folate: 218 mcg, pantothenic acid: 0.6 mg, vitamin B_{12}: 0 mcg, vitamin A: 18 mcg, vitamin C: 47 mg, vitamin E: 1 mg, omega-6 fatty acid: 0.4 g, omega-3 fatty acid: 0.2 g

Percentage of calories from: protein 15%, fat 11%, carbohydrates 74%

Tacos are a nutritionally balanced and nearly instant meal. Just warm the shells and beans, chop the veggies, and set out the colorful fillings in pretty bowls. Guests can each take one or more taco shells and create their favorite combinations. If you prefer burritos, replace the taco shells with soft tortillas. Check the label to make sure the refried beans do not contain lard.

TIMESAVING Tacos

10 taco shells or soft tortillas

14 ounces (400 g) canned vegan refried beans

2 cups (500 ml) shredded lettuce

1 ripe avocado, chopped

1 cup (250 ml) salsa

1 cup (250 ml) chopped fresh tomatoes

1 cup (250 ml) grated vegan cheese (optional)

1 carrot, grated

Preheat the oven to 250 degrees F (120 degrees C).

Put the refried beans in a small saucepan and cook over medium heat until warmed through. If the refried beans are too thick, thin with 1 tablespoon (15 ml) of water.

Put the taco shells on a baking sheet or directly on the oven rack and warm them for 1 to 2 minutes. Put the taco shells, beans, lettuce, avocado, salsa, tomato, optional vegan cheese, and carrot in serving bowls on the table. Leftover fillings can be refrigerated in covered dishes and used at another meal.

VARIATIONS:

- Replace the refried beans with 2 cups (500 ml) of mashed black beans or pinto beans.
- Put the avocado in a small bowl and mash with a fork. Stir in 2 teaspoons (10 ml) of freshly squeezed lemon juice.

Per taco: calories: 145, protein: 4 g, fat: 7 g, carbohydrates: 19 g (1 g from sugar), dietary fiber: 5 g, calcium: 52 mg, iron: 2 mg, magnesium: 42 mg, phosphorus: 91 mg, potassium: 397 mg, sodium: 293 mg, zinc: 1 mg, thiamin: 0.1 mg, riboflavin: 0.1 mg, niacin: 1 mg, vitamin B_6: 0.2 mg, folate: 55 mcg, pantothenic acid: 0.4 mg, vitamin B_{12}: 0 mcg, vitamin A: 102 mcg, vitamin C: 13 mg, vitamin E: 1 mg, omega-6 fatty acid: 1.5 g, omega-3 fatty acid: 0.1 g

Percentage of calories from: protein 11%, fat 39%, carbohydrates 50%

The firmness of tofu determines how readily it absorbs marinade. Medium- to extra-firm varieties work best (see below). This tofu can be used for Spicy Marinated Tofu Salad (page 118), Stir-Fry 101 (page 138), or Vegetable Kabobs (page 140).

Marinated TOFU

MAKES FOUR ½-CUP (125-ML) SERVINGS

12 ounces (350 g) **medium-firm, firm, or extra-firm tofu, cubed**

1 cup (250 ml) **Tofu Marinade** (page 184)

Put the tofu in a container with a lid. Pour the marinade over the tofu so that it covers the cubes on all sides. Cover and refrigerate for 6 hours. Drain excess marinade before using the tofu.

Per ½ cup (125 ml): calories: 139, protein: 14 g, fat: 9 g, carbohydrates: 4 g (0 g from sugar), dietary fiber: 2 g, calcium: 599 mg, iron: 9 mg, magnesium: 53 mg, phosphorus: 174 mg, potassium: 228 mg, sodium: 296 mg, zinc: 1 mg, thiamin: 0.1 mg, riboflavin: 0.1 mg, niacin: 4 mg, vitamin B_6: 0.1 mg, folate: 27 mcg, pantothenic acid: 0.1 mg, vitamin B_{12}: 0 mcg, vitamin A: 18 mcg, vitamin C: 1 mg, vitamin E: 0 mg, omega-6 fatty acid: 4 g, omega-3 fatty acid: 1 g

Percentage of calories from: protein 38%, fat 51%, carbohydrates 11%

Note: Because the tofu will not absorb all of the marinade, the analysis is based on ¼ cup (60 ml) of marinade being absorbed by 12 ounces (350 g) of tofu. Calcium content depends on the brand of tofu used.

Marinating Tofu

Tofu has a spongelike texture, so it absorbs flavor well when marinated. Tofu can be cut into cubes of different sizes depending on how it is to be used in a recipe. For example, for the Spicy Marinated Tofu Salad (page 118), the cube will be smaller than for the Vegetable Kabobs (page 140). Smaller cubes will soak up more marinade than larger cubes, which can result in a higher sodium content.

Though sufficient marinade is required to cover the tofu cubes, only part of the marinade is absorbed. Leftover marinade can be heated and served over brown rice or thickened with arrowroot starch or cornstarch and used as a stir-fry sauce for Stir-Fry 101 (page 138). One tablespoon (15 ml) of starch is needed to thicken 1 cup (250 ml).

The optimal time for marinating depends on the type of tofu and the marinade. Medium-firm tofu soaks up the marinade fastest, followed by firm tofu, then extra-firm tofu. Tofu can marinate at room temperature for up to one hour. For longer periods than that, the tofu should marinate in the refrigerator to prevent bacterial growth and spoilage.

If you want to introduce tofu to family or friends, this is a form they'll likely enjoy. Crispy Tofu Slices can be used as the high-protein part of a meal, as an appetizer, in a salad, in a sandwich, and even as a pizza topping. This tofu has a southern-fried quality; it can be either moist or crispy and dry, depending on the cooking time.

CRISPY Tofu Slices

2 tablespoons (30 ml) **low-sodium or regular tamari**

⅓ cup (85 ml) **nutritional yeast flakes**

1 teaspoon (5 ml) **salt-free or regular Spike** (see note and variation)

12 ounces (340 g) **extra-firm or firm tofu, cut into ¼-inch** (5-mm) **slices**

1 tablespoon (15 ml) **coconut oil or extra-virgin olive oil**

Pour the tamari onto a small plate. Put the nutritional yeast and Spike in a shallow bowl and stir until combined. Dip each tofu slice into the tamari, coating both sides. Then dip each slice into the nutritional yeast mixture, coating both sides.

Heat the oil in a large skillet over medium heat. Add the tofu and cook for 3 to 4 minutes, or until crisp and brown. Turn the tofu over and cook until the other side is crisp and brown, about 3 minutes.

NOTE: Spike is a brand of bottled dry seasoning sold at supermarkets and natural food stores.

VARIATION: Replace the Spike with ground ginger, cumin, or another seasoning, such as Mrs. Dash.

Per serving (about 6 slices): calories: 238, protein: 27 g, fat: 11 g, carbohydrates: 13 g (0 g from sugar), dietary fiber: 7 g, calcium: 789 mg, iron: 13 mg, magnesium: 93 mg, phosphorus: 417 mg, potassium: 634 mg, sodium: 859 mg, zinc: 5 mg, thiamin: 11 mg, riboflavin: 11 mg, niacin: 67 mg, vitamin B_6: 10 mg, folate: 286 mcg, pantothenic acid: 1.3 mg, vitamin B_{12}: 8.3 mcg, vitamin A: 19 mcg, vitamin C: 0 mg, vitamin E: 0 mg, omega-6 fatty acid: 5 g, omega-3 fatty acid: 1 g

Percentage of calories from: protein 43%, fat 37%, carbohydrates 20%

Note: Analysis was done using calcium-set tofu and Red Star Vegetarian Support Formula nutritional yeast flakes.

Tofu, Asia's top fast food, has become popular in the West as a versatile source of protein for breakfast, lunch, or dinner. Tofu readily takes on the flavors of the other ingredients it is cooked with, so it can be used in all types of cuisines. The following sauces are based on favorite flavor combinations from around the world. Teriyaki Sauce (page 183) or a store-bought sauce can also be used. Adjust the quantity of sauce if using larger or smaller amounts of tofu.

EASY TOFU Entrées

MAKES ABOUT 3 SERVINGS

12 ounces (350 g) **firm or extra-firm tofu, drained, rinsed, and cut into ⅓-inch** (8-mm) **slices**

½ cup sauce of choice (see options that follow)

Preheat the oven to 350 degrees F (180 degrees C).

Arrange the tofu slices in a single layer in a 13 x 9-inch (33 x 23-cm) baking dish. To make the sauce, put all the ingredients except the topping or garnish in a small bowl and stir until well combined. Pour the sauce over the tofu, arrange the topping over it, cover, and bake for 30 minutes.

HAWAIIAN-STYLE SAUCE

Makes ½ cup (125 ml), not including the pineapple topping

¼ cup (60 ml) frozen orange juice concentrate, thawed

¼ cup (60 ml) unsweetened pineapple juice

1 tablespoon (15 ml) peeled and minced fresh ginger

2 teaspoons (10 ml) tamari

2 cloves garlic, minced

1 cup (250 ml) diced fresh pineapple or canned pineapple packed in juice, for topping

MEXICAN-STYLE SAUCE

Makes ½ cup (125 ml)

½ cup (125 ml) salsa

1 to 2 teaspoons (5 to 10 ml) chili powder

2 cloves garlic, minced

1 teaspoon (5 ml) ground toasted cumin seeds (see sidebar, page 100)

½ onion, sliced, for topping

½ jalapeño chile, minced, for garnish

MEDITERRANEAN-STYLE SAUCE

Makes ½ cup (125 ml)

½ cup (125 ml) tomato sauce

2 cloves garlic, minced

1 teaspoon (5 ml) dried rosemary, crushed

1 teaspoon (5 ml) grated lemon zest

½ teaspoon (2 ml) dried marjoram

¼ teaspoon (1 ml) salt

Pinch ground pepper

1 cup (250 ml) chopped water-packed or thawed frozen
artichoke hearts, for topping

THAI-STYLE SAUCE

Makes ½ cup (125 ml)

⅓ cup (85 ml) coconut milk

2 tablespoons (30 ml) freshly squeezed lime juice

1 to 2 teaspoons (5 to 10 ml) Thai curry paste

1 teaspoon (5 ml) dried basil

½ teaspoon (2 ml) salt

¼ teaspoon (1 ml) dried mint

1 cup (250 ml) sliced red bell peppers, for topping

Per serving (about 3 slices): calories: 166, protein: 11 g, fat: 5 g, carbohydrates: 22 g (8 g from sugar), dietary fiber: 2 g, calcium: 257 mg, iron: 2 mg, magnesium: 64 mg, phosphorus: 170 mg, potassium: 454 mg, sodium: 243 mg, zinc: 1 mg, thiamin: 0.2 mg, riboflavin: 0.1 mg, niacin: 3 mg, vitamin B_6: 0.2 mg, folate: 73 mcg, pantothenic acid: 0.4 mg, vitamin B_{12}: 0 mcg, vitamin A: 2 mcg, vitamin C: 61 mg, vitamin E: 0.1 mg, omega-6 fatty acid: 2 g, omega-3 fatty acid: 0.2 g

Percentage of calories from: protein 25%, fat 25%, carbohydrates 50%

Note: Analysis was done using Hawaiian-Style Sauce. Calcium content depends on the brand of tofu used.

This mineral- and vitamin-rich dish provides a delightful blend of colors, flavors, and textures. It is best served with basmati rice, although it also goes well with other types of rice, millet, or quinoa. For a change, make this curry without the tofu and serve it with Chickpeas with Indian Spices (page 155). Half of the sugar in this recipe is from the natural fruit sugar in raisins; the other half is in the vegetables.

CURRIED VEGETABLES with Tofu

MAKES SIX 1-CUP (250-ML) SERVINGS

2 tablespoons (30 ml) **coconut oil or extra-virgin olive oil**

1 onion, **diced**

1 tablespoon (15 ml) **peeled and minced fresh ginger**

2 cloves garlic, **minced**

1 teaspoon (5 ml) **ground cumin**

1 teaspoon (5 ml) **curry powder**

½ teaspoon (2 ml) **ground coriander**

½ teaspoon (2 ml) **salt**

12 ounces (340 g) **firm tofu, diced**

1 cup (250 ml) **diced red bell pepper**

1 cup (250 ml) **broccoli florets**

1 cup (250 ml) **diced carrots**

1 cup (250 ml) **cauliflower florets**

7 ounces (210 ml) **coconut milk**

¼ cup (60 ml) **raisins, soaked in ¼ cup** (60 ml) **boiling water for 15 minutes**

1 tablespoon (15 ml) **freshly squeezed lime juice**

2 tablespoons (30 ml) **chopped fresh cilantro or parsley, for garnish**

Heat the oil in a large skillet over medium heat. Add the onion and cook, stirring occasionally, for 3 to 5 minutes, until soft. Add the ginger and garlic and cook, stirring occasionally, for 1 minute. Add the cumin, curry powder, coriander, and salt and cook for 1 minute, stirring frequently to avoid scorching. Stir in the tofu, bell pepper, broccoli, carrots, cauliflower, coconut milk, raisins, and the raisin soaking liquid. Cover and cook until the vegetables are tender-crisp, 5 to 7 minutes. Stir in the lime juice. Garnish with the cilantro.

Per cup (250 ml): calories: 266, protein: 12 g, fat: 18 g, carbohydrates: 21 g (9 g from sugar), dietary fiber: 5 g, calcium: 437 mg, iron: 8 mg, magnesium: 72 mg, phosphorus: 200 mg, potassium: 592 mg, sodium: 198 mg, zinc: 1.5 mg, thiamin: 0.2 mg, riboflavin: 0.2 mg, niacin: 4 mg, vitamin B_6: 0.3 mg, folate: 61 mcg, pantothenic acid: 0.5 mg, vitamin B_{12}: 0 mcg, vitamin A: 250 mcg, vitamin C: 76 mg, vitamin E: 1 mg, omega-6 fatty acid: 3 g, omega-3 fatty acid: 0.4 g

Percentage of calories from: protein 16%, fat 55%, carbohydrates 29%

Note: Calcium content depends on the brand of tofu used.

Rice vinegar is less acidic than vinegars made from fruit, such as apples. Here, the use of rice vinegar creates a dish that is more smooth than sharp. Little sweetener is needed, and the inherent sweetness of the vegetables shines through. Serve Sweet-and-Sour Tofu on a bed of rice for two hungry adults; if additional items are included in the meal, this dish can serve four.

Sweet-and-Sour TOFU

MAKES FOUR 1-CUP (250-ML) SERVINGS

1 tablespoon (15 ml) **coconut oil or extra-virgin olive oil**

1 cup (250 ml) **diced onion**

1 cup (250 ml) **diagonally sliced carrots**

1 tablespoon (15 ml) **peeled and minced fresh ginger**

2 cloves **garlic, minced**

¾ cup (185 ml) **unsweetened pineapple juice**

½ cup (125 ml) **diced fresh pineapple**

¼ cup (60 ml) **brown sugar or other granulated sweetener**

¼ cup (60 ml) **rice vinegar**

2 tablespoons (30 ml) **tamari**

1 tablespoon (15 ml) **arrowroot starch or cornstarch**

1 cup (250 ml) **diced green bell pepper**

1 cup (250 ml) **diced red or yellow bell pepper**

1 cup (250 ml) **diced firm tofu**

1 tablespoon (15 ml) **chopped fresh parsley, for garnish**

Heat the oil in a large skillet over medium heat. Add the onion and cook, stirring occasionally, for 3 to 5 minutes, or until soft and starting to brown. Add the carrots, ginger, and garlic and cook, stirring occasionally, for 3 minutes.

Put the pineapple juice, pineapple, sugar, vinegar, tamari, and arrowroot starch in a small bowl and stir until combined. Put the pineapple mixture, bell peppers, and tofu in the skillet with the onion mixture. Stir constantly until thickened, then cover and cook for 3 minutes. Garnish with the parsley.

VARIATION: Replace the carrots with cauliflower and some of the bell peppers with snow peas or bok choy. Stir in the snow peas or bok choy during the last minute of cooking.

Per cup (250 ml): calories: 305, protein: 16 g, fat: 11 g, carbohydrates: 40 g (16 g from sugar), dietary fiber: 5 g, calcium: 632 mg, iron: 10 mg, magnesium: 83 mg, phosphorus: 225 mg, potassium: 678 mg, sodium: 545 mg, zinc: 2 mg, thiamin: 0.3 mg, riboflavin: 0.2 mg, niacin: 2 mg, vitamin B$_6$: 0.5 mg, folate: 68 mcg, pantothenic acid: 0.6 mg, vitamin B$_{12}$: 0 mcg, vitamin A: 319 mcg, vitamin C: 156 mg, vitamin E: 2 mg, omega-6 fatty acid: 4 g, omega-3 fatty acid: 1 g

Percentage of calories from: protein 20%, fat 31%, carbohydrates 49%

Note: Analysis was done using calcium-set tofu.

Teriyaki Sauce (page 183), a sweet and salty staple in Japanese cuisine, can be high in sodium, so reserve it for an occasional treat. Served over a bed of brown rice or your favorite noodles, Teriyaki Tofu with Vegetables is a fully satisfying and attractive meal. It is also an excellent source of iron, and the abundant vitamin C in this dish substantially improves iron absorption.

Teriyaki Tofu **WITH VEGETABLES**

1 tablespoon (15 ml) **coconut oil or extra-virgin olive oil**

½ **onion, diced**

1 cup (250 ml) **diced red bell pepper**

1 cup (250 ml) **diced carrots**

1 cup (250 ml) **diced daikon radish**

1 cup (250 ml) **diced sweet potato**

1 cup (250 ml) **diced firm tofu**

1 tablespoon (15 ml) **peeled and minced fresh ginger**

1 clove **garlic, minced**

¾ cup (185 ml) **Teriyaki Sauce** (page 183) **or store-bought sauce**

2 tablespoons (30 ml) **chopped fresh cilantro or parsley, for garnish**

Heat the oil in a large skillet over medium heat. Add the onion and cook, stirring occasionally, for 3 to 5 minutes, until soft. Add the bell pepper, carrots, daikon radish, sweet potato, tofu, ginger, and garlic and cook, stirring frequently, for 5 minutes. Stir in the Teriyaki Sauce. Decrease the heat to low, cover, and cook for 3 minutes. Garnish with the cilantro.

Per cup (250 ml): calories: 255, protein: 10 g, fat: 8 g, carbohydrates: 34 g (20 g from sugar), dietary fiber: 4 g, calcium: 349 mg, iron: 6 mg, magnesium: 56 mg, phosphorus: 148 mg, potassium: 557 mg, sodium: 584 mg, zinc: 1 mg, thiamin: 0.2 mg, riboflavin: 0.2 mg, niacin: 4 mg, vitamin B_6: 0.3 mg, folate: 41 mcg, pantothenic acid: 0.7 mg, vitamin B_{12}: 0 mcg, vitamin A: 595 mcg, vitamin C: 83 mg, vitamin E: 1 mg, omega-6 fatty acid: 2 g, omega-3 fatty acid: 0.3 g

Percentage of calories from: protein 15%, fat 25%, carbohydrates 51%, alcohol 9%

Note: Calcium content depends on the brand of tofu used.

Tempeh, a traditional, fermented Indonesian food that is made with soybeans, is easy to digest and has abundant protein, minerals (calcium, iron, magnesium, and zinc), and B vitamins. Tempeh is stored in the freezer section of natural food stores. In addition to soybeans, some tempeh includes cereal grains, vegetables, and various seasonings.

LEMON-GINGER Tempeh

MAKES TWO 4-OUNCE (113-G) SERVINGS

8 ounces (227 gm) **tempeh, cut into eight 2 x 2 x ½-inch** (2.5 x 2.2 x 1-cm) **slices**

3 tablespoon (45 ml) **freshly squeezed lemon juice**

4 teaspoons (20 ml) **tamari**

2 teaspoons (10 ml) **peeled and minced fresh ginger**

1 teaspoon (5 ml) **minced garlic**

½ teaspoon (2 ml) **onion powder**

Put the tempeh in a pie pan or 8 x 8-inch (20 x 20-cm) baking dish. Put the lemon juice, tamari, ginger, garlic, and onion powder in a small bowl and stir until combined. Pour the lemon juice mixture over the tempeh, cover, and refrigerate for 2 to 6 hours, turning occasionally to marinate both sides of the tempeh.

Preheat the broiler for 5 minutes. Transfer the tempeh to a broiler-safe pan and broil for 2 minutes. Turn the tempeh over and broil the other side for 2 minutes. Alternatively, bake in a 350 degree F (180 degree C) oven for 15 minutes.

Fried Lemon-Ginger Tempeh: Heat 2 teaspoons (10 ml) of oil in a large skillet over medium heat. Add the marinated tempeh and cook for 3 minutes on each side, or until brown.

Tempeh with Tofu Marinade: Marinate the tempeh with ¼ cup of Tofu Marinade (page 184) for 2 to 6 hours in the refrigerator. Broil for 2 minutes on each side or cook in a skillet for 3 minutes on each side, or until brown.

Per 4 ounces (113-g): calories: 238, protein: 23 g, fat: 12 g, carbohydrates: 15 g (1 g from sugar), dietary fiber: 7 g, calcium: 135 mg, iron: 3 mg, magnesium: 100 mg, phosphorus: 324 mg, potassium: 541 mg, sodium: 691 mg, zinc: 1 mg, thiamin: 0.1 mg, riboflavin: 0.4 mg, niacin: 9 mg, vitamin B_6: 0.3 mg, folate: 33 mcg, pantothenic acid: 0.4 mg, vitamin B_{12}: 0 mcg, vitamin A: 0 mcg, vitamin C: 11 mg, vitamin E: 0 mg, omega-6 fatty acid: 4 g, omega-3 fatty acid: 0.2 g

Percentage of calories from: protein 35%, fat 22%, carbohydrates 43%

Paella is a traditional Spanish dish that features medium-grain rice and saffron. Arborio rice is suggested for this dish, although Spanish varieties, such as Calasparra and bomba, are also excellent. The cooked rice should be dry and relatively firm, rather than creamy, like a risotto. With the addition of Gardein's vegan chicken, this version of paella is a satisfying entrée.

Vegan Chick'n Paella WITH ARTICHOKES AND SPINACH

MAKES SIX 1-CUP (250-ML) SERVINGS

1 to 2 tablespoons (15 to 30 ml) **coconut oil or extra-virgin olive oil**

½ onion, diced

2 cups (500 ml) **chopped fresh or canned tomatoes**

4 cloves garlic, thinly sliced

1 package (10 ounces/285 g) **Gardein Chick'n Scallopini, cut into 1-inch (2.5-cm) pieces**

2 cups (500 ml) **vegetable stock**

1 cup (250 ml) **arborio rice**

1⅔ cups (420 ml) **canned or thawed frozen artichoke hearts, quartered**

1 teaspoon (5 ml) **dried basil**

⅛ teaspoon (0.5 ml) **ground pepper**

pinch saffron

4 cups (1 L) **spinach leaves, chopped**

½ lemon

Heat the oil in a large skillet or a wide, shallow pot over medium heat. Add the onion and cook, stirring occasionally, for 5 minutes, or until soft. Add the tomatoes and garlic and cook, stirring occasionally, for 5 minutes, until the tomatoes start to break down. Stir in the Chick'n Scallopini, stock, rice, artichokes, basil, pepper, and saffron. Decrease the heat to medium-low and cook, stirring occasionally, for 10 minutes. Cook for 10 additional minutes without disturbing the rice. Remove from the heat, stir in the spinach, cover, and let rest for 5 minutes. Squeeze the lemon over the top just before serving.

Per cup (250 ml): calories: 272, protein: 16 g, fat: 5 g, carbohydrates: 43 g (2 g from sugar), dietary fiber: 6 g, calcium: 107 mg, iron: 2 mg, magnesium: 43 mg, phosphorus: 68 mg, potassium: 490 mg, sodium: 57 mg, zinc: 0.5 mg, thiamin: 0.1 mg, riboflavin: 0.1 mg, niacin: 2 mg, vitamin B_6: 0.2 mg, folate: 128 mcg, pantothenic acid: 0.2 mg, vitamin B_{12}: 0 mcg, vitamin A: 127 mcg, vitamin C: 20 mg, vitamin E: 1 mg, omega-6 fatty acid: 0.2 g, omega-3 fatty acid: 0.1 g

Percentage of calories from: protein 23%, fat 16%, carbohydrates 61%

Note: Analyzed using frozen artichoke hearts.

This is a vegan version of a creamy, cheesy, childhood favorite. One cup provides most of your B vitamins for the day, including vitamin B$_{12}$ when made with Red Star Vegetarian Support Formula nutritional yeast flakes, and 12 grams of protein. Some children prefer this dish without the onion or tomatoes, and some like it with vegan wieners (see variations).

Mac UNCHEESE

MAKES FOUR TO FIVE 1-CUP (250-ML) SERVINGS

1½ cups (375 ml) **elbow macaroni** (12 ounces/340 g)

1 tablespoon (15 ml) **coconut oil or extra-virgin olive oil**

½ **onion, finely chopped**

1¾ cups (435 ml) **fresh or canned diced tomatoes** (14 ounces/400 g)

1 tablespoon (15 ml) **nutritional yeast flakes**

1 cup (250 ml) **Gee Whiz Spread** (page 79) **or grated vegan cheese**

salt

ground pepper

Bring a large pot of water to a boil over high heat. Add the macaroni and cook, stirring occasionally, until tender but firm. Drain well.

Heat the oil in a medium saucepan over medium heat. Add the onion and cook, stirring occasionally, until soft. Stir in the tomatoes and nutritional yeast. Add the Gee Whiz Spread, stir until combined, and cook until heated through. Add the pasta and stir until well combined. Season with salt and pepper to taste.

Gluten-Free Mac Uncheese: Replace the macaroni with rice pasta or corn pasta.

Mac Uncheese and Wieners: Add 3 to 4 chopped vegan wieners at the same time as the tomatoes and heat through.

Simple Mac Uncheese: Omit the oil, onion, tomatoes, and pepper. Stir the Gee Whiz Spread or vegan cheese into the hot pasta with the optional nutritional yeast and salt.

Mac Uncheese with Zip: Add 1 teaspoon of minced garlic plus a dash of hot sauce or a pinch of cayenne along with the onion. Season to taste.

NOTE: As this dish cools or if leftovers are refrigerated, the macaroni will continue to absorb moisture from the sauce. When the dish is reheated, add a little tomato juice, water, nondairy milk, or chopped fresh tomatoes for added moisture.

Per cup (250 ml): calories: 268, protein: 12 g, fat: 6 g, carbohydrates: 44 g (4 g from sugar), dietary fiber: 5 g, calcium: 67 mg, iron: 3 mg, magnesium: 59 mg, phosphorus: 216 mg, potassium: 552 mg, sodium: 124 mg, zinc: 217 mg, thiamin: 3.9 mg, riboflavin: 3.7 mg, niacin: 26 mg, vitamin B$_6$: 3.5 mg, folate: 216 mcg, pantothenic acid: 0.8 mg, vitamin B$_{12}$: 2.7 mcg, vitamin A: 21 mcg, vitamin C: 22 mg, vitamin E: 1 mg, omega-6 fatty acid: 1.1 g, omega-3 fatty acid: 0.1 g

Percentage of calories from: protein 17%, fat 20%, carbohydrates 63%

Note: Analysis was done using Red Star Vegetarian Support Formula nutritional yeast flakes, a source of vitamin B$_{12}$.

Cashews provide a cheesy-tasting topping for this delicious lasagne. Each serving is rich in protein; iron, zinc, and other minerals; and B vitamins. For the best flavor, use fresh lemon juice for the topping; however, high-quality frozen or bottled lemon juice will also work.

Cashew Cheese LASAGNE

MAKES 12 SERVINGS (EACH ABOUT 4 X 2 INCHES/11 X 6 CM)

12 ounces (324 g) **lasagna noodles** (12 noodles)

2 tablespoons (30 ml) **coconut oil or extra-virgin olive oil**

1 onion, diced

3 cups (750 ml) **chopped mushrooms**

2 cups (500 ml) **diced celery**

1 teaspoon (5 ml) **dried basil**

1 teaspoon (5 ml) **dried oregano**

½ teaspoon (2 ml) **salt** (optional)

¼ teaspoon (1 ml) **ground pepper**

36 ounces (1,020 g) **extra-firm silken tofu, or 2⅓ pounds** (1,043 g) **firm tofu**

1½ cups (375 ml) **raw cashew pieces**

1½ cups (375 ml) **water**

⅓ cup (85 ml) **freshly squeezed lemon juice**

⅓ cup (85 ml) **nutritional yeast flakes**

4 teaspoons (20 ml) **tamari**

2 teaspoons (10 ml) **onion powder**

1 teaspoon (5 ml) **celery seeds**

½ teaspoon (2 ml) **garlic powder**

3 cups (750 ml) **low-sodium tomato sauce**

1 large tomato, sliced

Bring a large pot of water to a boil over high heat. Add the noodles and cook, stirring occasionally, until tender but firm. Fill a large bowl with cold water. Drain the noodles in a colander, then immediately plunge the noodles into the cold water to stop the cooking. Drain the noodles again in the colander. Arrange the noodles side by side on baking sheets to prevent them from sticking together. If you stack the noodles, put plastic wrap between the layers.

Heat the oil in a large skillet over medium heat. Add the onion and cook, stirring occasionally, for 5 minutes. Stir in the mushrooms, celery, basil, oregano, optional salt, and pepper and cook for 5 minutes, or until the liquid from the mushrooms evaporates.

Put the tofu in a large bowl and mash it well with a potato masher or fork.
Add the vegetable mixture to the tofu and stir until well combined.

Put the cashews, water, lemon juice, nutritional yeast, tamari, onion powder, celery seeds, and garlic powder in a blender. Process on high speed for 1 minute, or until smooth.

Preheat the oven to 350 degrees F (180 degrees C).

To assemble the lasagne, spread 1 cup of the tomato sauce evenly over the bottom of a 13 x 9-inch (33 x 23-cm) baking dish (this will prevent the noodles from sticking to the dish). Arrange 3 noodles over the sauce. Arrange one-third of the tofu mixture over the noodles in an even layer, followed by 3 more noodles. Spoon 1 more cup of the tomato sauce over the noodles, followed by another one-third of the tofu mixture and 3 more noodles. Repeat this sequence (sauce, tofu, noodles) one more time. Pour the cashew mixture evenly over the last layer of noodles. Arrange the tomato slices on top. Bake for 30 to 40 minutes, or until the topping has set and the sides of the dish begin to bubble.

Per serving: calories: 316, protein: 17 g, fat: 13 g, carbohydrates: 37 g (5 g from sugar), dietary fiber: 4 g, calcium: 72 mg, iron: 4 mg, magnesium: 117 mg, phosphorus: 319 mg, potassium: 774 mg, sodium: 582 mg, zinc: 3 mg, thiamin: 2.3 mg, riboflavin: 2.2 mg, niacin: 17 mg, vitamin B_6: 2 mg, folate: 129 mcg, pantothenic acid: 0.9 mg, vitamin B_{12}: 1.5 mcg, vitamin A: 12 mcg, vitamin C: 11 mg, vitamin E: 1.4 mg, omega-6 fatty acid: 1.6 g, omega-3 fatty acid: 0 g

Percentage of calories from: protein 20%, fat 35%, carbohydrates 45%

Note: Analysis was done using Red Star Vegetarian Support Formula nutritional yeast flakes, a source of vitamin B_{12}. Calcium content depends on the brand of tofu used.

This dough can be used for Pesto Pizza (page 173), Tapenade Pizza (page 174), and Vegan Pepperoni Pizza (page 176). If you do not have a thermometer, water that is 100 degrees F (38 degrees C) is just slightly warm to the touch. We suggest making Pizza Dough in a glass or ceramic bowl because these materials retain warmth better than stainless steel. Soymilk is not essential but will promote the growth of the yeast.

Pizza DOUGH

MAKES 2 THIN 12-INCH (30-CM) CRUSTS (6 SERVINGS)

2 tablespoons (30 ml) **soymilk or hempseed milk** (optional)

1 tablespoon (15 ml) **extra-virgin olive oil**

1 teaspoon (5 ml) **brown sugar or other granulated sweetener**

1 cup (250 ml) **warm water** (100 degrees F; 38 degrees C)

1 package (1 tablespoon/15 ml) **active dry yeast**

2¾ cups (685 ml) **unbleached all-purpose flour, plus more for kneading**

1 teaspoon (5 ml) **salt**

Warm a large glass or ceramic bowl by running hot water over it for 2 minutes. Put the soymilk, oil, sugar, and warm water in the bowl and stir until thoroughly combined. Sprinkle the yeast over the soymilk mixture.

Fill a sink one-quarter full with warm water (about 100 degrees F/38 degrees C). Put the bowl in the warm water and leave it for 10 minutes, or until the yeast appears to have doubled in size. Remove the bowl from the water.

Slowly stir 1 cup (250 ml) of the flour into the yeast mixture, until it is the consistency of porridge, then add the salt. Gradually add the remaining 1¾ cups flour and form a ball of dough. Knead the dough on a lightly floured countertop for 5 to 10 minutes. Form it into a ball. Lightly oil the bottom of the bowl and the surface of the dough ball and return the dough ball to the bowl. Cover the dough with a clean dish towel. Replace the water in the sink with fresh warm water and put the bowl in the sink for 30 minutes while the dough rises. Use the dough to make the pizza of your choice.

Wrapped tightly in plastic wrap and put in a ziplock storage bag, Pizza Dough will keep for 4 days in the refrigerator or 6 months in the freezer.

Whole Wheat Pizza Crust: Replace the unbleached all-purpose flour with whole wheat flour and add 3 extra tablespoons (45 ml) of water.

Per serving: calories: 247, protein: 7 g, fat: 3 g, carbohydrates: 47 g (2 g from sugar), dietary fiber: 2 g, calcium: 12 mg, iron: 3 mg, magnesium: 15 mg, phosphorus: 85 mg, potassium: 97 mg, sodium: 396 mg, zinc: 0.5 mg, thiamin: 0.5 mg, riboflavin: 0.4 mg, niacin: 6 mg, vitamin B$_6$: 0.1 mg, folate: 128 mcg, pantothenic acid: 0.5 mg, vitamin B$_{12}$: 0 mcg, vitamin A: 0 mcg, vitamin C: 0 mg, vitamin E: 0 mg, omega-6 fatty acid: 0.2 g, omega-3 fatty acid: 0 g

Percentage of calories from: protein 11%, fat 11%, carbohydrates 78%

Pizza is so ingrained in American culture that the familiar aroma can be found on any city block. This version will tingle your taste buds and warm your soul. If you like, garnish the top with chopped fresh basil after baking.

Pesto PIZZA

1 recipe Pizza Dough (page 172)

unbleached all-purpose flour, for rolling

2 cups (500 ml) Pesto the Besto (page 82)

8 fresh tomatoes, cut into ¼-inch (½-cm) slices

extra-virgin olive oil (optional)

Preheat the oven to 375 degrees F (190 degrees C).

Roll out the pizza dough on a lightly floured surface into two 12-inch (30-cm) round crusts. Transfer the crusts to two 12-inch (30-cm) round pizza pans or baking pans. Spread 1 cup (250 ml) of the pesto sauce evenly over the crusts. Arrange the tomato slices evenly over the pizzas. If you like, drizzle a thin line of oil on the edges of the crusts. Bake for 10 to 12 minutes, until the edges and bottoms of the crusts are golden brown.

Pita Pesto Pizza: To make an individual pita bread pizza, preheat the oven to 375 degrees F (190 degrees C). Put one 6-inch (15-cm) pita bread on a baking sheet. Spread 2½ tablespoons (37 ml) of Pesto the Besto (page 82) on the pita bread and top with 1 sliced tomato. Bake for 6 minutes, or until the bottom starts to brown.

Per serving: calories: 616, protein: 15 g, fat: 37 g, carbohydrates: 62 g (7 g from sugar), dietary fiber: 8 g, calcium: 143 mg, iron: 6 mg, magnesium: 122 mg, phosphorus: 277 mg, potassium: 878 mg, sodium: 954 mg, zinc: 2 mg, thiamin: 0.7 mg, riboflavin: 0.5 mg, niacin: 9 mg, vitamin B_6: 0.5 mg, folate: 214 mcg, pantothenic acid: 1 mg, vitamin B_{12}: 0 mcg, vitamin A: 195 mcg, vitamin C: 34 mg, vitamin E: 3 mg, omega-6 fatty acid: 12 g, omega-3 fatty acid: 3 g

Percentage of calories from: protein 9%, fat 52%, carbohydrates 39%

Making pizza dough and sauce from scratch might seem like a daunting task, but nothing beats hot homemade pizza right out of the oven. Serve this tasty pizza for lunch or dinner or try it as an appetizer at your next gourmet dinner party.

Tapenade PIZZA

MAKES TWO 12-INCH (30-CM) PIZZAS (6 SERVINGS)

1 recipe Pizza Dough (page 172)

unbleached all-purpose flour, for rolling

1¼ cups Walnut, Olive, and Sun-Dried Tomato Tapenade (page 77)

2 onions, sliced and caramelized (see sidebar, page 175)

14 ounces (400 ml) fresh, canned, or thawed frozen artichoke hearts, sliced

½ cup (125 ml) roasted garlic, sliced (see sidebar, page 175)

extra-virgin olive oil (optional)

½ teaspoon (2 ml) fresh thyme leaves, for garnish

Preheat the oven to 375 degrees F (190 degrees C).

Roll out the pizza dough on a lightly floured surface into two 12-inch (30-cm) round crusts. Transfer the crusts to two 12-inch (30-cm) round pizza pans or baking pans. Spread half the tapenade evenly over each crust. Distribute the onions, artichokes, and garlic evenly between the pizzas. If you like, drizzle a thin line of oil on the edges of the crusts. Bake for 10 to 12 minutes, or until the edges and bottoms of the crusts are golden brown. Garnish with the thyme.

VARIATION: Replace the Pizza Dough with store-bought pizza shells and bake according to package directions.

Pita Tapenade Pizzas: Preheat the oven to 375 degrees F (190 degrees C). Put eight 6-inch (15-cm) pita breads on two baking sheets. For each pizza, use 2½ tablespoons (37 ml) of tapenade, 2 tablespoons (30 ml) of caramelized onion, 3 tablespoons (45 ml) of artichoke hearts, and 1 tablespoon (15 ml) of roasted garlic. Bake at 375 degrees F (190 degrees C) for 6 minutes, or until the bottoms start to brown.

Spinach Pizza: Replace the artichoke hearts with 2 cups (500 ml) of washed, stemmed, and steamed spinach leaves (squeeze out excess water). Arrange 1 cup of spinach over each pizza. If you like, sprinkle ½ cup (125 ml) of grated vegan cheese over each pizza. Bake as directed.

Per serving: calories: 374, protein: 11 g, fat: 9 g, carbohydrates: 65 g (6 g from sugar), dietary fiber: 7 g, calcium: 95 mg, iron: 5 mg, magnesium: 70 mg, phosphorus: 195 mg, potassium: 573 mg, sodium: 737 mg, zinc: 1.3 mg, thiamin: 0.6 mg, riboflavin: 0.5 mg, niacin: 7 mg, vitamin B_6: 0.4 mg, folate: 170 mcg, pantothenic acid: 1 mg, vitamin B_{12}: 0 mcg, vitamin A: 12 mcg, vitamin C: 16 mg, vitamin E: 0.6 mg, omega-6 fatty acid: 2.4 g, omega-3 fatty acid: 0.5 g

CARAMELIZING ONIONS. Caramelized red, yellow, or white onions deepen the flavor of soups or stews, are a flavorful topping for pizza, or are terrific alone as a sweet and nutty side dish. Sweet onions, such as the maui, vidalia, or Walla Walla varieties, will caramelize more quickly than others because they have a higher sugar content.

Cut the onions in half and then into crescent-shaped slices. Heat a small amount of coconut oil or extra-virgin olive oil in a large skillet over medium heat. Add the onions and a pinch of salt and cook, stirring occasionally, allowing the onions to brown. If the onions start to stick, add 1 or 2 tablespoons (15 to 30 ml) of water to loosen them and release the flavorful brown bits stuck to the skillet. Continue cooking until the onions are golden brown and very sweet, 10 to 15 minutes. Add 1/2 teaspoon (2 ml) of dried basil, rosemary, or thyme per onion for added flavor. For an even deeper sweet taste, add a dash of balsamic vinegar at the end of cooking.

Roasting Garlic

Roasting garlic is a simple procedure that transforms the pungent vegetable into an aromatic and sweet-tasting morsel for which garlic lovers find many uses. For example, roasted garlic can be mashed and spread over toast or stirred into mashed potatoes, chopped and cooked in soups or added as a garnish, scattered over pizzas, added to salad dressings, sprinkled over salads, or served on a vegetable platter alongside raw or grilled vegetables. Any oil that remains after roasting can be used for cooking or salad dressings.

There are many ways to roast garlic. Following are three methods. Stored in a sealed container in the refrigerator, roasted garlic will keep for 3 to 4 weeks.

ROASTING A WHOLE GARLIC HEAD IN AN OVEN

Preheat the oven to 300 degrees F (150 degrees C).

Using your fingers, remove most of the papery skin from the head of garlic while keeping the head intact. Slice off 1/4 inch (5 mm) from the top and put the head of garlic on a sheet of aluminum foil, cut-end facing up. Drizzle a small amount of extra-virgin olive oil over the top and tightly wrap in the foil. Put in an ovenproof skillet or on a baking sheet and roast in the oven for 45 to 60 minutes. The garlic is done when the skin is golden and the cloves are soft. When cool, remove the cloves from the head and squeeze out the contents into a bowl.

Alternatively, put the head of garlic in an ovenproof dish, drizzle extra-virgin olive oil over the top, cover the dish, and proceed as above.

ROASTING PEELED GARLIC CLOVES IN A SKILLET

Put peeled garlic cloves in a skillet and add enough extra-virgin olive oil to cover them. Heat the skillet over medium heat. When the oil starts to bubble around the garlic, decrease the heat to medium and cook, stirring occasionally, until golden brown, 10 to 15 minutes. (Note: Individually peeled garlic cloves are now sold by the pound or kilo in many grocery stores, which can be a time-saver.)

ROASTING PEELED GARLIC CLOVES IN AN OVEN

Preheat the oven to 300 degrees F (150 degrees C).

Put peeled garlic cloves in an ovenproof ovenproof dish with just enough extra-virgin olive oil to coat the cloves and roast, stirring occasionally, until golden brown, 20 to 30 minutes.

Children love to help make pizzas, and they readily eat vegetables, such as bell peppers, mushrooms, and tomatoes, that are used as pizza toppings. To keep the pizza from getting too chunky, thinly slice the vegetable toppings. Spooning the sauce over the pepperoni will prevent it from drying out. Extra-virgin olive oil carries a wealth of flavor and can give a crisp, delicious edge to the baked crust.

VEGAN PEPPERONI Pizza

MAKES TWO 12-INCH (30-CM) PIZZAS (6 SERVINGS)

1 recipe Pizza Dough (page 172)

unbleached all-purpose flour, for rolling

3 cups (750 ml) pizza sauce

8½ ounces (240 g) vegan pepperoni

2 cups (500 ml) thinly sliced mushrooms

1 red bell pepper, thinly sliced

1 cup (250 ml) thinly sliced black or green olives

1 cup (250 ml) thinly sliced red onion

2 to 3 cups (500 to 750 ml) grated vegan cheese

extra-virgin olive oil (optional)

Preheat the oven to 375 degrees F (190 degrees C).

Roll out the pizza dough on a lightly floured surface into two 12-inch (30-cm) round crusts. Transfer the crusts to two 12-inch (30-cm) round pizza pans or baking pans. Spread one-quarter of the sauce evenly over each crust. Distribute the vegan pepperoni slices evenly over the sauce, followed by the mushrooms, bell pepper, olives, and onions. Spoon the remaining tomato sauce evenly over the toppings. Sprinkle the vegan cheese on top. If you like, drizzle a thin line of oil on the edges of the crusts. Bake for 10 to 12 minutes, until the edges and bottoms of the crusts are golden brown.

Pineapple, Green Bell Pepper, and Vegan Ham Pizza: Instead of the pepperoni, mushrooms, red bell pepper, and olives, use pineapple chunks, green bell pepper, and vegan ham as toppings.

Individual Pita Pizzas: To make an individual vegan pepperoni pizza with a pita bread crust, preheat the oven to 375 degrees F (190 degrees C). Put one 6-inch (15-cm) pita bread on a baking sheet. Spread ¾ cup (185 ml) of the sauce over the pita bread. Top with 2 ounces (60 g) of vegan pepperoni, ½ cup (125 ml) of sliced mushrooms, ¼ cup of sliced red bell pepper, ¼ cup (60 ml) of sliced black or green olives, and ¼ cup (60 ml) of sliced red onion. Sprinkle ¼ cup (60 ml) of the vegan cheese on top. Bake at 375 degrees F (190 degrees C) for 6 minutes, or until the bottom starts to brown.

Per serving: calories: 556, protein: 23 g, fat: 16 g, carbohydrates: 78 g (10 g from sugar), dietary fiber: 11 g, calcium: 77 mg, iron: 6 mg, magnesium: 24 mg, phosphorus: 125 mg, potassium: 384 mg, sodium: 1,720 mg, zinc: 1 mg, thiamin: 0.8 mg, riboflavin: 0.5 mg, niacin: 7 mg, vitamin B_6: 0.2 mg, folate: 141 mcg, pantothenic acid: 2 mg, vitamin B_{12}: 1 mcg, vitamin A: 36 mcg, vitamin C: 42 mg, vitamin E: 1 mg, omega-6 fatty acid: 0.5 g, omega-3 fatty acid: 0 g

Percentage of calories from: protein 17%, fat 26%, carbohydrates 57%

Sauces and Gravies

This easy-to-make sauce goes beautifully on Whole Wheat Pancakes (page 71), Vegan Dazs Ice Cream (page 217), or other vegan ice creams. Arrowroot starch dissolves well in cold, not hot, liquids. Use the smaller amount if you want a sauce that can be poured or the larger amount to make a thicker sauce.

BLUEBERRY-ORANGE Sauce

MAKES TEN ¼-CUP (60-ML) SERVINGS

2 cups (500 ml) **fresh or frozen blueberries**

1 cup (250 ml) **unsweetened apple juice**

½ teaspoon (2 ml) **ground cinnamon**

¾ cup (185 ml) **frozen orange juice concentrate, thawed**

2 to 3 tablespoons (30 to 45 ml) **arrowroot starch or cornstarch**

¼ cup (60 ml) **maple syrup or other sweetener** (optional)

Put the blueberries, apple juice, and cinnamon in a medium saucepan and cook, stirring occasionally, over medium heat for about 5 minutes, until the berries soften and begin to lose their shape.

Put the orange juice concentrate and arrowroot starch in a small bowl and stir until well combined. Stir the orange juice mixture into the blueberry mixture. Bring to a boil over medium-high heat. Decrease the heat to low and simmer for 2 to 3 minutes. Serve warm or cold. Stored in a sealed container in the refrigerator, Blueberry-Orange Sauce will keep for about 3 days.

Per ¼ cup (60 ml): calories: 72, protein: 1 g, fat: 0.2 g, carbohydrates: 18 g (6 g from sugar), dietary fiber: 1 g, calcium: 13 mg, iron: 0.3 mg, magnesium: 10 mg, phosphorus: 18 mg, potassium: 206 mg, sodium: 2 mg, zinc: 0.1 mg, thiamin: 0.1 mg, riboflavin: 0 mg, niacin: 0.4 mg, vitamin B_6: 0.1 mg, folate: 37 mcg, pantothenic acid: 0.2 mg, vitamin B_{12}: 0 mcg, vitamin A: 1 mcg, vitamin C: 37 mg, vitamin E: 0.2 mg, omega-6 fatty acid: 0 g, omega-3 fatty acid: 0 g

Percentage of calories from: protein 4%, fat 2%, carbohydrates 94%

Cranberries are indigenous to North America and were used by early Native Americans for food and medicine. The bright crimson berries are very tart; if you like tangy relish, add the smaller amount of sugar. Cranberry relish is a popular side dish at winter holiday gatherings and pairs perfectly with Holiday Stuffed Winter Squash (page 142).

Cranberry-Ginger **RELISH**

MAKES TWELVE ¼-CUP (60-ML) SERVINGS

12 ounces (340 g) **fresh or frozen cranberries**

2 oranges, peeled, seeded, and chopped

⅓ to ½ cup (85 to 125 ml) **brown sugar or other granulated sweetener**

¼ cup (60 ml) **finely diced red onion**

¼ cup (60 ml) **orange juice**

1 tablespoon (15 ml) **peeled and minced fresh ginger**

1 teaspoon (5 ml) **grated orange zest**

½ teaspoon (2 ml) **ground cinnamon**

Put all the ingredients in a medium saucepan and bring to a boil over medium heat. Decrease the heat to low, cover, and simmer, stirring occasionally, for 15 to 20 minutes, or until the cranberries have popped open and have almost disintegrated. Stored in a sealed container in the refrigerator, Cranberry-Ginger Relish will keep for 7 to 10 days.

Per ¼ cup (60 ml): calories: 53, protein: 0.4 g, fat: 0.1g, carbohydrates: 14 g (10 g from sugar), dietary fiber: 2 g, calcium: 20 mg, iron: 0.3 mg, magnesium: 7 mg, phosphorus: 10 mg, potassium: 105 mg, sodium: 3 mg, zinc: 0.1 mg, thiamin: 0 mg, riboflavin: 0 mg, niacin: 0 mg, vitamin B_6: 0 mg, folate: 9 mcg, pantothenic acid: 0.2 mg, vitamin B_{12}: 0 mcg, vitamin A: 1 mcg, vitamin C: 19 mg, vitamin E: 0.4 mg, omega-6 fatty acid: 0 g, omega-3 fatty acid: 0 g

Percentage of calories from: protein 3%, fat 1%, carbohydrates 96%

Apples and plums are harvested in autumn, the perfect time to make this spicy, warm, and ruby-red chutney. Serve it with any of the dishes listed on the Indian Menu (page 54). This chutney also works well as a topping for Lem-Un-Cheesecake with Crumb Crust (page 232) or Vegan Dazs Ice Cream (page 217).

Apple-Plum CHUTNEY

MAKES NINE ¼-CUP (60-ML) SERVINGS

3 cups (750 ml) **unpeeled diced red apples**

3 cups (750 ml) **quartered prune plums**
(about 15 plums)

3 tablespoons (45 ml) **freshly squeezed lemon juice**

2 tablespoons (30 ml) **maple syrup**

1½ teaspoons (7 ml) **grated lemon zest**

2 teaspoons (10 ml) **vanilla extract**

½ teaspoon (2 ml) **cinnamon**

⅛ teaspoon (0.5 ml) **ground cloves**

Put all the ingredients in a medium saucepan and bring to a boil over medium heat. Decrease the heat to low, cover, and simmer, stirring occasionally, for 20 minutes, or until the plums have almost disintegrated. Stored in a sealed container, Apple-Plum Chutney will keep for 2 weeks in the refrigerator or 6 months in the freezer.

Per ¼ cup (60 ml): calories: 68, protein: 1 g, fat: 0.4 g, carbohydrates: 17 g (13 g from sugar), dietary fiber: 2 g, calcium: 10 mg, iron: 0.2 mg, magnesium: 7 mg, phosphorus: 11 mg, potassium: 159 mg, sodium: 1 mg, zinc: 0.3 mg, thiamin: 0 mg, riboflavin: 0.1 mg, niacin: 0.3 mg, vitamin B$_6$: 0.1 mg, folate: 3 mcg, pantothenic acid: 0.1 mg, vitamin B$_{12}$: 0 mcg, vitamin A: 1 mcg, vitamin C: 10 mg, vitamin E: 0.4 mg, omega-6 fatty acid: 0.10 g, omega-3 fatty acid: 0 g

Percentage of calories from: protein 4%, fat 5%, carbohydrates 88%, alcohol (from vanilla extract) 3%

Native to India, tamarind is a fruit that grows in a pod. This sauce, made from the fruit's pulp, adds a unique sweet and lemony sharpness to recipes. Serve it with Aloo Gobi (page 202), Potato Subji (page 205), Seasoned Potato Wedges (page 206), samosas (small stuffed vegetable turnovers served as appetizers or snacks), or any curried dish. It is also delicious in an Indonesian Roll-Up (page 145). Tamarind paste can be purchased at Indian groceries, where you can stock up on almonds, curry paste, papadums, and spices, such as cumin, curry powder, and garam masala.

TAMARIND-DATE Sauce

MAKES 1¼ CUPS (310 ML)

¾ cup (185 ml) **chopped dates**

¾ cup (185 ml) **boiling water**

3 tablespoons (45 ml) **tamarind pulp**

2 tablespoons (30 ml) **cider vinegar**

1 tablespoon (15 ml) **peeled and minced fresh ginger**

2 teaspoons (10 ml) **frozen orange juice concentrate, thawed**

½ teaspoon (2 ml) **garam masala**

pinch salt

Put the dates, water, and tamarind pulp in a small bowl and let soak for 30 minutes. Remove and discard any tamarind seeds.

Put the dates, tamarind pulp, soaking water, vinegar, ginger, orange juice concentrate, garam masala, and salt in a food processor. Process until smooth, occasionally stopping to scrape down the sides of the work bowl. Stored in a sealed container in the refrigerator, Tamarind-Date Sauce will keep for about 3 weeks.

Per 2 tablespoons (30 ml): calories: 41, protein: 0.4 g, fat: 0.1 g, carbohydrates: 11 g (9 g from sugar), dietary fiber: 1 g, calcium: 8 mg, iron: 0.2 mg, magnesium: 8 mg, phosphorus: 11 mg, potassium: 102 mg, sodium: 2 mg, zinc: 0 mg, thiamin: 0 mg, riboflavin: 0 mg, niacin: 0.2 mg, vitamin B_6: 0 mg, folate: 3 mcg, pantothenic acid: 0.1 mg, vitamin B_{12}: 0 mcg, vitamin A: 1 mcg, vitamin C: 2 mg, vitamin E: 0 mg, omega-6 fatty acid: 0 g, omega-3 fatty acid: 0 g

Percentage of calories from: protein 4%, fat 2%, carbohydrates 94%

Peanut sauce is widely used in Chinese, Indonesian, Malaysian, Thai, and Vietnamese cuisines. It can be made mild or hot by adjusting the amount of chili paste, garlic, and ginger. This delectable blend can be used as a stir-fry sauce; as a dip for Vietnamese Salad Roll (page 110); as a dressing for Thai Pasta Salad (page 115); or served over hot rice, noodles, or steamed vegetables.

Spicy Peanut SAUCE

MAKES 1¾ CUPS (435 ML)

½ cup (125 ml) **coconut milk**

½ cup (125 ml) **salt-free unsweetened peanut butter**

¼ cup (60 ml) **peeled and chopped fresh ginger**

¼ cup (60 ml) **tamari**

3 tablespoons (45 ml) **brown sugar**

3 tablespoons (45 ml) **freshly squeezed lime juice**

2 teaspoons (10 ml) **toasted sesame oil**

1 teaspoon (5 ml) **chili paste**

2 cloves garlic, chopped

Put all the ingredients in a food processor or blender and process for 1 minute, or until smooth. Stored in a sealed container in the refrigerator, Spicy Peanut Sauce will keep for 2 weeks. If it thickens after refrigeration, simply stir in a bit of warm water until the desired consistency is achieved.

Per 2 tablespoons (30 ml): calories: 98, protein: 3 g, fat:7 g, carbohydrates: 6 g (4 g from sugar), dietary fiber: 1 g, calcium: 11 mg, iron: 1 mg, magnesium: 24 mg, phosphorus: 49 mg, potassium: 127 mg, sodium: 296 mg, zinc: 0.4 mg, thiamin: 0 mg, riboflavin: 0 mg, niacin: 2 mg, vitamin B$_6$: 0.1 mg, folate: 12 mcg, pantothenic acid: 0.2 mg, vitamin B$_{12}$: 0 mcg, vitamin A: 0.2 mcg, vitamin C: 2 mg, vitamin E: 1 mg, omega-6 fatty acid: 2 g, omega-3 fatty acid: 0 g

Percentage of calories from: protein 12%, fat 64%, carbohydrates 24%

Teriyaki sauce, a staple in Japanese cuisine, adds both sweet and salty flavors and is fat-free. This recipe calls for sake, a Japanese rice wine that has a clean but distinctive taste and adds a lot of character. If you prefer not to use alcohol in this sauce, replace the sake with vegetable stock, preferably unsalted. Teriyaki Sauce can be added to stir-fries or poured over tofu and baked for 45 minutes at 350 degrees F (180 degrees C).

TERIYAKI Sauce

MAKES 2 CUPS (500 ML)

½ cup (125 ml) **mirin**

½ cup (125 ml) **sake or vegetable stock**

½ cup (125 ml) **packed brown sugar**

½ cup (125 ml) **tamari**

½ **onion, chopped**

3 tablespoons (45 ml) **unpeeled and thinly sliced ginger**

4 cloves garlic, chopped

1 tablespoon (15 ml) **arrowroot starch or cornstarch**

1 tablespoon (15 ml) **cold water**

Put the mirin, sake, sugar, tamari, onion, ginger, and garlic in a saucepan and bring to a boil over high heat. Decrease the heat to medium-low and cook, stirring occasionally, for 10 minutes.

Put the arrowroot starch and water in a small bowl and stir until well combined. Stir the arrowroot starch mixture into the mirin mixture and cook and stir for 3 minutes. Strain the sauce. Stored in a sealed container in the refrigerator, Teriyaki Sauce will keep for about 3 weeks.

Per 2 tablespoons (30 ml): calories: 64, protein: 1 g, fat: 0 g, carbohydrates: 11 g (10 g from sugar), dietary fiber: 0 g, calcium: 11 mg, iron: 0 mg, magnesium: 6 mg, phosphorus: 13 mg, potassium: 52 mg, sodium: 353 mg, zinc: 0 mg, thiamin: 0 mg, riboflavin: 0 mg, niacin: 0.3 mg, vitamin B_6: 0 mg, folate: 2 mcg, pantothenic acid: 0 mg, vitamin B_{12}: 0 mcg, vitamin A: 0 mcg, vitamin C: 0 mg, vitamin E: 0 mg, omega-6 fatty acid: 0 g, omega-3 fatty acid: 0 g

Percentage of calories from: protein 5%, fat 0%, carbohydrates 70%, alcohol 25%*

* The alcohol content reflects the amount alcohol before cooking. However, most of the alcohol in the sake is burned off during cooking, leaving behind only its taste and aroma.

Here's a marinade that will make tofu seriously tasty. It can also be used to marinate tempeh, thickened and used as a sauce for stir-fries or to baste vegetables on a barbecue, served as a light salad dressing, or simply heated and poured over brown rice.

TOFU Marinade

MAKES ABOUT 2 CUPS (470 ML)

½ cup (125 ml) **tamari**

½ cup (125 ml) **fresh or canned tomatoes**

½ cup (125 ml) **water**

¼ cup (60 ml) **rice vinegar or cider vinegar**

2 tablespoons (30 ml) **toasted sesame oil**

1 tablespoon (15 ml) **peeled and minced fresh ginger**

1 clove garlic

½ teaspoon (5 ml) **ground turmeric**

Put all the ingredients in a blender and process for 15 seconds, or until smooth. Stored in a sealed container in the refrigerator, Tofu Marinade will keep for 2 to 3 weeks.

Per tablespoon (15 ml): calories: 12, protein: 0.6 g, fat: 1 g, carbohydrates: 0.5 g (0 g from sugar), dietary fiber: 0 g, calcium: 2 mg, iron: 0.1 mg, magnesium: 3 mg, phosphorus: 8 mg, potassium: 20 mg, sodium: 284 mg, zinc: 0 mg, thiamin: 0 mg, riboflavin: 0 mg, niacin: 0.4 mg, vitamin B_6: 0 mg, folate: 1 mcg, pantothenic acid: 0 mg, vitamin B_{12}: 0 mcg, vitamin A: 3 mcg, vitamin C: 0 mg, vitamin E: 0 mg, omega-6 fatty acid: 0 g, omega-3 fatty acid: 0 g

Percentage of calories from: protein 18%, fat 67%, carbohydrates 15%

There are over four thousand varieties of tomatoes, which are easy to grow, delicious, and packed with vitamin C, iron, and potassium but very few calories. This easy and versatile tomato sauce can be used in Cashew Cheese Lasagne (page 170), Easy Tofu Entrées (page 162), and Tuscan Minestrone (page 104), or as a base for many other Italian dishes.

Marinara SAUCE

MAKES THREE TO FOUR 1-CUP (250-ML) SERVINGS

½ to 1 tablespoon (7 to 15 ml) **extra-virgin olive oil**

½ **onion, diced**

3⅓ cups (796 ml) **chopped canned tomatoes,** or 4 cups (1 L) **chopped fresh tomatoes**

1 tablespoon (15 ml) **dried basil**

4 cloves garlic, chopped

1 teaspoon (5 ml) **dried oregano**

½ teaspoon (2 ml) **crushed red pepper flakes** (optional)

salt

ground pepper

Heat the oil in a medium saucepan over medium heat. Add the onion and cook, stirring occasionally, for 3 to 5 minutes, or until soft. Stir in the tomatoes, basil, garlic, oregano, optional crushed red pepper flakes, and salt and pepper to taste. Cover and cook over medium-low heat, stirring occasionally, for 15 to 20 minutes. Stored in a sealed container in the refrigerator, Marinara Sauce will keep for 1 week.

Per cup (250 ml): calories: 80, protein: 3 g, fat: 2 g, carbohydrates: 14 g (7 g from sugar), dietary fiber: 3 g, calcium: 108 mg, iron: 2 mg, magnesium: 37 mg, phosphorus: 60 mg, potassium: 608 mg, sodium: 360 mg, zinc: 0.5 mg, thiamin: 0.1 mg, riboflavin: 0.1 mg, niacin: 2 mg, vitamin B$_6$: 0.3 mg, folate: 27 mcg, pantothenic acid: 0.4 mg, vitamin B$_{12}$: 0 mcg, vitamin A: 84 mcg, vitamin C: 38 mg, vitamin E: 1 mg, omega-6 fatty acid: 0.3 g, omega-3 fatty acid: 0.1 g

Percentage of calories from: protein 12%, fat 24%, carbohydrates 64%

This gravy is ideal over Holiday Stuffed Winter Squash (page 142), baked or mashed potatoes, or vegan burgers. If you use vegetable stock cubes or powder, experiment with different brands, because the flavor of the stock will make all the difference. Stocks vary in saltiness, so adjust the amount of tamari or salt accordingly.

LIGHT MUSHROOM Gravy

MAKES SIXTEEN ¼-CUP (60-ML) SERVINGS

1 tablespoon (15 ml) **coconut oil or extra-virgin olive oil**

2 cups (500 ml) **thinly sliced mushrooms**

½ cup (125 ml) **finely diced onion**

2 cloves garlic, minced

4 cups (1 L) **vegetable stock** (for homemade, see page 92) **or water**

½ cup (125 ml) **unbleached all-purpose flour or whole wheat flour**

2 tablespoons (30 ml) **tamari** (optional)

1 tablespoon (15 ml) **nutritional yeast flakes**

¼ teaspoon (1 ml) **dried sage**

¼ teaspoon (1 ml) **dried thyme**

2 tablespoons (30 ml) **chopped fresh parsley**

pinch ground pepper

salt (optional)

Heat the oil in a saucepan over medium heat. Add the mushrooms and onion and cook, stirring occasionally, for 5 minutes, or until the mushrooms have lost nearly all of their moisture. Add the garlic and cook, stirring occasionally, for 1 to 2 minutes.

Put 1 cup (250 ml) of the stock, the flour, optional tamari, nutritional yeast, sage, and thyme in a jar, seal with a lid, and shake until blended. Stir the flour mixture and the remaining 3 cups (750 ml) of the stock into the mushroom mixture. Bring to a boil over medium-high heat. Decrease the heat to low, cover, and simmer, stirring frequently, for 15 to 20 minutes. Stir in the parsley and pepper and season with salt to taste. If the gravy is too thick, add a little more stock. If it is too thin, simmer uncovered to let moisture evaporate until the desired consistency is achieved.

Per ¼ cup (60 ml): calories: 32, protein: 1 g, fat: 1 g, carbohydrates: 5g (0.5 g from sugar), dietary fiber: 0.5 g, calcium: 6 mg, iron: 0.4 mg, magnesium: 3 mg, phosphorus: 20 mg, potassium: 62 mg, sodium: 73 mg, zinc: 0.2 mg, thiamin: 0.3 mg, riboflavin: 0.3 mg, niacin: 2 mg, vitamin B_6: 0.3 mg, folate: 16 mcg, pantothenic acid: 0.1 mg, vitamin B_{12}: 0.2 mcg, vitamin A: 11 mcg, vitamin C: 1 mg, vitamin E: 0 mg, omega-6 fatty acid: 0 g, omega-3 fatty acid: 0 g

Percentage of calories from: protein 13%, fat 31%, carbohydrates 56%

Note: Analysis was done using Red Star Vegetarian Support Formula nutritional yeast flakes, a source of vitamin B_{12}.

Miso is a thick, sweet, and salty paste made from fermented soybeans that adds a tangy taste to dips, gravies, sauces, and soups. If you can't find it in the refrigerated section of your super-market, look for it in Asian markets or natural food stores. Miso contains live microorganisms that may be beneficial to our digestion and health. It is typically added after cooking to preserve enzyme activity. This gravy works great as a complement to Seasoned Potato Wedges (page 206), as a dipping sauce, or served over cooked brown rice.

Miso **GRAVY**

MAKES ELEVEN ¼-CUP (60-ML) SERVINGS

2 cups (500 ml) **vegetable stock**
(for homemade, see page 92)

1 tablespoon (15 ml) **maple syrup or other sweetener**

1 tablespoon (15 ml) **toasted sesame oil**

1 tablespoon (15 ml) **cider vinegar**

½ teaspoon (2 ml) **chili paste, or**
¼ teaspoon (1 ml) **cayenne**

2 cloves garlic, crushed

pinch turmeric

¼ cup (60 ml) **unbleached all-purpose flour**

½ cup (125 ml) **water**

¼ cup (60 ml) **miso**

Put the stock, maple syrup, oil, vinegar, chili paste, garlic, and turmeric in a medium saucepan over medium-high heat and simmer for 2 minutes, stirring occasionally.

Put the flour and water in a small bowl and stir until well blended. Add the flour mixture to the stock mixture and stir with a whisk or fork until well combined. Bring to a boil. Decrease the heat to low, cover, and simmer, stirring occasionally, for 5 minutes.

Remove from the heat and whisk in the miso until well incorporated. Strain and serve.

Per ¼ cup (60 ml): calories: 42, protein: 1 g, fat: 2 g, carbohydrates: 6 g (2 g from sugar), dietary fiber: 0.5 g, calcium: 8 mg, iron: 0.4 mg, magnesium: 4 mg, phosphorus: 15 mg, potassium: 30 mg, sodium: 290 mg, zinc: 0.3 mg, thiamin: 0 mg, riboflavin: 0 mg, niacin: 0 mg, vitamin B_6: 0 mg, folate: 6 mcg, pantothenic acid: 0 mg, vitamin B_{12}: 0 mcg, vitamin A: 1 mcg, vitamin C: 0 mg, vitamin E: 0 mg, omega-6 fatty acid: 0.2 g, omega-3 fatty acid: 0 g

Percentage of calories from: protein 11%, fat 38%, carbohydrates 51%

Can vegan gravy taste outstanding? Yes! Rosemary, sage, and thyme make this aromatic gravy a welcome feature at festive holiday meals. This gravy builds on a roux, a classic mixture of flour and oil, to thicken the vegetable stock.

Rosemary GRAVY

MAKES FOURTEEN ¼-CUP (60-ML) SERVINGS

¼ **cup** (60 ml) **coconut oil or extra-virgin olive oil**

¼ **cup** (60 ml) **diced carrot**

¼ **cup** (60 ml) **diced celery**

¼ **cup** (60 ml) **diced onion**

2 cloves garlic, chopped

½ **cup** (125 ml) **unbleached all-purpose flour or whole wheat flour**

3 cups (750 ml) **vegetable stock** (for homemade, see page 92)

2 to 3 tablespoons (30 to 45 ml) **tamari**

2 tablespoons (30 ml) **chopped fresh parsley**

2 teaspoons (10 ml) **dried rosemary**

1 teaspoon (5 ml) **dried thyme**

½ **teaspoon** (2ml) **dried sage**

¼ **teaspoon** (1 ml) **ground pepper**

salt

Heat the oil in a medium saucepan over medium heat. Add the carrot, celery, onion, and garlic and cook, stirring occasionally, for 5 minutes, or until the onion is soft.

To make the roux, stir the flour into the vegetable mixture and cook over medium heat for 3 minutes, stirring frequently to prevent the flour from burning. Gradually stir in the stock until it is well incorporated. Stir in the tamari, parsley, rosemary, thyme, sage, pepper, and salt to taste. Bring to a boil over high heat, decrease the heat to low and simmer, stirring occasionally, for 10 to 15 minutes. If the gravy is too thick, add a little more stock. If it is too thin, simmer uncovered to let moisture evaporate until the desired consistency is achieved. Strain and serve.

Per ¼ cup (60 ml): calories: 59, protein: 1 g, fat: 4 g, carbohydrates: 5 g (0 g from sugar), dietary fiber: 0 g, calcium: 10 mg, iron: 0.5 mg, magnesium: 4 mg, phosphorus: 12 mg, potassium: 41 mg, sodium: 211 mg, zinc: 0.1 mg, thiamin: 0 mg, riboflavin: 0 mg, niacin: 0.6 mg, vitamin B$_6$: 0 mg, folate: 11 mcg, pantothenic acid: 0 mg, vitamin B$_{12}$: 0 mcg, vitamin A: 22 mcg, vitamin C: 1 mg, vitamin E: 0 mg, omega-6 fatty acid: 0.1 g, omega-3 fatty acid: 0 g

Percentage of calories from: protein 6%, fat 61%, carbohydrates 33%

Side Dishes

Greens have an outstanding nutritional profile—just look at the protein, calcium, iron, and vitamin A content listed in the analysis. Make this robustly flavored dish using a single leafy green, such as calcium-rich kale, or a combination of greens. Spinach or Swiss chard produce a sweeter dish, but their calcium content is far less easily absorbed by the body. Wash the greens well and remove and discard tough stems and stalks. Note that mature kale leaves may take a little longer to cook than younger greens.

SAUTÉED Garden Greens

MAKES ABOUT THREE 1-CUP (250-ML) SERVINGS

1 tablespoon (15 ml) **coconut oil or extra-virgin olive oil**

½ **yellow onion, diced**

2 cloves **garlic, minced**

12 cups (3 L) **fresh greens** (kale; spinach; Swiss chard; or beet, collard, dandelion, or mustard greens), **stemmed and cut or torn into bite-sized pieces**

2 teaspoons (10 ml) **ground cumin**

1 teaspoon (5 ml) **paprika**

½ teaspoon (2 ml) **dried thyme**

¼ teaspoon (1 ml) **salt**

1 tablespoon (15 ml) **freshly squeezed lemon juice**

Heat the oil in a large pot over medium heat. Add the onion and cook for 2 to 3 minutes, until soft. Stir in the garlic. Add the greens, cumin, paprika, thyme, and salt, stirring well to coat the greens with the seasonings. Cover and cook for 2 to 5 minutes (depending on how tough the greens are), or until the greens are warmed through, wilted, and tender. Remove from the heat and stir in the lemon juice. Serve warm or at room temperature.

Per cup (250 ml): calories: 192, protein: 9 g, fat: 7 g, carbohydrates: 31 g (1 g from sugar), dietary fiber: 6 g, calcium: 387 mg, iron: 6 mg, magnesium: 99 mg, phosphorus: 166 mg, potassium: 1266 mg, sodium: 276 mg, zinc: 1 mg, thiamin: 0.3 mg, riboflavin: 0.4 mg, niacin: 5 mg, vitamin B_6: 1 mg, folate: 83 mcg, pantothenic acid: 0.3 mg, vitamin B_{12}: 0 mcg, vitamin A: 2,062 mcg, vitamin C: 326 mg, vitamin E: 3 mg, omega-6 fatty acid: 0.8 g, omega-3 fatty acid: 0.5 g

Percentage of calories from: protein 17%, fat 28%, carbohydrates 55%

Note: Analysis was done using kale.

First the bad news: after this meal, you will have a lot of dishes, including a blender, steamer, and skillet, to wash. Now the good news: when you serve this exquisitely seasoned vegan version of the Indian dish *palak paneer*, people's eyes will light up. In the Hindi language, garam masala means "warm mixture." The name arose because this spice mix, which is typically composed of black pepper, cardamom, cinnamon, cloves, mace, and nutmeg, has a warming effect. Steaming the greens allows you to retain the maximum amount of nutrients.

SPINACH WITH Tofu and Garam Masala

MAKES THREE ½-CUP (125-ML) SERVINGS

10 cups (2.5L) **fresh spinach**
(10 ounces/284 g)

1 tablespoon (15 ml) **coconut oil or extra-virgin olive oil**

1 small onion, diced

1 teaspoon (5 ml) **garam masala**

½ teaspoon (2 ml) **ground coriander**

¼ teaspoon (1 ml) **garlic powder**

¼ teaspoon (1 ml) **salt**

½ teaspoon (2 ml) **freshly squeezed lemon juice**

¼ cup (60 ml) **diced firm tofu**

Steam the spinach over medium-high heat for about 3 minutes, or just until tender.

Heat the oil in a large skillet over medium heat. Add the onion and cook, stirring occasionally, for 3 to 5 minutes, or until soft. Add the garam masala, coriander, garlic powder, and salt and cook for 2 to 3 minutes, stirring frequently to prevent the spices from sticking to the pan.

Transfer the steamed spinach and the onion mixture to a blender or food processor. Add the lemon juice and process until smooth. Transfer the spinach mixture back to the skillet. Stir in the tofu and cook over medium heat until the tofu is heated through. Serve hot.

VARIATIONS

- Make this dish without the tofu.
- Replace the spinach with stemmed and chopped collard greens and add 3 tablespoons (45 ml) of the cooking liquid from the steamer when processing the greens. The calcium in collard greens is more readily absorbed than the calcium in spinach.

Per ½ cup (125 ml): calories: 90, protein: 5 g, fat: 6 g, carbohydrates: 7 g (2 g from sugar), dietary fiber: 3 g, calcium: 150 mg, iron: 3 mg, magnesium: 91 mg, phosphorus: 84 mg, potassium: 636 mg, sodium: 240 mg, zinc: 1 mg, thiamin: 0.1 mg, riboflavin: 0.2 mg, niacin: 2 mg, vitamin B_6: 0.3 mg, folate: 204 mcg, pantothenic acid: 0.2 mg, vitamin B_{12}: 0 mcg, vitamin A: 469 mcg, vitamin C: 30 mg, vitamin E: 2 mg, omega-6 fatty acid: 0.5 g, omega-3 fatty acid: 0.2 g

Percentage of calories from: protein 20%, fat 53%, carbohydrates 27%

Note: Much of the calcium and iron in spinach is bound by oxalates and unavailable for absorption.

With about 200 milligrams of highly available calcium per cup, this nutritionally well-balanced recipe is one you'll turn to again and again. The vitamin C in the tomatoes helps the body absorb the abundant amount of iron in the kale. There is also plenty of potassium, folate, and antioxidant vitamins (A, C, and E). Best of all, the combination tastes very good indeed.

Stewed Tomatoes WITH KALE AND GARLIC

MAKES FOUR TO FIVE 1-CUP (250-ML) SERVINGS

1 tablespoon (15 ml) **coconut oil or extra-virgin olive oil**

1 **onion, cubed**

4 cups (1 L) **chopped fresh or canned tomatoes**

4 cloves **garlic, chopped**

1 teaspoon (5 ml) **dried basil**

1 teaspoon (5 ml) **dried thyme**

½ **teaspoon** (2 ml) **salt**

¼ **teaspoon** (1 ml) **ground pepper**

8 cups (2 L) **stemmed and sliced kale**

Heat the oil in a large pot over medium heat. Add the onion and cook, stirring occasionally, for 3 minutes, or until soft. Stir in the tomatoes, garlic, basil, thyme, salt, and pepper. Cover and cook for 3 to 5 minutes, or until the tomatoes have a chunky, saucelike texture. Stir in the kale. Cover and cook for 3 to 5 minutes, or until the kale is tender.

Per cup (250 ml): calories: 136, protein: 6 g, fat: 4 g, carbohydrates: 23 g (6 g from sugar), dietary fiber: 5 g, calcium: 210 mg, iron: 3 mg, magnesium: 67 mg, phosphorus: 124 mg, potassium: 1,024 mg, sodium: 274 mg, zinc: 1 mg, thiamin: 0.2 mg, riboflavin: 0.2 mg, niacin: 3 mg, vitamin B_6: 0.6 mg, folate: 68 mcg, pantothenic acid: 0.3 mg, vitamin B_{12}: 0 mcg, vitamin A: 1,041 mcg, vitamin C: 175 mg, vitamin E: 2 mg, omega-6 fatty acid: 0.6g, omega-3 fatty acid: 0.3 g

Percentage of calories from: protein 16%, fat 25%, carbohydrates 59%

The combination of carrots, Dijon mustard, and tarragon is classic. This simple recipe is delicious and provides an easy way to get vitamin A, calcium, iron, and potassium. Dijon mustard contains plenty of salt, so no additional salt is needed.

CARROTS with Dijon Mustard and Tarragon

MAKES TWO 1-CUP (250-ML) SERVINGS

3 cups (750 ml) **scrubbed and sliced carrots**

2 tablespoons (30 ml) **Dijon mustard**

1 tablespoon (15 ml) **freshly squeezed lemon juice**

1 teaspoon (5 ml) **dried tarragon, crushed**

Steam the carrots over medium-high heat for 5 to 7 minutes, or until tender yet firm. Put the mustard, lemon juice, and tarragon in a large bowl and stir until combined. Add the carrots to the mustard mixture and toss until well coated. Serve immediately.

Per cup (250 ml): calories: 89, protein: 3 g, fat: 2 g, carbohydrates: 17 g (8 g from sugar), dietary fiber: 5 g, calcium: 81 mg, iron: 1 mg, magnesium: 22 mg, phosphorus: 57 mg, potassium: 528 mg, sodium: 440 mg, zinc: 0.4 mg, thiamin: 0.1 mg, riboflavin: 0.1 mg, niacin: 2 mg, vitamin B_6: 0.2 mg, folate: 33 mcg, pantothenic acid: 0.4 mg, vitamin B_{12}: 0 mcg, vitamin A: 1,298 mcg, vitamin C: 13 mg, vitamin E: 1 mg, omega-6 fatty acid: 0.2 g, omega-3 fatty acid: 0 g

Percentage of calories from: protein 11%, fat 16%, carbohydrates 73%

What a pleasure it is when fresh corn season arrives. To remove corn kernels from the ear, slice off the stem and place the ear of corn, stem-end down, on a damp cloth to avoid slipping. Hold a knife at the top of the ear and slice from top to bottom. Slightly rotate the ear and repeat until all the kernels are removed. One large ear will produce about one cup (250 ml) of corn.

CORN WITH RED BELL PEPPERS and Pesto

MAKES THREE 1-CUP (250-ML) SERVINGS

1½ teaspoons (7 ml) **coconut oil or extra-virgin olive oil**

½ **red onion, cubed**

3 cups (750 ml) **fresh, frozen, or canned corn kernels, rinsed if canned**

¼ cup (125 ml) **diced red bell pepper**

2 cloves **garlic, minced**

¼ cup (60 ml) **Pesto the Besto** (page 82) **or other pesto**

1 tablespoon (15 ml) **freshly squeezed lime juice**

Heat the oil in a large skillet over medium heat. Add the onion and cook, stirring occasionally, for 3 to 5 minutes, or until soft. Stir in the corn, bell pepper, and garlic. Cover and cook for 3 minutes, or until the corn is hot. Put the pesto and lime juice in a small bowl and stir until combined. Remove the corn from the heat and stir in the pesto mixture. Serve immediately.

Per cup (250 ml): calories: 262, protein: 8 g, fat: 12 g, carbohydrates: 37 g (8 g from sugar), dietary fiber: 6 g, calcium: 40 mg, iron: 2 mg, magnesium: 88 mg, phosphorus: 197 mg, potassium: 632 mg, sodium: 163 mg, zinc: 1 mg, thiamin: 0.4 mg, riboflavin: 0.2 mg, niacin: 4 mg, vitamin B$_6$: 0.3 mg, folate: 99 mcg, pantothenic acid: 1.4 mg, vitamin B$_{12}$: 0 mcg, vitamin A: 89 mcg, vitamin C: 68 mg, vitamin E: 1 mg, omega-6 fatty acid: 4 g, omega-3 fatty acid: 0.7 g

Percentage of calories from: protein 11%, fat 38%, carbohydrates 51%

Parsnips are similar to potatoes in nutritional value but have more fiber and natural sugar. On the other hand, potatoes contain a little more protein. This recipe is a fabulous autumn and winter side dish and goes very well alongside Holiday Stuffed Winter Squash (page 142).

MASHED Parsnips and Apple WITH TOASTED WALNUTS

MAKES THREE 1-CUP (250-ML) SERVINGS

4 cups (1 L) **peeled and chopped parsnips**

1 red apple, peeled, cored, and cubed

2 tablespoons (30 ml) **hempseed oil or extra-virgin olive oil**

½ teaspoon (2 ml) **grated lemon zest**

½ teaspoon (2 ml) **ground nutmeg**

½ teaspoon (2 ml) **salt**

¼ teaspoon (1 ml) **ground white pepper**

½ cup (125 ml) **toasted walnuts, chopped** (see sidebar, page 100)

¼ cup (60 ml) **chopped fresh parsley**

Steam the parsnips and apple over medium-high heat for 5 minutes, or until the parsnips are tender when pierced with a knife. Retain ⅓ cup (85 ml) of the cooking liquid from the steamer. Transfer the parsnips and apple to a food processor. Add the oil, zest, nutmeg, salt, and pepper. Gradually add enough cooking liquid while processing until smooth. Transfer to a serving bowl. Stir in the walnuts and parsley until evenly distributed.

Per cup (250 ml): calories: 367, protein: 6 g, fat: 23 g, carbohydrates: 43 g (14 g from sugar), dietary fiber: 9 g, calcium: 99 mg, iron: 2 mg, magnesium: 92 mg, phosphorus: 213 mg, potassium: 863 mg, sodium: 337 mg, zinc: 2 mg, thiamin: 0.2 mg, riboflavin: 0.1 mg, niacin: 2 mg, vitamin B$_6$: 0.3 mg, folate: 153 mcg, pantothenic acid: 1 mg, vitamin B$_{12}$: 0 mcg, vitamin A: 23 mcg, vitamin C: 41 mg, vitamin E: 0.2 mg, omega-6 fatty acid: 13 g, omega-3 fatty acid: 4 g

Percentage of calories from: protein 6%, fat 52%, carbohydrates 42%

Vegetables in the cabbage, or *Brassica*, family provide valuable phytochemicals that help protect against cancer. The oils in walnuts are rich in essential omega-3 fatty acid. These health-supportive ingredients are enhanced by the sweet, smooth taste of balsamic vinegar, which is aged in wooden casks for up to ten years.

Red Cabbage WITH WALNUTS

MAKES THREE TO FOUR 1-CUP (250-ML) SERVINGS

1 tablespoon (15 ml) **coconut oil or extra-virgin olive oil**

4 cups (1 L) **thinly sliced red cabbage** (about ¼ head)

½ cup (125 ml) **chopped walnuts**

2 tablespoons (30 ml) **balsamic vinegar**

1 to 2 teaspoons (5 to 10 ml) **extra-virgin olive oil**

1 to 2 teaspoons (5 to 10 ml) **tamari**

Heat the coconut oil in a large pan over medium heat. Add the cabbage and cook, stirring occasionally, for 5 to 8 minutes, or until wilted. Remove from the heat and stir in the walnuts, vinegar, olive oil, and tamari. Serve warm, or let cool and serve as a salad.

Per cup (250 ml): calories: 173, protein: 4 g, fat: 15 g, carbohydrates: 8 g (4 g from sugar), dietary fiber: 3 g, calcium: 51 mg, iron: 1 mg, magnesium: 37 mg, phosphorus: 78 mg, potassium: 265 mg, sodium: 119 mg, zinc: 1 mg, thiamin: 0.1 mg, riboflavin: 0.1 mg, niacin: 0.6 mg, vitamin B_6: 0.2 mg, folate: 30 mcg, pantothenic acid: 0.2 mg, vitamin B_{12}: 0 mcg, vitamin A: 45 mcg, vitamin C: 46 mg, vitamin E: 1 mg, omega-6 fatty acid: 6 g, omega-3 fatty acid: 1.5 g

Percentage of calories from: protein 8%, fat 75%, carbohydrates 17%

Maintaining Vibrant Color in Green and Red Vegetables

Green vegetables, such as bok choy, broccoli, and green beans, contain the pigment chlorophyll, which turns an even brighter and more vivid green when heat is first applied. During cooking, green vegetables release acids. If these acids are not allowed to escape, particularly when greens are cooked in a pot with a lid, such as a steamer, the unstable chlorophyll molecule turns grayish yellow. To avoid discoloration, leave the pot lid slightly askew to release the acids, and immediately plunge the cooked greens into cold water to stop the cooking and to preserve, or stabilize, the chlorophyll pigment.

Green pigments also become dull when acids, such as lemon juice or vinegar, are added. To avoid discoloration, add acidic dressings to greens immediately before serving.

In contrast, red vegetables and fruit, such as red cabbage, red radishes, and grapes, not only retain their appealing color in the presence of acids but become even brighter. These foods contain a red pigment (anthocyanin) and a blue pigment (betacyanin), both of which are stabilized in the presence of citrus juice, wine, vinegar, and other acids.

The autumn harvest of root vegetables provides a great deal of nourishment and warmth. Vary the recipe by including other chopped root vegetables, such as parsnips, sweet potatoes, turnips, or winter squash. Just be sure to use a total of eight to nine cups (2 to 2.25 L) of vegetables. Those with deep yellow and orange hues are particularly rich in vitamin A.

ROASTED Root Vegetables

MAKES ABOUT EIGHT 1-CUP (250-ML) SERVINGS

2 carrots, cut into 1-inch (2.5-cm) pieces

2 gold or red-skinned potatoes, scrubbed and cut into 1-inch (2.5-cm) pieces

2 yams, scrubbed and cut into 1-inch (2.5-cm) pieces

1 large red, yellow, or white onion, cut into 1-inch (2.5-cm) pieces

2 tablespoons (30 ml) extra-virgin olive oil

1 tablespoon (15 ml) chopped fresh herbs (such as basil, thyme, oregano, or dill)

¼ teaspoon (1 ml) salt

pinch ground pepper

Heat the oven to 375 degrees F (190 degrees C).

Put the carrots, potatoes, yams, and onion in large bowl. Sprinkle with the oil, herbs, salt, and pepper and toss until the vegetables are well coated. Transfer to a 13 x 9-inch (33 x 23-cm) baking dish. Bake uncovered for 35 to 40 minutes, or until the vegetables are tender yet firm.

Per cup (250 ml): calories: 162, protein: 2 g, fat: 4 g, carbohydrates: 31 g (1 g from sugar), dietary fiber: 4 g, calcium: 24 mg, iron: 1 mg, magnesium: 29 mg, phosphorus: 71 mg, potassium: 885 mg, sodium: 79 mg, zinc: 0.4 mg, thiamin: 0.1 mg, riboflavin: 0.1 mg, niacin: 2 mg, vitamin B_6: 0.4 mg, folate: 28 mcg, pantothenic acid: 0.5 mg, vitamin B_{12}: 0 mcg, vitamin A: 129 mcg, vitamin C: 24 mg, vitamin E: 0.2 mg, omega-6 fatty acid: 0.1 g, omega-3 fatty acid: 0 g

Percentage of calories from: protein 6%, fat 20%, carbohydrates 74%

Yams are good sources of antioxidants, including vitamins C and E and the orange carotenoids that our bodies convert to vitamin A. This recipe cooks well in a glass baking dish. Alternatively, use a metal baking sheet and turn the yams over halfway through the cooking time.

Baked Yams WITH LEMON AND GREEN CHILES

MAKES SEVEN 1-CUP (250-ML) SERVINGS

2.5 pounds (1 kg) **peeled yams, cut into ¼-inch** (5-mm) **slices** (about 4 yams)

1 tablespoon (15 ml) **coconut oil or extra-virgin olive oil**

1 teaspoon (5 ml) **crushed coriander seeds,** or **½ teaspoon** (2 ml) **ground coriander**

¼ teaspoon (1 ml) **salt**

2 tablespoons (30 ml) **freshly squeezed lemon juice**

2 serrano chiles, seeded and minced

1 teaspoon (5 ml) **grated lemon zest**

Preheat the oven to 350 degrees F (180 degrees C).

Put the yams, oil, coriander seeds, and salt in a medium bowl and toss until the yams are coated. Transfer to a 13 x 9-inch (33 x 23-cm) glass baking dish and bake for 25 minutes, or until the yams are tender when pierced with a knife. Check the yams frequently near the end of the baking time to avoid burning. Return the yams to the bowl and add the lemon juice, chiles, and zest. Toss gently until well combined.

Per cup (250 ml): calories: 186, protein: 2 g, fat: 2 g, carbohydrates: 40 g (1 g from sugar), dietary fiber: 6 g, calcium: 25 mg, iron: 1 mg, magnesium: 30 mg, phosphorus: 78 mg, potassium: 1,162 mg, sodium: 80 mg, zinc: 0.4 mg, thiamin: 0.2 mg, riboflavin: 0 mg, niacin: 1 mg, vitamin B_6: 0.4 mg, folate: 33 mcg, pantothenic acid: 0.4 mg, vitamin B_{12}: 0 mcg, vitamin A: 10 mcg, vitamin C: 30 mg, vitamin E: 1 mg, omega-6 fatty acid: 0.3 g, omega-3 fatty acid: 0.3 g

Percentage of calories from: protein 5%, fat 11%, carbohydrates 84%

A portobello mushroom is a mature brown cremini mushroom that is four to six inches (10 to 15 cm) in diameter. In France, they are known as *champignons de Paris* (mushrooms of Paris), and in Italy, they are known as *capellone* (big hat). These large mushrooms can be sautéed, as in this recipe or Simple Sautéed Portobello Mushrooms (page 200), or they can be stuffed, as in Portobello Mushroom Burgers with Chickpea Topping (page 148).

Portobello Mushrooms WITH MARJORAM & BALSAMIC VINEGAR

MAKES THREE 1-CUP (250-ML) SERVINGS

1 to 2 tablespoons (15 to 30 ml) **vegan buttery spread, coconut oil, or extra-virgin olive oil**

3 large portobello mushrooms, stemmed and cut into ¼-inch (5-mm) **slices** (about 6 cups/1.5 L)

1 teaspoon (5 ml) **dried marjoram**

2 cloves garlic, minced

1 tablespoon (15 ml) **tamari**

1 tablespoon (15 ml) **balsamic vinegar**

Heat the vegan buttery spread in a large skillet over medium heat. Add the mushrooms and marjoram, cover, and cook for 4 to 5 minutes. Add the garlic and cook for 1 minute, stirring occasionally. Remove from the heat and stir in the tamari and vinegar.

Per cup (250 ml): calories: 66, protein: 3 g, fat: 4 g, carbohydrates: 6 g (2 g from sugar), dietary fiber: 2 g, calcium: 16 mg, iron: 1 mg, magnesium: 13 mg, phosphorus: 122 mg, potassium: 435 mg, sodium: 347 mg, zinc: 1 mg, thiamin: 0.1 mg, riboflavin: 0.4 mg, niacin: 4 mg, vitamin B$_6$: 0.1 mg, folate: 20 mcg, pantothenic acid: 1 mg, vitamin B$_{12}$: 0 mcg, vitamin A: 1 mcg, vitamin C: 1 mg, vitamin E: 0 mg, omega-6 fatty acid: 0.1 g, omega-3 fatty acid: 0 g

Percentage of calories from: protein 17%, fat 49%, carbohydrates 34%

These whole, sautéed mushrooms have a delicate flavor that shines through whether you serve them whole on a plate or on a fresh whole wheat hamburger bun.

SIMPLE SAUTÉED Portobello Mushrooms

MAKES 2 SERVINGS

1 to 2 tablespoons (15 to 30 ml) **vegan buttery spread or extra-virgin olive oil**

2 large portobello mushrooms, stemmed

salt

ground pepper

Heat the vegan buttery spread in a large skillet over medium heat. Add the mushrooms and season with salt and pepper to taste. Cook for 4 to 5 minutes, until slightly browned. Turn and cook the other side for 2 minutes, until heated through.

Variation: Cut the mushrooms into ¼-inch (5-mm) slices and cook for a total of 6 minutes, or until slightly browned. Serve as a salad topping.

Per serving: calories: 69, protein: 2 g, fat: 6 g, carbohydrates: 4 g (1 g from sugar), dietary fiber: 2 g, calcium: 6 mg, iron: 0.4 mg, magnesium: 8 mg, phosphorus: 91 mg, potassium: 339 mg, sodium: 4 mg, zinc: 0.4 mg, thiamin: 0.1 mg, riboflavin: 0.3 mg, niacin: 3 mg, vitamin B$_6$: 0.1 mg, folate: 15 mcg, pantothenic acid: 1 mg, vitamin B$_{12}$: 0 mcg, vitamin A: 0 mcg, vitamin C: 0 mg, vitamin E: 0 mg, omega-6 fatty acid: 0 g, omega-3 fatty acid: 0 g

Percentage of calories from: protein 10%, fat 70%, carbohydrates 20%

Note: Analyzed without salt and pepper.

Shiitake mushrooms are native to China and Japan, where they are featured extensively in the local cuisine. Now popular around the world, shiitake mushrooms can be found in most supermarkets. Known for their possible anticancer benefits, shiitake mushrooms have a meaty texture and a strong earthy flavor that is perfectly complemented by a few drops of tamari. Always remove the stems before using shiitakes; if you like, save the stems for making stock (see page 92) for miso soup.

Shiitake Mushrooms, KALE, AND SESAME

MAKES TWO TO THREE 1-CUP (250-ML) SERVINGS

2 teaspoons (10 ml) **coconut oil or extra-virgin olive oil**

1 teaspoon (5 ml) **toasted sesame oil**

2 cups (500 ml) **stemmed and sliced shiitake mushrooms**

6 cups (1.5 L) **stemmed and sliced kale leaves**

1 cup (250 ml) **chopped red bell pepper**

1 tablespoon (15 ml) **mirin or other Japanese cooking wine**

1 tablespoon (15 ml) **tamari**

1 tablespoon (15 ml) **rice vinegar**

1 tablespoon (15 ml) **toasted sesame seeds** (see sidebar, page 100)

Heat the coconut oil and toasted sesame oil in a large skillet over medium heat. Add the mushrooms, cover, and cook, stirring frequently, for 3 to 5 minutes, until slightly browned. Stir in the kale and bell pepper, cover, and cook for 3 to 5 minutes, or until the kale is tender. Remove from the heat and stir in the mirin, tamari, and vinegar until well combined. Sprinkle with the sesame seeds.

Per cup (250 ml): calories: 196, protein: 8 g, fat: 9 g, carbohydrates: 26 g (5 g from sugar), dietary fiber: 5 g, calcium: 273 mg, iron: 4 mg, magnesium: 82 mg, phosphorus: 146 mg, potassium: 926 mg, sodium: 483 mg, zinc: 1 mg, thiamin: 0.2 mg, riboflavin: 0.3 mg, niacin: 4 mg, vitamin B_6: 1 mg, folate: 66 mcg, pantothenic acid: 0.4 mg, vitamin B_{12}: 0 mcg, vitamin A: 1406 mcg, vitamin C: 324 mg, vitamin E: 2 mg, omega-6 fatty acid: 1 g, omega-3 fatty acid: 0.4 g

Percentage of calories from: protein 15%, fat 36%, carbohydrates 46%, alcohol (from mirin) 3%

This popular Indian dish is a superb combination of potatoes (*aloo*) and cauliflower (*gobi*). The seasonings include golden-hued turmeric and curry powder, which is a mixture of spices that varies from one household, and one region, to another. The saucepan must be covered with a tight-fitting lid because the potatoes and cauliflower cook in the steam they release.

ALOO Gobi

1½ **tablespoons** (22 ml) **coconut oil or extra-virgin olive oil**

1 **large onion, chopped**

1 **tablespoon** (15 ml) **peeled and minced fresh ginger**

2 **teaspoons** (10 ml) **curry powder**

½ **teaspoon** (2 ml) **ground turmeric**

2 **cups** (500 ml) **cauliflower florets**

2 **cups** (500 ml) **scrubbed and diced russet, gold, or red-skinned potatoes** (about 2 potatoes)

½ **teaspoon** (2 ml) **salt**

¾ **cup** (185 ml) **water**

2 **teaspoons** (10 ml) **freshly squeezed lemon juice**

Heat the oil in a large saucepan over medium heat. Add the onion and cook, stirring occasionally, until translucent. Add the ginger, curry powder, and turmeric and cook for 1 minute, stirring frequently to prevent the spices from burning. Add the cauliflower, potatoes, and salt. Cook and stir until the vegetables are coated with the spices and turn yellow. Stir in the water. Decrease the heat to low, cover with a tight-fitting lid, and cook for 20 to 25 minutes, or until the vegetables are fork-tender. Stir in the lemon juice. Serve hot.

VARIATION: Replace the curry powder with 2 teaspoons (10 ml) of Patak's Mild Curry Paste or another Indian curry paste to taste.

Per cup (250 ml): calories: 142, protein: 3 g, fat: 5 g, carbohydrates: 22 g (4 g from sugar), dietary fiber: 3 g, calcium: 31 mg, iron: 1 mg, magnesium: 32 mg, phosphorus: 75 mg, potassium: 675 mg, sodium: 258 mg, zinc: 1 mg, thiamin: 0.1 mg, riboflavin: 0.1 mg, niacin: 2 mg, vitamin B$_6$: 0.4 mg, folate: 50 mcg, pantothenic acid: 1 mg, vitamin B$_{12}$: 0 mcg, vitamin A: 1 mcg, vitamin C: 44 mg, vitamin E: 1 mg, omega-6 fatty acid: 0.5 g, omega-3 fatty acid: 0.1 g

Percentage of calories from: protein 9%, fat 32%, carbohydrates 59%

Scalloped potatoes are typically made with plenty of milk, cream, and butter. This version is dairy-free and low in fat. The combination of miso and Dijon mustard enlivens this dish, which is thickened with a roux, a classical French cooking technique in which wheat flour and fat are cooked together.

Dijon Scalloped POTATOES

MAKES SIX 1-CUP (250-ML) SERVINGS

2 cups (500 ml) **low-sodium vegetable broth or stock** (for homemade, see page 92)

⅓ cup (85 ml) **unbleached all-purpose flour**

3 tablespoons (45 ml) **coconut oil or extra-virgin olive oil**

2 pounds (900 g) **russet, gold, or red-skinned potatoes, scrubbed**

½ **red onion, thinly sliced**

3 tablespoons (45 ml) **miso**

1½ tablespoons (22 ml) **Dijon mustard**

¼ teaspoon (1 ml) **ground pepper**

Put the broth in a small saucepan and heat over medium-high heat until hot. Cover and set aside.

Put the flour and oil in a large saucepan over medium heat. Stir until well combined to make a roux. Cook for 3 minutes, stirring frequently to prevent the flour from burning. Remove from the heat and let cool for 1 minute. (Slightly cooling the roux will prevent it from clumping when the hot broth is added.)

Gradually stir the hot broth into the roux with a whisk or wooden spoon until it is well incorporated. Return to the heat. Bring to a boil over medium-high heat, decrease the heat to low, and simmer, stirring occasionally, for 10 minutes.

Preheat the oven to 375 degrees F (190 degrees C). Lightly oil a 13 x 9-inch (33 x 23-cm) baking dish.

Cut the potatoes into ¼-inch (½-cm) slices. Layer half of the potatoes in the prepared baking dish. Arrange the onion slices evenly over the potatoes. Arrange the remaining potatoes evenly over the onions.

Put the miso, mustard, and pepper in small bowl and stir until the miso dissolves. Remove the sauce from the heat and stir in the miso mixture. Pour over the potatoes. Cover and bake for 30 minutes. Uncover and bake for 20 minutes longer, or until the potatoes are fork-tender.

Per cup (250 ml): calories: 223, protein: 5 g, fat: 8 g, carbohydrates: 34 g (3 g from sugar), dietary fiber: 5 g, calcium: 25 mg, iron: 1.5 mg, magnesium: 38 mg, phosphorus: 118 mg, potassium: 658 mg, sodium: 463 mg, zinc: 1 mg, thiamin: 0.2 mg, riboflavin: 0.1 mg, niacin: 3 mg, vitamin B_6: 0.3 mg, folate: 42 mcg, pantothenic acid: 0.5 mg, vitamin B_{12}: 0 mcg, vitamin A: 37 mcg, vitamin C: 30 mg, vitamin E: 1 mg, omega-6 fatty acid: 1 g, omega-3 fatty acid: 0.1 g

Percentage of calories from: protein 10%, fat 30%, carbohydrates 60%

The Greeks use lemon and olive oil to make spectacular roasted potatoes, but traditional recipes are very high in fat. This version keeps the lemon and herb flavors but eliminates much of the oil and salt. Yukon gold or nugget potatoes work best in this recipe, although russets work well too.

LEMON ROASTED Potatoes

6 cups (1.5 L) **peeled and cubed gold or red-skinned potatoes** (about 6 potatoes)

3 tablespoons (45 ml) **freshly squeezed lemon juice**

3 tablespoons (45 ml) **extra-virgin olive oil**

1 tablespoon chopped fresh oregano or thyme, or 1 teaspoon (5 ml) **dried**

½ teaspoon (2 ml) **salt**

¼ teaspoon (1 ml) **ground pepper**

2 tablespoons (30 ml) **chopped fresh parsley, for garnish**

Preheat the oven to 400 degrees F (200 degrees C).

Put the potatoes, lemon juice, oil, oregano, salt, and pepper in a large bowl and toss to mix well. Transfer the potato mixture to a 13 x 9-inch (33 x 23-cm) baking dish and bake uncovered for 20 minutes. Remove from the oven and stir. Bake for 15 to 20 minutes longer, or until the potatoes are tender. Garnish with the parsley. Serve hot.

Per cup (250 ml): calories: 209, protein: 3 g, fat: 9 g, carbohydrates: 29 g (3 g from sugar), dietary fiber: 3 g, calcium: 15 mg, iron: 1 mg, magnesium: 35 mg, phosphorus: 75 mg, potassium: 880 mg, sodium: 168 mg, zinc: 1 mg, thiamin: 0.1 mg, riboflavin: 0.1 mg, niacin: 3 mg, vitamin B_6: 0.4 mg, folate: 24 mcg, pantothenic acid: 1 mg, vitamin B_{12}: 0 mcg, vitamin A: 6 mcg, vitamin C: 37 mg, vitamin E: 1 mg, omega-6 fatty acid: 1 g, omega-3 fatty acid: 0.1 g

Percentage of calories from: protein 6%, fat 39%, carbohydrates 55%

India's vegetarian tradition has roots in antiquity, and Indian cooking has a great deal to offer in terms of color, depth, richness, and variety. For example, this subji ("vegetable dish") is one of the tastiest potato recipes ever created. Use a heavy pan when making Potato Subji to spread the heat evenly and prevent burning.

POTATO Subji

MAKES SEVEN 1-CUP (250-ML) SERVINGS

2 tablespoons (30 ml) **coconut oil or extra-virgin olive oil**

1 tablespoon (15 ml) **brown mustard seeds**

2 cups (500 ml) **diced onion**

2 teaspoons (10 ml) **ground turmeric**

2.3 pounds (1 kg) **russet, gold, or red-skinned potatoes, scrubbed and cubed** (about 4 potatoes)

¼ cup (60 ml) **water, plus more if necessary**

1 teaspoon (5 ml) **salt**

Heat the oil and mustard seeds in a large saucepan over medium heat. Once the seeds begin to pop, cover and cook for 1 to 2 minutes, until you hear that the seeds have stopped popping. Stir in the onion and cook until soft, 3 to 5 minutes. Add the turmeric and cook for 1 minute. Stir in the potatoes, water, and salt. Cover and cook for 20 minutes, or until the potatoes are fork-tender, adding more water if necessary to prevent the potatoes from drying out.

Per cup (250 ml): calories: 177, protein: 4 g, fat: 5 g, carbohydrates: 31 g (4 g from sugar), dietary fiber: 3 g, calcium: 30 mg, iron: 2 mg, magnesium: 40 mg, phosphorus: 93 mg, potassium: 872 mg, sodium: 348 mg, zinc: 1 mg, thiamin: 0.2 mg, riboflavin: 0.1 mg, niacin: 3 mg, vitamin B$_6$: 0.5 mg, folate: 29 mcg, pantothenic acid: 0.6 mg, vitamin B$_{12}$: 0 mcg, vitamin A: 0 mcg, vitamin C: 31 mg, vitamin E: 1 mg, omega-6 fatty acid: 0.4 g, omega-3 fatty acid: 0.1 g

Percentage of calories from: protein 8%, fat 23%, carbohydrates 69%

You may be surprised to discover that these easy-to-prepare potato wedges are a good source of antioxidants, protein, minerals, vitamin C, and B vitamins. They are a delicious and low-fat alternative to French fries and can be served alone or with Miso Gravy (page 187), Spicy Peanut Sauce (page 182), or other dipping sauces. Experiment by trying different herb and spice combinations in the nutritional yeast mixture. If any of the nutritional yeast mixture is left over, sprinkle it over casseroles, popcorn, or salad.

SEASONED Potato Wedges

MAKES 3 SERVINGS

3 russet, gold, or red-skinned potatoes, scrubbed

¼ cup (60 ml) **nondairy milk**

½ teaspoon (2 ml) **salt**

⅓ cup (85 ml) **nutritional yeast flakes**

2 teaspoons (10 ml) **chili powder**

2 teaspoons (10 ml) **onion powder**

¾ teaspoon (4 ml) **garlic powder**

¼ teaspoon (1 ml) **ground pepper**

Preheat the oven to 400 degrees F (200 degrees C).

Cut each potato in half lengthwise, then cut each half into thirds or quarters, depending on the size of the potato. Pour the nondairy milk into a flat-bottomed bowl. Stir in the salt until dissolved. Put the nutritional yeast, chili powder, onion powder, garlic powder, and pepper in a shallow bowl and stir to combine. Dip the potato wedges into the nondairy milk, then into the nutritional yeast mixture until coated. Arrange the wedges on a nonstick baking sheet and bake for 30 minutes, or until the potatoes are soft when pierced with a fork.

VARIATION: For crispy wedges, lightly oil a baking sheet and arrange the potato wedges cut-side down. Bake at 400 degrees F (200 degrees C) for 15 minutes. Use a fork or metal tongs to turn the wedges. Bake for 15 minutes longer, or until the potatoes are soft when pierced with a fork.

Per serving (one potato): calories: 228, protein: 10 g, fat: 1.5 g, carbohydrates: 45 g (3 g from sugar), dietary fiber: 7 g, calcium: 68 mg, iron: 2 mg, magnesium: 70 mg, phosphorus: 286 mg, potassium: 1,245 mg, sodium: 357 mg, zinc: 3 mg, thiamin: 7 mg, riboflavin: 7 mg, niacin: 45 mg, vitamin B_6: 7 mg, folate: 241 mcg, pantothenic acid: 2 mg, vitamin B_{12}: 6 mcg, vitamin A: 35 mcg, vitamin C: 23 mg, vitamin E: 0.1 mg, omega-6 fatty acid: 0.3 g, omega-3 fatty acid: 0g

Percentage of calories from: protein 17%, fat 6%, carbohydrates 77%

Note: Analysis was done using fortified soymilk and Red Star Vegetarian Support Formula nutritional yeast flakes, both of which are sources of vitamin B_{12}.

A pilaf is a dish that contains a grain, such as rice, that is sautéed in vegetable oil containing fragrant ingredients, then cooked in a seasoned broth. The oil coats each individual grain, which keeps the grains from sticking together. Brown Rice, Mushroom, and Walnut Pilaf can be cooked on the stovetop or in the oven (see the variation).

Brown Rice, MUSHROOM, AND WALNUT PILAF

MAKES FOUR 1-CUP (250-ML) SERVINGS

1 tablespoon (15 ml) **coconut oil or extra-virgin olive oil**

2 cups (500 ml) **sliced white mushrooms**

½ **onion, diced**

1 cup (250 ml) **brown rice**

½ cup (125 ml) **coarsely chopped walnuts**

1 teaspoon (5 ml) **ground cumin**

2 cups (500 ml) **water or vegetable stock** (for homemade, see page 92)

½ teaspoon (2 ml) **salt**

chopped fresh parsley, for garnish

Heat the oil in a large skillet over medium heat. Add the mushrooms and onions and cook and stir for 5 minutes, or until the liquid from the mushrooms has evaporated. Add the rice, walnuts, and cumin and stir for 30 seconds, until the rice is coated with the oil. Stir in the water and salt. Bring to a boil. Decrease the heat to low, cover, and cook for 45 minutes, or until the rice is tender and all the water is absorbed. Garnish with parsley.

Baked Brown Rice, Mushroom, and Walnut Pilaf: For a baked version of this recipe, preheat the oven to 350 degrees F (180 degrees C). After cooking the mushrooms and onion in a skillet as directed in the recipe, add the rice, walnuts, cumin, water, and salt. Bring the liquid to a boil over medium-high heat, then transfer the mixture to a 6-cup (1.5-L) baking dish. Cover with a lid or foil and bake for 45 to 50 minutes, or until the rice is tender and all the water is absorbed.

Per cup (250 ml): calories: 309, protein: 7 g, fat: 14 g, carbohydrates: 41 g (2 g from sugar), dietary fiber: 3 g, calcium: 42 mg, iron: 2 mg, magnesium: 98 mg, phosphorus: 211 mg, potassium: 334 mg, sodium: 230 mg, zinc: 2 mg, thiamin: 0.3 mg, riboflavin: 0.2 mg, niacin: 5 mg, vitamin B_6: 0.4 mg, folate: 33 mcg, pantothenic acid: 1 mg, vitamin B_{12}: 0 mcg, vitamin A: 4 mcg, vitamin C: 3 mg, vitamin E: 0.4 mg, omega-6 fatty acid: 6g, omega-3 fatty acid: 1.3 g

Percentage of calories from: protein 9%, fat 40%, carbohydrates 51%

The combination of ingredients in this simple dish creates a very special blend of flavors. Coconut milk is a good source of iron and potassium. Canned coconut milk separates on standing, so you may need to stir or shake it before you measure and use it. Rinse the white rice, which may have been "polished" with talc powder, to remove any residue and the slight cloudiness it can impart to a rice dish. Add the rice after the liquid has come to a boil to keep the grains separate.

Coconut-Saffron Rice WITH CARDAMOM AND LIME

MAKES THREE TO FOUR 1-CUP (250-ML) SERVINGS

1 cup (250 ml) **white basmati rice**

1 cup (250 ml) **coconut milk**

¾ cup (185) **water**

2 **cardamom pods, crushed, or ⅛ teaspoon**
(0.5 ml) **ground cardamom**

¼ **teaspoon** (1 ml) **salt**

pinch saffron

2 **tablespoons** (30 ml) **freshly squeezed
lime juice**

**chopped fresh cilantro or parsley,
for garnish**

Put the rice in a fine-mesh strainer and rinse it under cold water, stirring with your fingers, until the water runs clear. Drain well.

Put the coconut milk, water, cardamom, salt, and saffron in a medium saucepan and bring to a boil over medium-high heat. Stir in the rice. Decrease the heat to low, cover, and cook for 20 minutes, or until the rice is tender and all the water is absorbed. Sprinkle the lime juice evenly over the rice, then fluff with a fork. Garnish with cilantro.

Per cup (250 ml): calories: 363, protein: 5 g, fat: 15 g, carbohydrates: 58 g (0 g from sugar), dietary fiber: 2 g, calcium: 18 mg, iron: 4 mg, magnesium: 36 mg, phosphorus: 72 mg, potassium: 179 mg, sodium: 146 mg, zinc: 0.4 mg, thiamin: 0.2 mg, riboflavin: 0 mg, niacin: 2 mg, vitamin B_6: 0 mg, folate: 12 mcg, pantothenic acid: 0.1 mg, vitamin B_{12}: 0 mcg, vitamin A: 5 mcg, vitamin C: 5 mg, vitamin E: 0 mg, omega-6 fatty acid: 0.3 g, omega-3 fatty acid: 0 g

Percentage of calories from: protein 5%, fat 36%, carbohydrates 59%

This rice is a popular staple in Spain but can also be found in Latin American and American Tex-Mex cuisine. The tomatoes make Spanish Rice very moist, and the bell pepper, herbs, and spices provide a deep, rich flavor. Try Spanish Rice as a stuffing for International Roll-Ups (page 144) or Timesaving Tacos (page 159). Alternatively, serve it alongside warmed black beans and a salad for a pleasant color and taste combination.

Spanish RICE

MAKES FOUR 1-CUP (250-ML) SERVINGS

1 tablespoon (15 ml) **coconut oil** or **extra-virgin olive oil**

½ **onion, diced**

2 cups (500 ml) **chopped fresh or drained canned tomatoes**

½ cup (125 ml) **diced green bell pepper**

1 clove **garlic, minced**

½ teaspoon (2 ml) **chili powder**

½ teaspoon (2 ml) **ground cumin**

½ teaspoon (2 ml) **dried oregano**

¼ teaspoon (1 ml) **ground pepper**

¼ teaspoon (1 ml) **salt**

2 cups (500 ml) **vegetable stock** (for homemade, see page 92) **or water**

1 cup (250 ml) **brown rice**

Heat the oil in a large saucepan over medium heat. Add the onion and cook for 3 to 5 minutes, or until soft. Add the tomatoes, bell pepper, garlic, chili powder, cumin, oregano, pepper, and salt and cook, stirring occasionally, for 5 minutes, or until the tomatoes have released most of their liquid. Stir in the stock and rice. Bring to a boil. Decrease the heat to low, cover, and cook for 45 minutes, or until the rice is tender and all the stock is absorbed.

Per cup (250 ml): calories: 252, protein: 5 g, fat: 5 g, carbohydrates: 48 g (4 g from sugar), dietary fiber: 4 g, calcium: 38 mg, iron: 2 mg, magnesium: 88 mg, phosphorus: 167 mg, potassium: 432 mg, sodium: 420 mg, zinc: 1 mg, thiamin: 0.3 mg, riboflavin: 0.1 mg, niacin: 4 mg, vitamin B_6: 0.4 mg, folate: 30 mcg, pantothenic acid: 0.9 mg, vitamin B_{12}: 0 mcg, vitamin A: 61 mcg, vitamin C: 39 mg, vitamin E: 1 mg, omega-6 fatty acid: 0.6 g, omega-3 fatty acid: 0 g

Percentage of calories from: protein 8%, fat 18%, carbohydrates 74%

Note: Analyzed with stock that provided 292 milligrams of sodium per cup (250 ml) of Spanish Rice.

Sweet Treats

Use this thick, creamy topping on Apple-Pear Crumble (page 219), Creamy Rice Pudding (page 238), and other desserts. Cashew Cream Topping is rich in minerals—including copper, iron, magnesium, manganese, and zinc—and protein. Just two tablespoons (30 ml) provide 4 grams of protein.

CASHEW CREAM Topping

MAKES 1¼ CUPS (310 ML)

1 cup (250 ml) **raw cashews, soaked in hot water for 2 hours and drained**

½ cup (125 ml) **water**

¼ cup (60 ml) **pitted dates or maple syrup**

Put the cashews, water, and dates in a blender and process until smooth. For a thinner topping, add a little more water, 1 tablespoon at a time, until the desired consistency is achieved. Stored in a sealed container in the refrigerator, Cashew Cream Topping will keep for 1 week.

Per 2 tablespoons (30 ml): calories: 144, protein: 4 g, fat: 10 g, carbohydrates: 11 g (5 g from sugar), dietary fiber: 1 g, calcium: 11 mg, iron: 2 mg, magnesium: 70 mg, phosphorus: 139 mg, potassium: 191 mg, sodium: 3 mg, zinc: 1 mg, thiamin: 0.1 mg, riboflavin: 0 mg, niacin: 1 mg, vitamin B$_6$: 0.1 mg, folate: 7 mcg, pantothenic acid: 0.2 mg, vitamin B$_{12}$: 0 mcg, vitamin A: 0 mcg, vitamin C: 0 mg, vitamin E: 0.2 mg, omega-6 fatty acid: 2 g, omega-3 fatty acid: 0 g

Percentage of calories from: protein 11%, fat 59%, carbohydrates 30%

This low-fat alternative to whipped cream is a great accompaniment to Blueberry Mince Tarts or Pies (page 234), Pumpkin Spice Pie (page 237), or apple pie.

Holiday Pie TOPPING

MAKES ABOUT 2 CUPS (450 ML)

12 ounces (340 g) **firm silken tofu**

¼ cup (60 ml) **maple syrup**

1 tablespoon (15 ml) **freshly squeezed lemon juice**

1 teaspoon (5 ml) **vanilla extract**

Put all the ingredients in a blender or food processor and process for about 1 minute, or until completely smooth. Cover and refrigerate for 1 to 2 hours. Spread over a cooled pie, pass at the table, or put a dollop on each serving. Stored in a sealed container in the refrigerator, Holiday Pie Topping will keep for 1 week.

Per 2 tablespoons (30 ml): calories: 30, protein: 2 g, fat: 1 g, carbohydrates: 4 g (4 g from sugar), dietary fiber: 0 g, calcium: 11 mg, iron: 0.3 mg, magnesium: 7 mg, phosphorus: 58 mg, potassium: 58 mg, sodium: 9 mg, zinc: 0.4 mg, thiamin: 0 mg, riboflavin: 0 mg, niacin: 0.4 mg, vitamin B$_6$: 0 mg, folate: 0.1 mcg, pantothenic acid: 0 mg, vitamin B$_{12}$: 0 mcg, vitamin A: 0 mcg, vitamin C: 0.5 mg, vitamin E: 0.1 mg, omega-6 fatty acid: 0 g, omega-3 fatty acid: 0 g

Percentage of calories from: protein 22%, fat 20%, carbohydrates 58%

This glaze, or thin icing, is a lovely blend of sweet and sour tastes. It is particularly delicious on Apple Spice Cake (page 220) but will also add zing to many other homebaked goods.

LEMON Glaze

MAKES 1⅔ CUPS (420 ML)

¼ cup (60 ml) **vegan buttery spread**

2 cups (500 ml) **confectioners' sugar**

2 tablespoons (30 ml) **grated lemon zest**

1½ tablespoons (22 ml) **freshly squeezed lemon juice**

Put the vegan buttery spread in a medium bowl. Use a hand mixer or spoon to mix until creamy. Add the sugar and stir until most of it is incorporated, pressing out any lumps. Add the zest and lemon juice and stir until well combined.

Per 4 teaspoons (20 ml): calories: 70, protein: 0 g, fat: 2 g, carbohydrates: 13 g (13 g from sugar), dietary fiber: 0.1 g, calcium: 1 mg, iron: 0 mg, magnesium: 0.2 mg, phosphorus: 0.4 mg, potassium: 3 mg, sodium: 0.2 mg, zinc: 0.1 mg, thiamin: 0 mg, riboflavin: 0 mg, niacin: 0 mg, vitamin B_6: 0 mg, folate: 0.2 mcg, pantothenic acid: 0 mg, vitamin B_{12}: 0 mcg, vitamin A: 0 mcg, vitamin C: 1 mg, vitamin E: 0 mg, omega-6 fatty acid: 0 g, omega-3 fatty acid: 0 g

Percentage of calories from: protein 0%, fat 28%, carbohydrates 72%

Fruits: Nutritional Superstars

Fruits provide minerals that are essential to electrolyte balance, nerve transmission, and body function. Bananas, cantaloupe, grapefruit, and strawberries provide abundant amounts of potassium. Oranges and figs are high in calcium, and bananas, prunes, and raisins provide copper. In addition, fruits are loaded with health-promoting antioxidants and phytochemicals (plant chemicals), including the following:

- Anthocyanins are antioxidants that are found in blackberries, black currants, blueberries, cherries, and plums.

- Carotenoids, a group of protective compounds that are related to vitamin A, act as antioxidants, support communication between cells in the body, and may protect us against several cancers and macular degeneration. They provide the gorgeous hues in apricots, guavas, mangoes,

In the summer when locally grown produce is at its peak, fresh fruit is a superb dessert. In the winter, fresh fruit provides a healthful and refreshing finish to hearty meals. Any time of year, fresh fruit is the ideal dessert for people with food allergies or gluten sensitivities.

Following are several ideas for serving fresh fruit in season. Alternatively, try the Watermelon and Fresh Fruit Sculpture (page 216).

Fresh Fruit AS DESSERT

- Emulate upscale restaurants that serve a single large, ripe heirloom peach or other fruit at the peak of perfection. This dessert makes an attractive and thought-provoking presentation—it's a great way to start a conversation about the virtues of simple living.

- Create a fruit platter by choosing and organizing cut or sliced fruits by colors. For example, try blackberries, blueberries, or plums; strawberries or raspberries; mangoes, papayas, or mandarin oranges; apricots or peaches; grapefruit, guavas, or watermelons; honeydew melons or kiwifruit; and apples, bananas, or pears (sprinkle white fruits with a little lemon juice to prevent browning). For an elegant presentation, artistically arrange cut fruit on a mirror that has a frame or polished edges.

- Cut fruit into uniform pieces and thread the pieces on bamboo skewers to create a colorful presentation for a brunch, picnic, or potluck dinner.

- Slice a pineapple or melon in half and carefully remove the flesh of one half to create a cavity. Fill the cavity with fresh fruit salad.

- Arrange a dessert plate that will delight children by using pieces of fruit to compose a smiling face. For example, use a curve of melon for the mouth, the pointed end of a banana for a nose, and berries for eyes.

papayas, persimmons, pink grapefruit, pumpkins, and watermelons.

- Coumaric acid is an antioxidant and anticancer agent in grapes, pineapples, and strawberries.

- Ellagic acid is an anticancer agent in berries, grapes, and pomegranates.

- Flavonols, such as quercitin, help to keep the doctor away and are present in apples, berries, and cherries.

- Folate helps to build amino acids and DNA. Excellent sources are kiwifruit and oranges.

- Limonoids, which are found in citrus fruits, support heart health.

- Vitamin B_6 (pyridoxine), which is essential for protein metabolism, is present in many fruits. You can get your day's supply from three bananas.

- Vitamin C is a powerful antioxidant that helps our bodies resist disease and infection, absorb iron from food, and build essential compounds, such as carnitine, collagen, and the neurotransmitter norepinephrine. Sources include cantaloupes, citrus fruits, mangoes, papayas, and strawberries. The vitamin C content of organic foods has been shown to be higher than that of their nonorganic counterparts.

On a hot summer day, this is a great dessert to make with children. Free of allergens, such as eggs, dairy, and wheat, and low in calories, it is colorful, attractive, and thirst quenching. In addition to the fruits suggested in the recipe, many others could be used for decoration (see note below).

WATERMELON AND Fresh Fruit Sculpture

MAKES ABOUT 12 SERVINGS

½ **large** (about 5 pounds/2.25 kg) **seedless watermelon** (slice the watermelon in half lengthwise)

¼ **ripe pineapple, cored, peeled, and cut into ½-inch** (1-cm) **pieces**

1 cup (250 ml) **peeled and sliced kiwifruit** (cut into half-moons about ¼ inch/5 mm thick)

1 cup (250 ml) **stemmed and halved strawberries**

Slice about 1 inch (2.5 cm) from each end of the watermelon half. Hold the watermelon half on its end and cut off the peel, including the white inner part.

To assemble the sculpture, lay the watermelon half flat-side down on a platter. Skewer pieces of pineapple, kiwifruit, and strawberry with toothpicks, then stick the toothpicks into the watermelon, creating a decorative pattern. Arrange any leftover fruit around the base of the sculpture. If possible, allow the sculpture to chill for 1 to 2 hours before serving. To serve, slice into pieces.

NOTE: Many types of fruit can be used to decorate the watermelon. Use 3 to 4 cups (0.75 to 1L) total, such as combinations of the following:

- several blueberries threaded onto a single toothpick
- cantaloupe or honeydew melon pieces
- grapes (whole or halved)
- whole red or black raspberries
- star fruit (halved and thinly sliced); star fruit works particularly well when used to form a border along the base of the watermelon

Per serving: calories: 54, protein: 1 g, fat: 0 g, carbohydrates: 14 g (10 g from sugar), dietary fiber: 1 g, calcium: 17 mg, iron: 0.4 mg, magnesium: 17 mg, phosphorus: 21 mg, potassium: 207 mg, sodium:2 mg, zinc: 0.2 mg, thiamin: 0.1 mg, riboflavin: 0 mg, niacin: 1 mg, vitamin B_6: 0.1 mg, folate: 12 mcg, pantothenic acid: 0.3 mg, vitamin B_{12}: 0 mcg, vitamin A: 33 mcg, vitamin C: 35 mg, vitamin E: 0.3 mg, omega-6 fatty acid: 0.1 g, omega-3 fatty acid: 0 g

Percentage of calories from: protein 7%, fat 4%, carbohydrates 89%

If you have a masticating juicer (such as a Champion) or a twin gear juicer (such as a Green Power or Green Star), you can make the simplest nondairy ice cream imaginable. To make this ice cream in a food processor, see the variation that follows. The fat content is low and the potassium content is high because the only ingredient is bananas. Vegan Dazs Ice Cream will turn out thicker if the juicer parts and bowl are chilled before processing.

Vegan Dazs ICE CREAM

MAKES TWO TO THREE 1-CUP (250-ML) SERVINGS

4 peeled and frozen ripe bananas, cut in half

Feed frozen banana halves gradually into a juicer that is fitted with a blank (in place of the juicing screen) and process until smooth. Serve immediately.

VARIATIONS

Chocolate Ice Cream: Add 2 teaspoons (10 ml) of unsweetened cocoa powder or carob powder with each banana so that the cocoa powder is mixed in with the banana as it goes through the juicer. Serve immediately.

Mixed Fruit Ice Cream: Use 2 frozen bananas plus 2 cups (500 ml) of other frozen fruits, such as blueberries, mangoes, pineapple, strawberries, or a combination. Serve immediately.

Food Processor Method: Put 2 cups (500 ml) of frozen banana pieces or other frozen fruit in a food processor, add 1 cup (250 ml) of nondairy milk (such as almond milk, hempseed milk, or soymilk), and process until smooth. Serve immediately.

Freezing Bananas

Use frozen bananas in Vegan Dazs Ice Cream or smoothies. Select ripe bananas, as they are much sweeter and do not have a starchy aftertaste. Peel the bananas and leave them whole or break them into chunks. Sprinkle freshly squeezed lemon juice over the bananas to keep them from turning brown. Put the bananas in ziplock freezer bags or airtight containers and store them in the freezer. Frozen bananas will keep in the freezer for about three weeks before becoming brown (depending on their ripeness and the freezer temperature).

Per cup (250 ml): calories: 169, protein: 2 g, fat: 1 g, carbohydrates: 43 g (29 g from sugar), dietary fiber: 3 g, calcium: 11 mg, iron: 0.6 mg, magnesium: 53 mg, phosphorus: 37 mg, potassium: 726 mg, sodium: 2 mg, zinc: 0.3 mg, thiamin: 0.1 mg, riboflavin: 0.2 mg, niacin: 1 mg, vitamin B_6: 1 mg, folate: 35 mcg, pantothenic acid: 0.5 mg, vitamin B_{12}: 0 mcg, vitamin A: 15 mcg, vitamin C: 17 mg, vitamin E: 0.5 mg, omega-6 fatty acid: 0.1 g, omega-3 fatty acid: 0.1 g

Percentage of calories from: protein 4%, fat 4%, carbohydrates 92%

This recipe is equally tasty made with McIntosh apples, which cook quickly, or other varieties, such as Golden Delicious or Granny Smith, which may take longer to cook.

BAKED Stuffed Apples

4 apples

¼ **cup** (60 ml) **raisins**

¼ **cup** (60 ml) **tahini**

2 teaspoons (10 ml) **freshly squeezed lemon juice**

2 teaspoons (10 ml) **brown sugar, maple syrup, or other sweetener**

½ **teaspoon** (2 ml) **grated lemon zest**

¼ **teaspoon** (1 ml) **ground cinnamon**

Preheat the oven to 300 degrees F (150 degrees C).

Remove each apple stem by holding a paring knife at a 45-degree angle to the stem. Rotate the knife around the top of the apple to produce a small cone-shaped top. Set aside the apple tops. Remove the core from each apple using a melon baller or teaspoon, being careful not to pierce the bottoms.

Put the raisins, tahini, lemon juice, sugar, zest, and cinnamon in a small bowl and stir until well combined. Fill the apple cavities almost to the top with the raisin mixture. Replace the apple tops. Put the apples on a baking sheet and bake for 15 minutes, or until the apples are tender when pierced with a toothpick.

VARIATION: Replace the tahini with 3 stemmed dried figs that have been soaked in water for 8 hours, drained, and chopped.

Per serving: calories: 151, protein: 3 g, fat: 8 g, carbohydrates: 19 g (3 g from sugar), dietary fiber: 2 g, calcium: 33 mg, iron: 1 mg, magnesium: 20 mg, phosphorus: 135 mg, potassium: 199 mg, sodium: 7 mg, zinc: 1 mg, thiamin: 0.3 mg, riboflavin: 0 mg, niacin: 1 mg, vitamin B_6: 0.1 mg, folate: 17 mcg, pantothenic acid: 0 mg, vitamin B_{12}: 0 mcg, vitamin A: 31 mcg, vitamin C: 4 mg, vitamin E: 0.4 mg, omega-6 fatty acid: 3 g, omega-3 fatty acid: 0.1 g

Percentage of calories from: protein 8%, fat 45%, carbohydrates 47%

Many other fruits can be substituted for apples and pears in this recipe. For example, try peaches or nectarines with blueberries or raspberries. With any combination, use a total of seven to eight cups (1.75 to 2 L) of chopped fruits and berries. If using sour fruits, increase the amount of sweetener to taste.

Apple-Pear CRUMBLE

MAKES NINE 1-CUP (250-ML) SERVINGS

2 cups (500 ml) **old-fashioned rolled oats**

1 cup (250 ml) **orange juice**

6 tablespoons (45 ml) **maple syrup**

¼ cup (60 ml) **chopped walnuts**

1 tablespoon (15 ml) **grated orange zest**

½ teaspoon (2ml) **ground cinnamon**

⅛ teaspoon (0.5 ml) **ground nutmeg**

3 apples with peel, cored and chopped

3 pears with peel, cored and chopped

2 tablespoons (30 ml) **freshly squeezed lemon juice**

¼ cup (60 ml) **raisins**

Preheat the oven to 350 degrees F (175 degrees C).

Put the oats, orange juice, 3 tablespoons of the maple syrup, walnuts, zest, cinnamon, and nutmeg in a large bowl and stir until combined. Let sit for 10 minutes so the oats absorb the liquid.

Put the apples, pears, and lemon juice in a 9-inch (23-cm) square baking dish and toss until the fruit is coated with the juice. Drizzle the remaining 3 tablespoons of maple syrup and sprinkle the raisins on top. Spoon the oat mixture evenly over the fruit and bake for 30 to 35 minutes, or until the topping is golden brown.

VARIATION: Replace 1 cup (250 ml) of apples or pears with 1 cup (250 ml) of cranberries.

Per cup (250 ml): calories: 208, protein: 4 g, fat: 2 g, carbohydrates: 48 g (9 g from sugar), dietary fiber: 5 g, calcium: 40 mg, iron: 1 mg, magnesium: 64 mg, phosphorus: 111 mg, potassium: 377 mg, sodium: 5 mg, zinc: 1 mg, thiamin: 0.2 mg, riboflavin: 0.1 mg, niacin: 0.5 mg, vitamin B_6: 0.1 mg, folate: 34 mcg, pantothenic acid: 0.3 mg, vitamin B_{12}: 0 mcg, vitamin A: 10 mcg, vitamin C: 29 mg, vitamin E: 0.4 mg, omega-6 fatty acid: 0.5 g, omega-3 fatty acid: 0 g

Percentage of calories from: protein 7%, fat 7%, carbohydrates 86%

This cake can be dressed up and served as a birthday cake. Top it with Lemon Glaze (page 214), Vanilla Frosting (page 223), or Cashew Cream Topping (page 212) and strawberries (see variation). It also tastes great plain.

APPLE SPICE Cake

MAKES 20 PIECES (EACH 2¼ X 2½ INCHES/6 X 6 CM)

3 cups (750 ml) **whole wheat pastry flour**

1 tablespoon (15 ml) **baking powder**

2 teaspoons (10 ml) **ground cinnamon**

1 teaspoon (5 ml) **ground allspice**

1 teaspoon (5 ml) **baking soda**

1 teaspoon (5 ml) **ground cloves**

1 teaspoon (5 ml) **ground ginger**

1 teaspoon (5 ml) **ground nutmeg**

½ teaspoon (2 ml) **salt**

1 cup (250 ml) **hempseed milk or other nondairy milk**

1 cup (250 ml) **maple syrup**

⅔ cup (170 ml) **sunflower seed oil or melted coconut oil**

2 tablespoons (30 ml) **ground flaxseeds**

2 cups (500 ml) **peeled and grated apples**

1 cup (250 ml) **raisins**

1 cup (250 ml) **chopped walnuts or pecans**

Preheat the oven to 350 degrees F (180 degrees C). Oil and flour a 13 x 9-inch (33 x 23-cm) baking pan.

Put the flour, baking powder, cinnamon, allspice, baking soda, cloves, ginger, nutmeg, and salt in a medium bowl and stir with a dry whisk until combined.

Put the hempseed milk, maple syrup, oil, and flaxseeds in a large bowl and stir until combined. Stir in the flour mixture until just combined. Fold in the apples, raisins, and walnuts. Do not overmix. Pour into the prepared baking pan. Bake for 30 to 35 minutes, or until a toothpick inserted in the center comes out clean.

Cake, Strawberries, and "Cream": Make the Apple Spice Cake using either whole wheat or unbleached all-purpose flour and serve it with sliced strawberries and Cashew Cream Topping (page 212) or Holiday Pie Topping (page 213).

Per piece: calories: 255, protein: 4 g, fat: 12 g, carbohydrates: 35 g (17 g from sugar), dietary fiber: 4 g, calcium: 99 mg, iron: 2 mg, magnesium: 42 mg, phosphorus: 171 mg, potassium: 221 mg, sodium: 170 mg, zinc: 1.5 mg, thiamin: 0.1 mg, riboflavin: 0.1 mg, niacin: 2 mg, vitamin B_6: 0.1 mg, folate: 15 mcg, pantothenic acid: 0.2 mg, vitamin B_{12}: 0 mcg, vitamin A: 1 mcg, vitamin C: 1 mg, vitamin E: 0.3 mg, omega-6 fatty acid: 3 g, omega-3 fatty acid: 1 g

Percentage of calories from: protein 6%, fat 41%, carbohydrates 53%

This cake has a nice texture and is not too sweet. Top it with Chocolate Frosting (page 222) or Blueberry-Orange Sauce (page 178). The leavening used in this cake is baking soda, so it is best to mix the batter quickly and get it right into the oven. When wet ingredients come in contact with baking soda or baking powder, gases are instantly released, making the batter rise. Overmixing destroys the gas bubbles, resulting in a flatter cake.

Chocolate-Orange CAKE

MAKES 20 PIECES (EACH 2¼ X 2½ INCHES/6 X 6 CM)

1½ cups (375 ml) **brown sugar or other granulated sweetener**

1½ cups (375 ml) **whole wheat pastry flour**

1 cup (250 ml) **unbleached all-purpose flour**

½ cup (125 ml) **unsweetened cocoa powder, sifted to remove any lumps**

1 teaspoon (5 ml) **baking soda, sifted**

½ teaspoon (2 ml) **salt**

2 cups (500 ml) **orange juice**

⅓ cup (85 ml) **sunflower oil or other vegetable oil**

1 tablespoon (15 ml) **cider vinegar**

1 tablespoon (15 ml) **grated orange zest**

1 teaspoon (5 ml) **vanilla extract**

Preheat the oven to 350 degrees F (180 degrees C). Lightly oil a 13 x 9-inch (33 x 23-cm) baking pan.

Put the sugar, flours, cocoa powder, baking soda, and salt in a medium bowl and stir with a dry whisk until combined.

Put the orange juice, oil, vinegar, zest, and vanilla extract in a large bowl and stir until combined. Quickly stir in the flour mixture just until the dry ingredients are moist. Immediately pour into the prepared baking pan. Bake for 30 minutes, or until a toothpick inserted in the center comes out clean. Let cool completely before frosting.

VARIATION: Add ½ teaspoon (2 ml) cayenne to the dry ingredients for a cake that has a warming sensation after each bite.

Per piece: calories: 152, protein: 3 g, fat: 5 g, carbohydrates: 27 g (13 g from sugar), dietary fiber: 2 g, calcium: 20 mg, iron: 1 mg, magnesium: 32 mg, phosphorus: 64 mg, potassium: 173 mg, sodium: 181 mg, zinc: 0.5 mg, thiamin: 0.1 mg, riboflavin: 0.1 mg, niacin: 2 mg, vitamin B$_6$: 0.1 mg, folate: 23 mcg, pantothenic acid: 0.2 mg, vitamin B$_{12}$: 0 mcg, vitamin A: 3 mcg, vitamin C: 14 mg, vitamin E: 0.1 mg, omega-6 fatty acid: 0.2g, omega-3 fatty acid: 0 g

Percentage of calories from: protein 7%, fat 25%, carbohydrates 68%

Frosting, or icing, is a sweet topping for cakes, cookies, brownies, and pastries that prevents them from drying out too quickly. The minerals shown in the nutritional analysis are from cocoa powder, which gives this frosting a wonderful flavor. Chocolate Frosting was developed for Chocolate-Orange Cake (page 221).

Chocolate FROSTING

MAKES 1¼ CUPS (310 ML)

1 cup (250 ml) **nondairy chocolate chips, or 6 ounces** (180 g) **semisweet baking chocolate**

½ cup (125 ml) **confectioners' sugar**

½ cup (125 ml) **vegan buttery spread**

¼ cup (60 ml) **unsweetened cocoa powder**

1 teaspoon (5 ml) **vanilla extract**

Put the chocolate chips in the top of a double boiler over boiling water or in a small pan over medium-low heat. Stir until the chocolate chips melt and become a thick sauce. Remove from the heat. Stir in the sugar and vegan buttery spread until evenly distributed. Stir in the cocoa powder and vanilla extract until evenly distributed. Cool completely, then spread over a cake or other baked item.

Per 1 tablespoon (15 ml): calories: 100, protein: 0.6 g, fat: 7 g, carbohydrates: 9 g (8 g from sugar), dietary fiber: 1 g, calcium: 4 mg, iron: 0.4 mg, magnesium: 16 mg, phosphorus: 20 mg, potassium: 49 mg, sodium: 1 mg, zinc: 0.2 mg, thiamin: 0 mg, riboflavin: 0 mg, niacin: 0.2 mg, vitamin B_6: 0 mg, folate: 2 mcg, pantothenic acid: 0 mg, vitamin B_{12}: 0 mcg, vitamin A: 0 mcg, vitamin C: 0 mg, vitamin E: 0 mg, omega-6 fatty acid: 0.1 g, omega-3 fatty acid: 0 g

Percentage of calories from: protein 2%, fat 62%, carbohydrates 36%

The vegan buttery spreads found in the marketplace are delicious, healthful substitutes for butter, and they contain none of the hydrogenated fats commonly associated with margarine. Before using vegan buttery spread in frosting, bring it to room temperature.

VANILLA Frosting

MAKES 1⅔ CUP (420 ML)

⅔ **cup** (170 ml) **vegan buttery spread**

2 cups (500 ml) **confectioners' sugar**

1 teaspoon (5 ml) **vanilla extract**

Put the vegan buttery spread in a medium bowl and beat well using a hand mixer or spoon. Stir in the sugar until well incorporated, pressing out any lumps. Stir in the vanilla extract until well combined.

Per 4 teaspoons (20 ml): calories: 107, protein: 0 g, fat: 6 g, carbohydrates: 13 g (12 g from sugar), dietary fiber: 0 g, calcium: 0 mg, iron: 0 mg, magnesium: 0 mg, phosphorus: 0 mg, potassium: 1 mg, sodium: 0 mg, zinc: 0 mg, thiamin: 0 mg, riboflavin: 0 mg, niacin: 0 mg, vitamin B$_6$: 0 mg, folate: 0 mcg, pantothenic acid: 0 mg, vitamin B$_{12}$: 0 mcg, vitamin A: 0 mcg, vitamin C: 0 mg, vitamin E: 0 mg, omega-6 fatty acid: 0 g, omega-3 fatty acid: 0 g

Percentage of calories from: protein 0%, fat 53%, carbohydrates 47%

These nut butter balls are an ideal snack to take along on outdoor adventures, such as hiking, riding, or climbing. They are light, take up little space, and yet provide a generous number of nourishing calories. Four of these balls can fuel a person weighing 150 pounds (68 kg) for five miles (8 k) on an uphill hike. Note that the density and oil content of nut butters can vary, so you may need to adjust the amount of water to achieve the desired consistency.

Almond Butter **BALLS**

MAKES 30 BALLS (EACH ABOUT 2 TABLESPOONS/30 ML)

1 cup (250 ml) **old-fashioned rolled oats**

1 cup (250 ml) **almond butter or peanut butter**

½ cup (125 ml) **nondairy chocolate chips**

½ cup (125 ml) **chopped dried cranberries**

½ cup (125 ml) **dried currants**

½ cup (125 ml) **raw pumpkin seeds**

1 tablespoon (15 ml) **freshly squeezed lemon juice**

1 teaspoon (5 ml) **ground cinnamon**

½ teaspoon (2 ml) **ground cardamom**

½ teaspoon (2 ml) **vanilla extract**

½ teaspoon (2 ml) **lemon zest**

1 to 2 tablespoons (15 to 30 ml) **water**

Put the oats in a food processor and process for 20 seconds, or until finely ground. Transfer the oats to a medium bowl. Add the almond butter, chocolate chips, cranberries, currants, pumpkin seeds, lemon juice, cinnamon, cardamom, vanilla extract, and zest and stir with a fork until well combined. Stir in just enough water to hold the mixture together.

Scoop out 2 tablespoons (30 ml) of the mixture and form a ball. Put the balls on a sheet of waxed paper or parchment paper or directly in a storage container as they are made. Repeat until all the mixture has been used. Stored in a sealed container, Almond Butter Balls will keep for 2 weeks in the refrigerator or 6 months in the freezer.

Per ball: calories: 113, protein: 3 g, fat: 8 g, carbohydrates: 11 g (5 g from sugar), dietary fiber: 2 g, calcium: 33 mg, iron: 1 mg, magnesium: 44 mg, phosphorus: 82 mg, potassium: 151 mg, sodium: 41 mg, zinc: 0.5 mg, thiamin: 0 mg, riboflavin: 0.1 mg, niacin: 1 mg, vitamin B_6: 0 mg, folate: 8 mcg, pantothenic acid: 0 mg, vitamin B_{12}: 0 mcg, vitamin A: 2 mcg, vitamin C: 1 mg, vitamin E: 2 mg, omega-6 fatty acid: 2 g, omega-3 fatty acid: 0 g

Percentage of calories from: protein 9%, fat 56%, carbohydrates 35%

These raw macaroons are delicious and simple to make. If you have a dehydrator, try the variation that follows.

COCONUT Macaroons

MAKES 32 COOKIES (EACH ¾ INCH/2 CM)

1½ cups (375 ml) **pitted soft dates**

1 cup (250 ml) **raw cashew pieces, soaked in water for 4 hours, drained, and rinsed**

1 teaspoon (5 ml) **vanilla extract**

1¾ cups (435 ml) **unsweetened shredded dried coconut**

Put the dates, cashews, and vanilla extract in a food processor and process for 3 minutes, or until smooth. Add 1¼ cups (310 ml) of the coconut and pulse a few times, just until the coconut is evenly distributed. Put the remaining ½ cup (125 ml) of the coconut on a small plate.

Scoop out 1 tablespoon (15 ml) of the mixture and form a ball. Roll the ball in the coconut until coated. Put the balls on a sheet of waxed paper or parchment paper, on a serving platter, or directly in a storage container as they are made. Repeat until all the mixture has been used. Stored in a sealed container, Coconut Macaroons will keep for 1 month in the refrigerator or 6 months in the freezer.

VARIATIONS

Apricot Macaroons: Replace half the dates with unsulfured dried apricots.

Chocolate Macaroons: Increase the dates to 2 cups (500 ml). Add 2 tablespoons (30 ml) of unsweetened cocoa powder when processing the other ingredients.

Dehydrator Method: Put the cookies on one or two dehydrator trays lined with nonstick sheets. Dehydrate at 110 degrees F (43 degrees C) for about 12 hours.

Per cookie: calories: 70, protein: 1 g, fat: 4 g, carbohydrates: 8 g (5 g from sugar), dietary fiber: 1 g, calcium: 5 mg, copper: 140 mcg, iron: 0.5 mg, magnesium: 19 mg, phosphorus: 38 mg, potassium: 97 mg, sodium: 2 mg, zinc: 0.4 mg, thiamin: 0 mg, riboflavin: 0 mg, niacin: 0.4 mg, pyridoxine: 0 mg, folate: 3 mcg, pantothenic acid: 0.1 mg, vitamin B_{12}: 0 mcg, vitamin A: 0 mcg, vitamin C: 0 mg, vitamin E: 0.1 mg, vitamin K: 2 mcg, omega-6 fatty acid: 0.4 g, omega-3 fatty acid: 0 g.

Percentage of calories from: protein 7%, fat 52%, carbohydrates 41%

Reprinted by permission from *Becoming Raw* © Brenda Davis and Vesanto Melina (Summertown, TN: Book Publishing Company, 2010).

These delectable cookies have a moist cakelike texture and are a very pleasant dessert or snack. They go well with a hot cup of tea or a fresh fruit salad.

Lemon-Sesame COOKIES

MAKES 36 COOKIES (EACH 1 ½ INCHES/4 CM)

2 cups (500 ml) **unbleached all-purpose flour or whole wheat pastry flour**

½ cup (125 ml) **sesame seeds**

2 teaspoons (10 ml) **baking powder**

½ teaspoon (2 ml) **salt**

11 ounces (300 g) **soft tofu**

½ cup (125 ml) **maple syrup**

½ cup (125 ml) **sunflower oil or other vegetable oil**

¼ cup (60 ml) **brown sugar or other granulated sweetener**

2 teaspoons (10 ml) **grated lemon zest**

1½ teaspoons (7 ml) **lemon extract**

1 teaspoon (5 ml) **vanilla extract**

Preheat the oven to 350 degrees F (180 degrees C). Oil two baking sheets.

Put the flour, sesame seeds, baking powder, and salt in a medium bowl and stir with a dry whisk until combined.

Put the tofu in a large bowl and mash with a fork. Stir in the maple syrup, oil, sugar, zest, lemon extract, and vanilla extract until combined. Quickly stir in the flour mixture until well combined.

Drop the batter by rounded tablespoonfuls onto the prepared baking sheets. Bake for about 20 minutes, or until golden brown, rotating the baking sheets after 10 minutes for even baking. Transfer to a rack to cool. Stored in a sealed container, Lemon-Sesame Cookies will keep for 7 days in the refrigerator or 6 month in the freezer.

Per cookie: calories: 96, protein: 2 g, fat: 5 g, carbohydrates: 12 g (5 g from sugar), dietary fiber: 0.5 g, calcium: 37 mg, iron: 1 mg, magnesium: 14 mg, phosphorus: 33 mg, potassium: 59 mg, sodium: 43 mg, zinc: 0.5 mg, thiamin: 0.1 mg, riboflavin: 0.1 mg, niacin: 1 mg, vitamin B_6: 0 mg, folate: 13 mcg, pantothenic acid: 0 mg, vitamin B_{12}: 0 mcg, vitamin A: 0 mcg, vitamin C: 0 mg, vitamin E: 0 mg, omega-6 fatty acid: 2 g, omega-3 fatty acid: 0 g

Percentage of calories from: protein 8%, fat 44%, carbohydrates 48%

These muffins are delicious and good for you, making them the perfect choice for brunch, packed lunches, or afternoon tea. Paper liners will make the muffins easier to remove from the pan and will peel away easily after the muffins have cooled. Blueberry-Cornmeal Muffins freeze well.

BLUEBERRY-CORNMEAL Muffins

1½ cups (375 ml) **fortified nondairy milk**

1 cup (250 ml) **cornmeal**

⅓ cup (85 ml) **sunflower oil or other vegetable oil**

⅔ cup (170 ml) **granulated sweetener**

1 cup (250 ml) **unbleached all-purpose flour**

1 cup (250 ml) **whole wheat pastry flour**

1½ teaspoons (7 ml) **baking powder**

½ teaspoon (2 ml) **baking soda**

½ teaspoon (2 ml) **salt**

1½ cups (375 ml) **fresh or frozen blueberries**

Preheat the oven to 400 degrees F (200 degrees C). Line or lightly oil a 12-cup muffin pan.

Put the nondairy milk, cornmeal, oil, and sweetener in a large bowl and stir until well combined. Let sit for 3 minutes.

Put the flours, baking powder, baking soda, and salt in a medium bowl and stir until well combined. Add the flour mixture to the nondairy milk mixture and stir until just combined. Do not overmix. Fold in the blueberries.

Spoon into the prepared muffin pan and bake for 25 to 30 minutes, or until golden brown and a toothpick inserted in the center of a muffin comes out clean. If frozen blueberries are used, the longer baking time will be needed.

VARIATION: Instead of using a combination unbleached all-purpose and whole wheat pasty flours, use a total of 2 cups of either one.

Per muffin: calories: 245, protein: 4 g, fat: 8 g, carbohydrates: 40 g (13 g from sugar), dietary fiber: 3 g, calcium: 104 mg, iron: 2 mg, magnesium: 23 mg, phosphorus: 124 mg, potassium: 104 mg, sodium: 188 mg, zinc: 0.5 mg, thiamin: 0.2 mg, riboflavin: 0.2 mg, niacin: 2 mg, vitamin B_6: 0.1 mg, folate: 44 mcg, pantothenic acid: 0.3 mg, vitamin B_{12}: 0.4 mcg, vitamin A: 13 mcg, vitamin C: 2 mg, vitamin E: 0.2 mg, omega-6 fatty acid: 3 g, omega-3 fatty acid: 0.1 g

Percentage of calories from: protein 7%, fat 28%, carbohydrates 65%

Stock the freezer with cranberries if you are a muffin lover, because you'll want to make these often. Maple syrup offsets the tartness of the cranberries and provides a deep, sweet flavor.

CRANBERRY-PECAN Muffins

MAKES 12 MUFFINS

2½ cups (625 ml) **fresh or thawed frozen cranberries**

½ cup (125 ml) **maple syrup**

1 teaspoon (5 ml) **grated orange or lemon zest**

11 ounces (300 g) **soft tofu**

½ cup (125 ml) **nondairy milk**

½ cup (125 ml) **granulated sweetener**

⅓ cup (85 ml) **sunflower oil or melted coconut oil**

1 teaspoon (5 ml) **vanilla extract**

2 cups (500 ml) **whole wheat pastry flour**

2 teaspoons (10 ml) **baking powder**

2 teaspoons (10 ml) **ground cinnamon**

1 teaspoon (5 ml) **baking soda**

½ teaspoon (2 ml) **ground allspice**

½ teaspoon (2 ml) **ground cardamom** (optional)

½ teaspoon (2 ml) **ground cloves**

½ teaspoon (2 ml) **salt**

1 cup (250 ml) **chopped pecans**

Preheat the oven to 375 degrees F (190 degrees C). Line or lightly oil a 12-cup muffin pan.

Put 1½ cups (375 ml) of the cranberries, the maple syrup, and zest in a small saucepan over medium heat and cook for about 10 minutes, until the cranberries have popped and a thick liquid has formed. Chop the remaining cup (250 ml) of cranberries and stir into the cooked berries. Set aside and let cool for 5 minutes.

Put the tofu, nondairy milk, sweetener, oil, and vanilla extract in a large bowl and stir until combined.

Put the flour, baking powder, cinnamon, baking soda, allspice, optional cardamom, cloves, and salt in a medium bowl and stir with a dry whisk until combined.

Stir the cranberries into the tofu mixture until evenly distributed. Stir in the flour mixture and the pecans until just combined.

Spoon into the prepared muffin pan and bake for 30 to 35 minutes, or until a toothpick inserted in the center of a muffin comes out clean.

Per muffin: calories: 302, protein: 5 g, fat: 16 g, carbohydrates: 38 g (16 g from sugar), dietary fiber: 5 g, calcium: 108 mg, iron: 2 mg, magnesium: 27 mg, phosphorus: 75 mg, potassium: 158 mg, sodium: 240 mg, zinc: 1 mg, thiamin: 0.2 mg, riboflavin: 0.1 mg, niacin: 2 mg, vitamin B$_6$: 0.1 mg, folate: 24 mcg, pantothenic acid: 0.5 mg, vitamin B$_{12}$: 0.1 mcg, vitamin A: 2 mcg, vitamin C: 4 mg, vitamin E: 4 mg, omega-6 fatty acid: 7 g, omega-3 fatty acid: 0.2 g

Percentage of calories from: protein 7%, fat 45%, carbohydrates 48%

Note: Analysis was done using fortified nondairy milk, a source of vitamin B$_{12}$.

A pastry recipe that does not call for hydrogenated oils or saturated fats is a welcome addition to anyone's repertoire. The amount of water needed for this recipe can vary depending on the type of flour used. If you use whole wheat flour, you will need slightly more water because the extra bran will absorb more moisture. Letting the dough rest for a minimum of twenty minutes after it is made allows the gluten in the flour to relax, making the dough easier to roll.

Tart and Pie PASTRY

MAKES PASTRY FOR THIRTY 3-INCH (7.5-CM) TARTS OR TWO 8-INCH (20-CM) SINGLE-CRUST PIES

1½ cups (375 ml) **unbleached all-purpose flour**

1½ cups (375 ml) **whole wheat pastry flour or whole wheat flour**

1 tablespoon (15 ml) **baking powder**

½ teaspoon (2 ml) **salt**

½ cup (125 ml) **sunflower oil or other vegetable oil**

½ cup (125 ml) **ice water** (see note)

Put the flours, baking powder, and salt in a medium bowl and stir with a dry whisk until combined. Add the oil and toss the mixture with a fork or your fingers to form pea-size balls. Sprinkle the ice water over the mixture and use your hands to form a ball of dough. Use just enough water to hold the dough together. Divide the dough into two equal pieces and form two balls. Wrap tightly in plastic wrap, or ziplock bag, and refrigerate for 20 minutes or until needed. Stored in the refrigerator, Tart and Pie Pastry will keep for 6 months.

NOTE: To make ice water, put 2 or 3 ice cubes in a glass of water for about 7 minutes, or put cold water in the freezer for 15 minutes if you have no ice.

Per tart shell: calories: 81, protein: 2 g, fat: 4 g, carbohydrates: 10 g (0 g from sugar), dietary fiber: 1 g, calcium: 25 mg, iron: 0.1 mg, magnesium: 10 mg, phosphorus: 64 mg, potassium: 84 mg, sodium: 32 mg, zinc: 0.2 mg, thiamin: 0.1 mg, riboflavin: 0.1 mg, niacin: 1 mg, vitamin B_6: 0 mg, folate: 14 mcg, pantothenic acid: 0.1 mg, vitamin B_{12}: 0 mcg, vitamin A: 0 mcg, vitamin C: 0 mg, vitamin E: 2 mg, omega-6 fatty acid: 0.2 g, omega-3 fatty acid: 0 g

Percentage of calories from: protein 7%, fat 45%, carbohydrates 48%

Pie crusts are usually made with flour and baked in the oven. This raw crust is easy to make, gluten-free, and is an excellent source of the antioxidant vitamin E.

Almond, Date, and **COCONUT PIE CRUST**

MAKES ONE 8- OR 9-INCH (20- OR 23-CM) **PIE CRUST** (8 SERVINGS)

1 cup (250 ml) **almonds**

½ cup (125 ml) **unsweetened shredded dried coconut**

½ cup (125 ml) **pitted medjool dates**

Put the almonds in a food processor and process into a fine meal. Do not overprocess or the almonds will become oily and start to form a butter. Remove 1 tablespoon (15 ml) of the almond meal and set it aside. Add the coconut and dates and process until the mixture adheres to the work bowl, forming a wall.

Sprinkle the remaining tablespoon of almond meal into a 9-inch (23-cm) pie pan (this will prevent the crust from sticking to the pan). Press the mixture evenly onto the bottom and sides of the pan. Put the crust in the freezer for 15 minutes before filling.

Per serving: calories: 174, protein: 5 g, fat: 13 g, carbohydrates: 14 g (9 g from sugar), dietary fiber: 4 g, calcium: 56 mg, iron: 1 mg, magnesium: 63 mg, phosphorus: 107 mg, potassium: 246 mg, sodium: 2 mg, zinc: 1 mg, thiamin: 0.1 mg, riboflavin: 0.2 mg, niacin: 2 mg, vitamin B$_6$: 0.1 mg, folate: 8 mcg, pantothenic acid: 0.2 mg, vitamin B$_{12}$: 0 mcg, vitamin A: 1 mcg, vitamin C: 0 mg, vitamin E: 5 mg, omega-6 fatty acid: 2 g, omega-3 fatty acid: 0 g

Percentage of calories from: protein 10%, fat 61%, carbohydrates 29%

The ground flaxseeds in this recipe provide a nutty flavor and beneficial omega-3 fatty acids and vitamin E; they also help to hold the crust together. Good choices for the cold cereal are whole-grain corn flakes or rice flakes. This crust was created for Lem-Un-Cheesecake with Crumb Crust (page 232) and Pumpkin Spice Pie (page 237).

FLAX AND OATS Crumb Crust

MAKES ONE 8- OR 9-INCH (20- OR 23-CM) CRUST (8 SERVINGS)

1 cup (250 ml) **cold cereal flakes**

1 cup (250 ml) **old-fashioned rolled oats**

¼ cup (60 ml) **ground flaxseeds** (see page 20)

¼ cup (60 ml) **sunflower oil or other vegetable oil**

¼ cup (60 ml) **water**

2 teaspoons (10 ml) **vanilla extract**

Lightly oil an 8- or 9-inch (20- or 23-cm) pie pan.

Put the cold cereal flakes in a food processor and process for 30 seconds, or until ground. Transfer to a medium bowl. Put the oats in the food processor and process for 20 seconds, or until ground. Add the oats and the flaxseeds to the cereal flakes and stir until combined.

Put the oil, water, and vanilla extract in a small bowl and stir with a fork or whisk until combined. Quickly stir the oil mixture into the crumb mixture with the fork. Work the mixture well with your fingers for 5 to 10 seconds, until the mixture is crumbly. Press the mixture firmly and evenly onto the bottom and sides of the prepared pie pan. Fill and bake as directed.

Per serving: calories: 148, protein: 3 g, fat: 10 g, carbohydrates: 13 g (0.5 g from sugar), dietary fiber: 3 g, calcium: 16 mg, iron: 1 mg, magnesium: 16 mg, phosphorus: 27 mg, potassium: 94 mg, sodium: 22 mg, zinc: 0.2 mg, thiamin: 0.1 mg, riboflavin: 0 mg, niacin: 0.4 mg, vitamin B$_6$: 0 mg, folate: 4 mcg, pantothenic acid: 0 mg, vitamin B$_{12}$: 0 mcg, vitamin A: 0 mcg, vitamin C: 0 mg, vitamin E: 3 mg, omega-6 fatty acid: 0.5g, omega-3 fatty acid: 1 g

Percentage of calories from: protein 8%, fat 58%, carbohydrates 34%

This cheesecake is rich in protein and looks irresistible when topped with fresh fruit or a fruit sauce. Top the chilled cheesecake with blueberries or sliced kiwifruit, peaches, or strawberries. Alternatively, top with Apple-Plum Chutney (page 180) or Blueberry-Orange Sauce (page 178).

LEM-UN-CHEESECAKE with Crumb Crust

MAKES ONE 8- OR 9-INCH (20- TO 23-CM) PIE (8 SERVINGS)

24 ounces (680 g) **firm silken tofu**

⅓ cup (85 ml) **maple syrup or agave nectar**

¼ cup (60 ml) **freshly squeezed lemon juice**

4 teaspoons (20 ml) **grated lemon zest**

1½ teaspoons (7 ml) **vanilla extract**

1 Flax and Oats Crumb Crust (page 231)

Preheat the oven to 350 degrees F (180 degrees C).

Put the tofu, maple syrup, lemon juice, zest, and vanilla extract in a food processor and process until smooth, occasionally stopping to scrape down the sides of the work bowl. Pour into the prepared crust. Bake for 1 hour, or until a toothpick inserted in the center comes out clean. Cover and refrigerate for 1 to 2 hours before serving. Serve chilled. Covered and stored in the refrigerator, Lem-Un-Cheesecake with Crumb Crust will keep for 4 to 5 days.

Per serving: calories: 244, protein: 9 g, fat: 12 g, carbohydrates: 25 g (10 g from sugar), dietary fiber: 3 g, calcium: 56 mg, iron: 2 mg, magnesium: 42 mg, phosphorus: 106 mg, potassium: 305 mg, sodium: 55 mg, zinc: 1 mg, thiamin: 0.2 mg, riboflavin: 0.1 mg, niacin: 2 mg, vitamin B_6: 0 mg, folate: 5 mcg, pantothenic acid: 0.1 mg, vitamin B_{12}: 0 mcg, vitamin A: 0 mcg, vitamin C: 5 mg, vitamin E: 3 mg, omega-6 fatty acid: 0.5 g, omega-3 fatty acid: 1 g

Percentage of calories from: protein 15%, fat 44%, carbohydrates 41%

Blueberries and cranberries are combined in this mouthwatering and light tart filling. If you use frozen blueberries, the yield will be smaller because berries shrink when they thaw. For instructions on how to use this filling in a pie, see Blueberry Mince Tarts or Pie (page 234).

Blueberry Mince **TART OR PIE FILLING**

MAKES 8 CUPS (2 L) FILLING FOR 30 TARTS OR TWO 8-INCH (20-CM) PIES

1½ cups (375 ml) **dark raisins**

1½ cups (375 ml) **golden raisins**

½ cup (125 ml) **dried cranberries**

½ cup (125 ml) **brown sugar or other granulated sweetener**

⅓ cup (85 ml) **candied citrus peel**

2 tablespoons (30 ml) **arrowroot starch or cornstarch** (see note)

2 tablespoons (30 ml) **fruit juice or brandy**

1 tablespoon (15 ml) **freshly squeezed lemon juice**

1 teaspoon (5 ml) **ground cinnamon**

1 teaspoon (5 ml) **grated lemon zest**

½ teaspoon (2 ml) **ground ginger**

½ teaspoon (2 ml) **ground nutmeg**

¼ teaspoon (1 ml) **ground cloves**

4 cups (1 L) **fresh or frozen blueberries**

Put the dark and golden raisins, cranberries, sugar, citrus peel, arrowroot starch, fruit juice, lemon juice, cinnamon, zest, ginger, nutmeg, and cloves in a large bowl and stir until well combined. Stir in the blueberries until well incorporated. Blueberry Mince Tart or Pie Filling will keep in the refrigerator for 1 week or 6 months in the freezer.

NOTE: Omit the arrowroot starch or cornstarch if you plan to store the filling in the refrigerator or freezer before using; add the arrowroot starch or cornstarch just prior to making the tarts or pies.

Per ¼-cup (60-ml) serving: calories: 80, protein: 1 g, fat: 0.2 g, carbohydrates: 21 g (16 g from sugar), dietary fiber: 1 g, calcium: 11 mg, iron: 0 mg, magnesium: 4 mg, phosphorus: 11 mg, potassium: 136 mg, sodium: 7 mg, zinc: 0 mg, thiamin: 0 mg, riboflavin: 0 mg, niacin: 0 mg, vitamin B_6: 0.1 mg, folate: 2 mcg, pantothenic acid: 0 mg, vitamin B_{12}: 0 mcg, vitamin A: 1 mcg, vitamin C: 3 mg, vitamin E: 0 mg, omega-6 fatty acid: 0 g, omega-3 fatty acid: 0 g

Percentage of calories from: protein 3%, fat 2%, carbohydrates 95%

There are several ways to roll out pie dough. One method is to roll the dough between sheets of waxed paper, parchment paper, or two clean plastic produce bags that have been cut and opened up to create two pieces of plastic. Another is the old-fashioned method of rolling out the dough on a countertop or on a marble slab. All methods require a dusting of flour to prevent the dough from sticking.

Blueberry Mince TARTS OR PIES

MAKES 30 TARTS OR TWO 8 X 1¼-INCH (20 X 3-CM) SINGLE-CRUST PIES

2 crusts (1 recipe) **Tart and Pie Pastry** (page 229)

8 cups (2 L) **Blueberry Mince Tart or Pie Filling** (page 233)

For Tarts: Preheat the oven to 350 degrees F (180 degrees C). Lightly oil a nonstick muffin pan or tart pan.

Roll out one of the two pastry balls with a rolling pin to form a 12-inch (30 cm) circle. Cut the dough using a 3½-inch (9-cm) cutter or a lid for a widemouthed jar. Gently lift the rounds of dough with a metal spatula and press each into the prepared muffin cups or pan. Gather loose scraps and reroll until all the dough is used up. Repeat using the other ball of dough.

Spoon about 3 tablespoons (45 ml) of the blueberry filling into each shell. Bake for 20 to 25 minutes, until the crust is golden brown. Remove the tarts from the pan while they are still warm.

For Pies: Preheat the oven to 350 degrees F (180 degrees C). Lightly oil two 8-inch (20-cm) pie pans.

Roll out one of the pastry balls with a rolling pin to form a 12-inch (30-cm) circle. Carefully lift the circle of dough with one or two metal spatulas and press the dough into one of the oiled pie pans. Use small amounts of excess dough to fill any gaps and patch any broken areas. Trim any excess overhang with a knife and flute the edges. Repeat using the other ball of dough.

Spoon half of the Blueberry Mince Filling into each pie shell. Bake for 45 to 50 minutes, until the crust is golden brown.

Per tart: calories: 161, protein: 2 g, fat: 4 g, carbohydrates: 31 g (16 g from sugar), dietary fiber: 2 g, calcium: 37 mg, iron: 1 mg, magnesium: 15 mg, phosphorus: 75 mg, potassium: 220 mg, sodium: 39 mg, zinc: 0.3 mg, thiamin: 0.1 mg, riboflavin: 0.1 mg, niacin: 1 mg, vitamin B_6: 0.1 mg, folate: 17 mcg, pantothenic acid: 0.1 mg, vitamin B_{12}: 0 mcg, vitamin A: 1 mcg, vitamin C: 3 mg, vitamin E: 2 mg, omega-6 fatty acid: 0.2 g, omega-3 fatty acid: 0 g

Percentage of calories from: protein 5%, fat 23%, carbohydrates 72%

Per slice (8 per pie): calories: 302, protein: 4 g, fat: 8 g, carbohydrates: 57 g (30 g from sugar), dietary fiber: 5 g, calcium: 69 mg, iron: 2 mg, magnesium: 27 mg, phosphorus: 141 mg, potassium: 412 mg, sodium: 73 mg, zinc: 1 mg, thiamin: 0.2 mg, riboflavin: 0.1 mg, niacin: 3 mg, vitamin B_6: 0.2 mg, folate: 31 mcg, pantothenic acid: 0.2 mg, vitamin B_{12}: 0 mcg, vitamin A: 2 mcg, vitamin C: 6 mg, vitamin E: 3 mg, omega-6 fatty acid: 0.4 g, omega-3 fatty acid: 0 g

Percentage of calories from: protein 5%, fat 23%, carbohydrates 72%

This raw filling has the ideal balance of sweetness and tang. The Almond, Date, and Coconut Pie Crust adds a crunchy contrast. Avocado can become brown if overprocessed, so process this filling just until it is smooth. The pie slices will maintain a firmer edge when cut if you include the coconut oil, but the pie will still be excellent without it. Because this pie filling is so rich, so you might want to cut smaller pieces. (Then again, it's so delicious, you might want to cut larger pieces.)

LIME Pie

MAKES ONE 8- OR 9-INCH (20- OR 23-CM) PIE (8 SERVINGS)

4 ripe avocados

⅔ cup (170 ml) **freshly squeezed lime juice**

⅔ cup (170 ml) **maple syrup**

2 tablespoons (30 ml) **coconut oil, melted, or** 2 teaspoons (10 ml) **guar gum** (optional)

1 tablespoon (15 ml) **lime zest**

1 **Almond, Date, and Coconut Pie Crust** (page 230)

3 kiwifruit, peeled and sliced, for garnish

Put the avocado flesh, lime juice, maple syrup, and oil in a blender and process just until smooth and fluid. Add the zest and process just until incorporated. Pour into the prepared crust.

Cover and freeze for 1 to 2 hours or refrigerate for 8 to 12 hours until set. Garnish with the kiwifruit. Serve chilled so that the slices retain their shape. Covered and stored in the refrigerator, Lime Pie will keep for 2 to 3 days.

VARIATIONS

- Garnish with other sliced fruit or unsweetened shredded dried coconut.
- Serve as a pudding, without the pie crust.

Per serving: calories: 434, protein: 7 g, fat: 28 g, carbohydrates: 47 g (29 g from sugar), dietary fiber: 10 g, calcium: 100 mg, iron: 3 mg, magnesium: 113 mg, phosphorus: 161 mg, potassium: 1,022 mg, sodium: 16 mg, zinc: 2 mg, thiamin: 0.2 mg, riboflavin: 0.3 mg, niacin: 4 mg, vitamin B$_6$: 0.4 mg, folate: 79 mcg, pantothenic acid: 1 mg, vitamin B$_{12}$: 0 mcg, vitamin A: 66 mcg, vitamin C: 42 mg, vitamin E: 7 mg, omega-6 fatty acid: 4 g, omega-3 fatty acid: 0 g

Percentage of calories from: protein 6%, fat 54%, carbohydrates 40%

This raw pie will dazzle your family and friends. The pie slices will maintain a firmer edge when cut if you include the coconut oil. However, this filling is superb when made with mango alone.

Mango-Strawberry PIE

MAKES ONE 8- OR 9-INCH (20- OR 23-CM) PIE (8 SERVINGS)

1 cup (250 ml) **dried mangoes, soaked in water for 10 minutes**

3 cups (750 ml) **chopped fresh mangoes** (about 2 mangoes)

2 tablespoons (30 ml) **coconut oil, melted,** or 2 teaspoons (10 ml) **guar gum** (optional)

1 **Almond, Date, and Coconut Pie Crust** (page 230)

1 cup (250 ml) **sliced strawberries, for garnish**

Drain the dried mangoes well, then press them in a small sieve or with your hands to remove excess liquid. Put the dried mangoes, the fresh mangoes, and the optional coconut oil in a blender or food processor and process until smooth.

Spoon the mango mixture into the prepared crust. Garnish with the strawberries. Cover and refrigerate for 2 to 3 hours to set. Serve chilled so that the slices retain their shape. Covered and stored in the refrigerator, Mango-Strawberry Pie will keep for 2 to 3 days.

VARIATION: Garnish with other sliced fruit or unsweetened shredded dried coconut.

Per serving: calories: 277, protein: 5 g, fat: 13 g, carbohydrates: 41 g (22 g from sugar), dietary fiber: 6 g, calcium: 71 mg, iron: 1 mg, magnesium: 73 mg, phosphorus: 125 mg, potassium: 402 mg, sodium: 4 mg, zinc: 1 mg, thiamin: 0.1 mg, riboflavin: 0.2 mg, niacin: 3 mg, vitamin B_6: 0.2 mg, folate: 22 mcg, pantothenic acid: 0.4 mg, vitamin B_{12}: 0 mcg, vitamin A: 53 mcg, vitamin C: 37 mg, vitamin E: 6 mg, omega-6 fatty acid: 2 g, omega-3 fatty acid: 0 g

Percentage of calories from: protein 7%, fat 39%, carbohydrates 54%

Pumpkin pie has become a symbol of the harvest in North America, and it is usually eaten at fall and winter celebrations. Pumpkin Spice Pie is an excellent alternative to the traditional pie, which is made with eggs and dairy products. Serve with Cashew Cream Topping (page 212) or Holiday Pie Topping (page 213).

PUMPKIN SPICE Pie

MAKES ONE 8- OR 9-INCH (20- OR 23-CM) PIE (8 SERVINGS)

12 ounces (340 g) **firm silken tofu, or 1¾ cups** (435 ml) **mashed soft tofu**

2 cups (500 ml) **mashed cooked or canned pumpkin**

⅔ cup (170 ml) **maple syrup or other liquid sweetener**

1½ teaspoons (7 ml) **ground cinnamon**

1 teaspoon (5 ml) **vanilla extract**

¾ teaspoon (4 ml) **ground ginger**

¼ teaspoon (1 ml) **ground nutmeg**

⅛ teaspoon (0.5 ml) **ground cloves**

1 Flax and Oats Crumb Crust (page 231)

Preheat the oven to 375 degrees F (190 degrees C).

Put the tofu in a food processor or blender and process until creamy and smooth. Add the pumpkin, maple syrup, cinnamon, vanilla extract, ginger, nutmeg, and cloves and process until well combined. Pour into the prepared crust and bake for 50 to 60 minutes, or until a toothpick inserted in the center comes out clean and the pie just begins to crack. Cover and refrigerate. Serve chilled. Covered and stored in the refrigerator, Pumpkin Spice Pie will keep for 2 to 3 days.

Per serving: calories: 266, protein: 6 g, fat: 11 g, carbohydrates: 37 g (19 g from sugar), dietary fiber: 4 g, calcium: 65 mg, iron: 2 mg, magnesium: 39 mg, phosphorus: 87 mg, potassium: 392 mg, sodium: 42 mg, zinc: 2 mg, thiamin: 0.2 mg, riboflavin: 0.1 mg, niacin: 1 mg, vitamin B_6: 0.1 mg, folate: 10 mcg, pantothenic acid: 0.2 mg, vitamin B_{12}: 0 mcg, vitamin A: 162 mcg, vitamin C: 3 mg, vitamin E: 4 mg, omega-6 fatty acid: 0.5 g, omega-3 fatty acid: 1 g

Percentage of calories from: protein 10%, fat 36%, carbohydrates 54%

Use short- or medium-grain rice to create a soft, creamy, and comforting pudding. The medium-grain arborio rice is ideal. If you like, top individual servings with a dollop of Cashew Cream Topping (page 212) or Holiday Pie Topping (page 213) or a sprinkle of cinnamon. For a sweet morning treat, serve leftovers for breakfast.

CREAMY Rice Pudding

MAKES FOUR 1-CUP (250-ML) SERVINGS

2 cups (500 ml) **water**

1 cup (250 ml) **white arborio rice or short-grain brown rice**

2 cups (500 ml) **nondairy milk**

½ cup (125 ml) **raisins or chopped dates**

¼ cup (60 ml) **maple syrup or other sweetener**

1 teaspoon (5 ml) **vanilla extract**

½ teaspoon (2 ml) **ground cinnamon**

⅛ teaspoon (0.5 ml) **ground cloves or ground nutmeg**

Preheat the oven to 350 degrees F (180 degrees C).

Put the water and rice in a medium saucepan over medium-high heat. Bring to a boil. Decrease the heat to low, cover, and cook for 15 to 20 minutes if using white arborio rice or 45 minutes if using brown rice, or until all the water has been absorbed.

Transfer to a 6-cup (1.5-L) baking pan. Add the nondairy milk, raisins, maple syrup, vanilla extract, cinnamon, and cloves and stir until well combined. Bake for about 30 minutes, until all of the liquid has been absorbed.

VARIATION: Instead of baking Creamy Rice Pudding in the oven, put the cooked rice, nondairy milk, raisins, maple syrup, vanilla extract, cinnamon, and cloves in the top of a double boiler over simmering water and cook for 20 to 30 minutes, until all the liquid has been absorbed.

Per cup (250 ml): calories: 335, protein: 5 g, fat: 2 g, carbohydrates: 77 g (29 g from sugar), dietary fiber: 3 g, calcium: 133 mg, iron: 2 mg, magnesium: 25 mg, phosphorus: 117 mg, potassium: 323 mg, sodium: 88 mg, zinc: 2 mg, thiamin: 0.3 mg, riboflavin: 0.1 mg, niacin: 3 mg, vitamin B$_6$: 0.1 mg, folate: 206 mcg, pantothenic acid: 0.7 mg, vitamin B$_{12}$: 0 mcg, vitamin A: 0 mcg, vitamin C: 1 mg, vitamin E: 5 mg, omega-6 fatty acid: 0.1 g, omega-3 fatty acid: 0 g

Percentage of calories from: protein 6%, fat 5%, carbohydrates 89%

Note: Analysis was done using fortified almond milk.

Figs, one of the first cultivated fruits, have recently become popular because they are a good source of calcium. This recipe also provides iron, magnesium, potassium, and protein. The golden Calimyrna fig is suggested here because of its lighter color. Served in wide mouthed champagne glasses, Figgy Pudding makes an elegant dessert, especially when garnished with slivered almonds or mint sprigs.

Figgy **PUDDING**

MAKES FOUR ¾-CUP (185-ML) SERVINGS

1 cup (250 ml) **stemmed dried golden figs** (about 15 figs), **soaked in 1½ cups** (375 ml) **unsweetened apple juice in the refrigerator for 12 hours**

12 ounces (340 g) **firm silken tofu**

1 tablespoon (15 ml) **freshly squeezed lemon juice**

1 tablespoon (15 ml) **sweetener** (optional)

¼ teaspoon (1 ml) **ground cinnamon**

¼ teaspoon (1 ml) **vanilla extract**

pinch ground cloves

Drain the figs. Reserve the liquid for smoothies. Put the figs, tofu, lemon juice, optional sweetener, cinnamon, vanilla extract, and cloves in a blender and process for 2 to 3 minutes, or until completely smooth, stopping occasionally to scrape down the sides of the container. Scoop into four small serving bowls or glasses. Covered tightly and stored in the refrigerator, leftover Figgy Pudding will keep for 2 to 3 days.

Per ¾ cup (185 ml) serving: calories: 237, protein: 8 g, fat: 3 g, carbohydrates: 48 g (47 g from sugar), dietary fiber: 7 g, calcium: 113 mg, iron: 2 mg, magnesium: 58 mg, phosphorus: 122 mg, potassium: 668 mg, sodium: 41 mg, zinc: 1 mg, thiamin: 0.2 mg, riboflavin: 0.1 mg, niacin: 2 mg, vitamin B_6: 0.2 mg, folate: 5 mcg, pantothenic acid: 0.3 mg, vitamin B_{12}: 0 mcg, vitamin A: 7 mcg, vitamin C: 4 mg, vitamin E: 0.2 mg, omega-6 fatty acid: 0.3 g, omega-3 fatty acid: 0 g

Percentage of calories from: protein 12%, fat 11%, carbohydrates 77%

DIETARY REFERENCE INTAKES FOR MINERALS

	Calcium mg	Chromium mcg	Copper mcg	Fluoride mg	Iodine mcg	Iron mg	Magnesium mg	Manganese mg	Molybdenum mcg	Phosphorus mg	Selenium mcg	Zinc mg
INFANTS												
0–6 months	200	0.2	200	0.01	110	0.27	30	0.003	2	100	15	2
7–12 months	260	5.5	220	0.5	130	11	75	0.6	3	275	20	3
CHILDREN												
1–3 years	**700**	11	**340**	0.7	**90**	**7**	**80**	1.2	**17**	**460**	**20**	**3**
4–8 years	**1,000**	15	**440**	1	**90**	**10**	**130**	1.5	**22**	**500**	**30**	**5**
MALES												
9–13 years	**1,300**	25	**700**	2	**120**	**8**	**240**	19	**34**	**1,250**	**40**	**8**
14–18 years	**1,300**	35	**890**	3	**150**	**11**	**410**	2.2	**43**	**1,250**	**55**	**11**
19–30 years	**1,000**	35	**900**	4	**150**	**8**	**400**	2.3	**45**	**700**	**55**	**11**
31–50 years	**1,000**	35	**900**	4	**150**	**8**	**420**	2.3	**45**	**700**	**55**	**11**
51–70 years	**1,200**	30	**900**	4	**150**	**8**	**420**	2.3	**45**	**700**	**55**	**11**
> 70 years	**1,200**	30	**900**	4	**150**	**8**	**420**	2.3	**45**	**700**	**55**	**11**
FEMALES												
9–13 years	**1,300**	21	**700**	2	**120**	**8**	**240**	1.6	**34**	**1,250**	**40**	**8**
14–18 years	**1,300**	24	**890**	3	**150**	**15**	**360**	1.6	**43**	**1,250**	**55**	**9**
19–30 years	**1,000**	25	**900**	3	**150**	**18**	**310**	1.8	**45**	**700**	**55**	**8**
31–50 years	**1,000**	25	**900**	3	**150**	**18**	**320**	1.8	**45**	**700**	**55**	**8**
51–70 years	**1,200**	20	**900**	3	**150**	**8**	**320**	1.8	**45**	**700**	**55**	**8**
> 70 years	**1,200**	20	**900**	3	**150**	**8**	**320**	1.8	**45**	**700**	**55**	**8**
PREGNANCY												
< 18 years	**1,300**	29	**1,000**	3	**220**	**27**	**400**	2.0	**50**	**1,250**	**60**	**13**
19–30 years	**1,000**	30	**1,000**	3	**220**	**27**	**350**	2.0	**50**	**700**	**60**	**11**
31–50 years	**1,000**	30	**1,000**	3	**220**	**27**	**360**	2.0	**50**	**700**	**60**	**11**
LACTATION												
< 18 years	**1,300**	44	**1,300**	3	**290**	**10**	**360**	2.6	**50**	**1,250**	**70**	**14**
19–30 years	**1,000**	45	**1,300**	3	**290**	**9**	**310**	2.6	**50**	**700**	**70**	**12**
31–50 years	**1,000**	45	**1,300**	3	**290**	**9**	**320**	2.6	**50**	**700**	**70**	**12**

Key: Micrograms = mcg. Milligrams = mg. The symbol < means "less than or equal to."

Note: Recommended dietary allowances (RDAs) are in bold type and adequate intakes (AIs) are in roman type. Both RDAs and AIs can be used as goals for individual intake.

Source: See notes 1 and 2 (page 242).

	Vit A[a] mcg	Vit C mg	Vit D[b] IU	Vit E mg	Vit K mcg	Thiamin mg	Riboflavin mg	Niacin[c] mg	Vit B6 mg	Folate[d] mcg	Vit B12[e] mcg	Pantothenic Acid mg	Biotin mcg	Choline mg
INFANTS														
0–6 months	400	40	400	4	2.0	0.2	0.3	2	0.1	65	0.4	1.7	5	125
7–12 months	500	50	400	5	2.5	0.3	0.4	4	0.3	80	0.5	1.8	6	150
CHILDREN														
1–3 years	**300**	**15**	**600**	6	30	**0.5**	**0.5**	6	**0.5**	**150**	**0.9**	2	8	200
4–8 years	**400**	**25**	**600**	7	55	**0.6**	**0.6**	8	**0.6**	**200**	**1.2**	3	12	250
MALES														
9–13 years	**600**	**45**	**600**	11	60	**0.9**	**0.9**	12	**1**	**300**	**1.8**	4	20	375
14–18 years	**900**	**75**	**600**	15	75	**1.2**	**1.3**	16	**1.3**	**400**	**2.4**	5	25	550
19–30 years	**900**	**90**	**600**	15	120	**1.2**	**1.3**	16	**1.3**	**400**	**2.4**	5	30	550
31–50 years	**900**	**90**	**600**	15	120	**1.2**	**1.3**	16	**1.3**	**400**	**2.4**	5	30	550
51–70 years	**900**	**90**	**600**	15	120	**1.2**	**1.3**	16	**1.7**	**400**	**2.4**	5	30	550
> 70 years	**900**	**90**	**800**	15	120	**1.2**	**1.3**	16	**1.7**	**400**	**2.4**	5	30	550
FEMALES														
9–13 years	**600**	**45**	**600**	11	60	**0.9**	**0.9**	12	**1**	**300**	**1.8**	4	20	375
14–18 years	**700**	**65**	**600**	15	75	**1**	**1**	14	**1.2**	**400**	**2.4**	5	25	400
19–30 years	**700**	**75**	**600**	15	90	**1.1**	**1.1**	14	**1.3**	**400**	**2.4**	5	30	425
31–50 years	**700**	**75**	**600**	15	90	**1.1**	**1.1**	14	**1.3**	**400**	**2.4**	5	30	425
51–70 years	**700**	**75**	**600**	15	90	**1.1**	**1.1**	14	**1.5**	**400**	**2.4**	5	30	425
> 70 years	**700**	**75**	**800**	15	90	**1.1**	**1.1**	14	**1.5**	**400**	**2.4**	5	30	425
PREGNANCY														
18 years	**750**	**80**	**600**	15	75	**1.4**	**1.4**	18	**1.9**	**600**	**2.6**	6	30	450
19–30 years	**770**	**85**	**600**	15	90	**1.4**	**1.4**	18	**1.9**	**600**	**2.6**	6	30	450
31–50 years	**770**	**85**	**600**	15	90	**1.4**	**1.4**	18	**1.9**	**600**	**2.6**	6	30	450
LACTATION														
18 years	**1,200**	**115**	**600**	19	75	**1.4**	**1.6**	17	**2**	**500**	**2.8**	7	35	550
19–30 years	**1,300**	**120**	**600**	19	90	**1.4**	**1.6**	17	**2**	**500**	**2.8**	7	35	550
31–50 years	**1,300**	**120**	**600**	19	90	**1.4**	**1.6**	17	**2**	**500**	**2.8**	7	35	550

Key: Microgram = mcg. Milligrams = mg. The symbol < means "less than or equal to."

Notes: Recommended dietary allowances (RDAs) are in bold type and adequate intakes (AIs) are in roman type. Both RDAs and AIs can be used as goals for individual intake.

[a]Vitamin A as retinal activity equivalents (RAEs): 1 RAE = 1 mcg retinol, 12 mcg beta-carotene, or 24 mcg other provitamin A carotenoids in foods; [b]Vitamin D: 1 mcg cholecalciferol = 40 IU vitamin D; [c]Niacin as niacin equivalents (NE): 1 mg of niacin = 60 mg tryptophan. Infants younger than six months must receive preformed niacin, not NE; [d]Folate as dietary folate equivalents (DFE): 1 DFE = 1 mcg food folate = 0.6 mcg of folic acid from fortified food or a supplement consumed with food, or 0.5 mcg from a supplement consumed on an empty stomach; [e]Vitamin B12: 10 to 30 percent of people fifty years and older malabsorb vitamin B12. Consequently, they are advised to meet the RDA using B12-fortified foods or supplements.

Source: See notes 1 and 2 (page 242).

NOTES AND REFERENCES

NOTES

1. Institute of Medicine. *Dietary Reference Intakes for Energy, Carbohydrate, Fiber, Fat, Fatty Acids, Cholesterol, Protein, and Amino Acids (Macronutrients)*, accessed November 2011, iom.edu/reports.aspx.

2. Institute of Medicine. *Dietary Reference Intakes* (for vitamins and minerals), accessed November 2011, iom.edu/reports.aspx.

3. Messina V, The Vegan R.D. *Food Guide 4 Vegans*, accessed November 2011, theveganrd.com/food-guide-for-vegans.

4. Messina V, Melina V, Mangels R, "A new food guide for North American vegetarians," *J Am Diet Assoc* 103, no. 6 (2003): 771–775.

5. "MyPyramid poster," United States Department of Agriculture Center for Nutrition Policy and Promotion, accessed February 2011, mypyramid.gov/downloads/MiniPoster.pdf.

6. World Health Organization, "Diet, nutrition, and the prevention of chronic diseases," *WHO Technical Report Series 916* (2003).

REFERENCES

Davis B, Melina V. 2010. *Becoming Raw.* Summertown, TN: Book Publishing Company.

Davis B, Melina V. 2000. *Becoming Vegan.* Summertown, TN: Book Publishing Company.

Drewnowski A, Gomez-Carneros C. 2000. "Bitter taste, phytonutrients, and the consumer: a review." *Am J of Clin Nutr*, 72(6): 1424–1435.

Holick MF, Biancuzzo, RM, Chen TC, et al. 2008. "Vitamin D_2 is as effective as vitamin D_3 in maintaining circulating concentrations of 25-hydroxyvitamin D." *J Clin Endocrinol Metab* 93(3): 677–681.

Mangels, R, Messina V, Messina M. 2010. *The Dietitian's Guide to Vegetarian Diets: Issues and Applications.* Sudbury, MA: Jones and Bartlett.

Melina V, Stepaniak J, Aronson D. 2004. *Food Allergy Survival Guide.* Summertown, TN: Book Publishing Company.

Rodriguez NR, DiMarco NM, Langley S. 2009. "Position of the American Dietetic Association, Dietitians of Canada, and the American College of Sports Medicine: Nutrition and athletic performance." *J Am Diet Assoc* 109(3): 509–527.

Soria C, Davis B, Melina V. 2009. *The Raw Food Revolution Diet.* Summertown, TN: Book Publishing Company.

Stepaniak J, Melina V. 2003. *Raising Vegetarian Children.* New York: McGraw-Hill.

Stepaniak J, Melina V, Aronson D. 2010. *Food Allergies: Health and Healing.* Summertown, TN: Book Publishing Company.

United States Department of Agriculture. *National Nutrient Database for Standard Reference.* Online at http://www.nal.usda.gov/fnic/foodcomp/search/ Accessed November 2011.

World Health Organization and Food and Agriculture Organization of the United Nations. 2003. "Diet, nutrition, and the prevention of chronic diseases." *WHO Technical Report Series 916.*

INDEX

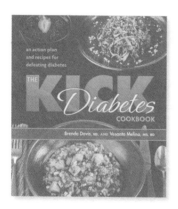